Software & Systems Requirements Engineering: In Practice

About the Authors

Brian Berenbach is the technical manager of the requirements engineering competency center at Siemens Corporate Research in Princeton, NJ. Prior to joining Siemens, he consulted for many of the Fortune 100 companies on large projects. For several years he was an architect at ABB Corporation and oversaw the installation of large software-based systems in power companies. Mr. Berenbach has graduate degrees from Emory University and the U.S. Air Force, and he is an ACM Distinguished Engineer.

Daniel J. Paulish is a Distinguished Member of Technical Staff at Siemens Corporate Research in Princeton, NJ, responsible for the Siemens Software Initiative in the Americas. He is a co-author of *Software Metrics: A Practitioner's Guide to Improved Product Development*, the author of *Architecture-Centric Software Project Management: A Practical Guide,* and a co-author of *Global Software Development Handbook*. He is formerly an industrial resident affiliate at the Software Engineering Institute (SEI), and he has done research on software measurement at Siemens Corporate Technology in Europe. He holds a Ph.D. in Electrical Engineering from the Polytechnic Institute of New York.

Juergen Kazmeier holds a major degree in Mathematics and a Ph.D. in Computer Science from the Technical University of Munich. He has worked at Siemens on software development processes, methods, and tools, and he has been a researcher and consultant on modeling languages and visualization methods. As a member of the Corporate Development Audit Unit, he analyzed and supported large product development and IT projects. Within the Intelligent Transportation Systems Division, he headed a global development group, as Vice President of R&D. Dr. Kazmeier has been responsible for the Software and Engineering Research Department at Siemens Corporate Research, where he started the Siemens Requirements Engineering Global Technology Field. Currently, he is Vice President of the Software Engineering Services Division of Siemens IT Solutions and Services, headquartered in Vienna, Austria.

Arnold Rudorfer holds an M.S. in Telematics degree from the University of Technology, Graz. Prior to joining Siemens, he worked as a developer, process consultant, and manager for user interface design and usability engineering at the European Software Institute (Spain), the Institute of Production Engineering Research (Sweden), and Meta4 (Spain), a French software multinational. At Siemens, he was responsible for building up Corporate Technology's first regional business unit in the United States, the User Interface Design Center. Since 2004, he is heading the Requirements Engineering (RE) Global Technology Field with Centers of Competence in Princeton (NJ, USA), Munich and Erlangen (Europe), as well as Beijing (China).

Software & Systems Requirements Engineering: In Practice

Brian Berenbach
Daniel J. Paulish
Juergen Kazmeier
Arnold Rudorfer

New York   Chicago   San Francisco
Lisbon   London   Madrid   Mexico City
Milan   New Delhi   San Juan
Seoul   Singapore   Sydney   Toronto

The McGraw·Hill Companies

Library of Congress Cataloging-in-Publication Data

Software & systems requirements engineering: in practice/Brian Berenbach ... [et al.].
    p. cm.
Includes bibliographical references and index.
ISBN 978-0-07-160547-2 (alk. paper)
    1. Software engineering. 2. System design. 3. Requirements engineering.
    I. Berenbach, Brian.
QA76.758.S6452 2009
005.1—dc22

2009002434

McGraw-Hill books are available at special quantity discounts to use as premiums and sales promotions, or for use in corporate training programs. To contact a special sales representative, please visit the Contact Us page at www .mhprofessional.com.

Software & Systems Requirements Engineering: In Practice

1234567890   FGR FGR   019

ISBN   978-0-07-160547-2
MHID   0-07-160547-9

Sponsoring Editor	**Copy Editor**	**Composition**
Wendy Rinaldi	Robert Campbell	International Typesetting and Composition
Editorial Supervisor	**Proofreader**	
Patty Mon	Paul Tyler	**Illustration**
Project Manager	**Indexer**	International Typesetting and Composition
Smita Rajan, International Typesetting and Composition	Karin Arrigoni	
	Production Supervisor	**Art Director, Cover**
	Jean Bodeaux	Jeff Weeks
Technical Editor		**Cover Designer**
Capers Jones		Pattie Lee

Contents at a Glance

Contents

Industrial Foreword

The last decade has seen a great deal of attention paid to requirements engineering by researchers, teachers, consultants, managers, and practitioners. Increasingly, people within information technology, commercial product development, services industries, nonprofits, government, and beyond regard good requirements as a key to project and product success. Requirements methods and practices are common subject matter for conferences, books, and classes. The business case for requirements is clear. It is in a sense a golden age for requirements.

So why then another book on the topic?

There is evidence from many sources to suggest that requirements engineering is not gaining much ground on the underlying problems of excessive rework, persistent scope creep, and finished products that fail to meet user expectations. So, despite the large investment made and the hard work done to this point, challenges still exist with regard to ever-increasing product complexity, time-to-market pressures, market segmentation, and globally diverse users.

It is here that books from practitioners, such as *Software & Systems Requirements Engineering: In Practice,* make a valuable contribution. Unlike most consultants and researchers, practitioners are deeply involved with individual projects. Moreover, they are present throughout the project and into the next one. In books from practitioners, we can see a set of requirements practices *and* the underlying setting; a detailed description of the philosophy and environment in which those practices work.

So, rather than being a compendium of possible practices, or a generic reference book, *Software & Systems Requirements Engineering: In Practice* provides readers a particular view into the world of product development and applied requirements engineering. Such windows provide a coherent and useful picture of requirements engineering.

For most practitioners, locating potential solutions to requirements engineering challenges is only part of the battle. When a method or practice is being considered for use, the question becomes "Will this work *for me*?" Understanding the experiences of other practitioners can be an incredibly valuable shortcut to the answer, and books like *Software & Systems Requirements Engineering: In Practice* are a great place to find that information.

Erik Simmons
Requirements Engineering Practice Lead
Corporate Platform Office
Intel Corporation

Academic Foreword

Requirements engineering has proven to be one of the most difficult and critical activities for the successful development of software and software-intensive systems. The reasons for that are obvious. If requirements are invalid, then even the most careful implementation of a system will not result in a product that is useful. Moreover, if requirements are included in the requirements specifications that are not actually valid, then the product or system becomes unnecessarily expensive. This shows that requirements engineering is important.

In fact, requirements engineering is also difficult. There are many reasons for this. One is that often software-intensive systems are innovative in providing new functionality. Then, learning curves have to be considered. It is often impossible to understand, in advance, what the requirements actually are. The people involved have quite different perspectives on their valid requirements. Therefore, it is difficult to arrive at an agreement. At the same time, important requirements might be overlooked and only discovered when gaining first experiences with the produced systems. Moreover, for large, long-term projects requirements may change due to changes in the environment, the market, or user needs.

Finally, requirements engineering is often underestimated or even neglected by project management. The core of requirements engineering is devoted to understand and work on the problem statement and not so much the solution. However, management may think that only when a team of developers starts to work on the solution will the project begin to show real progress. Therefore, both for management and even for experienced developers, there is always a tendency to rush too early into the solution domain. As a result, solutions are produced that miss requirements or do not explore the full range of possible solutions.

However, even having accepted that requirements engineering is difficult, error-prone, costly, but nevertheless important, a lot more has to be understood to be able to do professional requirements engineering. For most projects, the overall development process can be easily standardized after the requirements have been captured.

What is most difficult is to standardize the process of requirements engineering, since requirements engineering is at the very beginning of a project when so much is unclear. Therefore, in industrial software development, it is important to come up with a requirements engineering approach that is on the one hand flexible but on the other hand gives enough methodological guidance.

In scientific research, exploring requirements engineering has been an active field for many years. However, at least in the beginning, requirements engineering was sometimes misunderstood as a discipline, which only has to document and specify requirements but neglects the necessary decision making. This ignores the difficulty of coming up with a requirements specification that takes into account all issues from functionality to quality and cost. There are even process development issues to consider, such as certification requirements or product constraints dealing with given operating systems or software reuse.

As a result of all these considerations, the software engineering group of Siemens Corporate Research in Princeton, New Jersey, decided a few years ago to concentrate their research on a broad spectrum of requirements engineering themes. I had the privilege to work extensively with this group of engineers and researchers, who gained a lot of experience in requirements engineering on coaching, teaching, and consulting methods in ongoing Siemens projects. Some of the projects are very large scale. It is helpful that the software engineering group in Princeton is not just focused on the core topics of requirements engineering but also covers closely related aspects such as architectural design, quality assurance, testing, model-based software development, and prototyping. Doing so, the group is looking at a systematic foundation to requirements engineering by creating a requirements engineering reference model, which helps to list all the necessary content in the requirements engineering process while at the same time providing flexibility by tailoring and by a choice of methods.

It is a pleasure to see the results of the requirements engineering research and practice at Siemens Corporate Research documented in this book. It describes a lot of precious experiences, principles, and the state of the practice in industry. As such, it is quite unique and complements existing academic books on requirements engineering, which look more at the basic terminology and approaches.

I hope that this book will help in many respects development teams around the world to improve their industrial requirements engineering. It is a pleasure for me to thank the authors and the members of Siemens Corporate Research for a scientifically fruitful cooperation over the last six years and to congratulate them on this book, which is a milestone in the field of industrial requirements engineering.

Manfred Broy
Professor of Software and Systems Engineering
Technical University of Munich

Preface

Today's software and systems engineers are facing an increasing number of challenges as they attempt to develop new products and systems faster, with higher quality and rich feature content. Part of these challenges are created by advances in computing technology, as processors and memory become faster and less expensive. Along with increased processing capability, there is an expectation that today's systems will do more. As more features are being defined for a product or system, the discipline of *requirements engineering* has increased in importance to help manage the development of the features throughout the product life cycle.

This book was written to help provide an understanding of the challenges in requirements engineering (RE) that are facing industrial practitioners and to present some best practices for coping with those challenges. Many texts on RE generally do a good job covering the basics of RE, but they may not adequately discuss the real-world problems that can make requirements elicitation, analysis, and management difficult. For example, Siemens products are typically defined with at least several thousand recorded requirements. Complex Department of Defense projects are sometimes reported as having 100,000 requirements or more in their project database. Managing projects of this size is very difficult, and managing the requirements on such a project can be quite daunting. The trend is toward defining more requirements, but developers often struggle with managing them, especially as requirements are added or changed during the development life cycle. Unfortunately, problems of scale often do not always appear on a project until it is too late to easily change process, tooling, or infrastructure. It is hoped that some of the techniques described in this book will be of use to industrial practitioners for helping to make project managers aware of potential problems before they happen, and providing techniques and guidance for successfully navigating the many pitfalls associated with large, complex projects.

Background

The Software and Systems Engineering Department of Siemens Corporate Research is involved with many software development projects with Siemens organizations working across a broad spectrum of application domains in the business sectors of industrial, health care, and energy. In our dual role of an industrial research and development laboratory, we have many opportunities for observing how requirements engineers do their work. Over time we can classify certain requirements engineering practices as "best practices," and we also learn from the not-so-best practices that were not as effective in achieving project goals.

This book was written to summarize our requirements engineering experiences, and to describe them in a form that would be useful to software and systems engineering practitioners; i.e., methods, processes, and rules of thumb that can be applied to new development projects. We are not so naïve as to believe that engineers who follow what is described in this book will work only on successful projects. We know too well that a practice that worked well in Princeton may not work so well in Poland, and much like our children, engineers sometimes learn best from their own mistakes. But, if software and systems engineers can learn from our experiences and increase the probability of a successful project outcome, our efforts will be worthwhile.

Requirements engineering is most critically applied in the early phases of a systems development project, but it is a decision-making process that is applied across the entire product development life cycle. Thus, the requirements engineer must work effectively with software and systems engineers working on other tasks such as architecture design and test procedures. Indeed, our research in requirements engineering was initiated based on the observation that the first task for an architect on a new project is to understand the product requirements.

We have worked on projects for a broad range of application domains; e.g., medical equipment, factory automation, transportation, communications, automotive. The number of requirements that must be defined, analyzed, and managed in the projects may range from a few thousand to one hundred thousand. Many of our projects are distributed over multiple development sites, involving engineers living in many different countries. These software and systems engineers are often working under great pressure to deliver the product quickly, with good quality and a rich feature set. Most of the products contain both hardware and embedded software; thus, there are dependencies on electrical and mechanical characteristics, reliability, usability engineering, and requirements that must be considered by many different stakeholders. We often work within regulated domains such as medical devices where requirements must be carefully documented, traced, reviewed, and tested. We have also had to develop expertise on subjects that are not commonly taught at universities, such as hazard analysis.

Requirements engineering has become more complicated over time as the complexity of the products we desire to develop has increased. Thus, the requirements engineer is continually challenged by issues of scale, unstable requirements, product complexity, and managing change. Our experience has resulted from the opportunities to work on, for example, a project that is defining the requirements for an automobile infotainment system and then a few months later a project that is defining the requirements for a medical imaging system.

How to Use This Book

Our experience is with requirements engineering for products, systems, and services; typically (but not always) with high software content. This book contains RE methods, processes, and rules of thumb that have been derived from observed best practices of RE across many such projects. Thus, this book is meant for software and systems engineering professionals who are interested in learning new or validating their current techniques for RE. Such professionals include practicing requirements engineers, who should benefit most from the best practices discussed. But, the book material may also be useful to other engineering professionals, such as system architects, testers, developers, and engineering managers. The book may be useful to "not quite yet" practitioners such as graduate students in software engineering, systems engineering, or computer science. We would also hope that product or marketing managers would receive valuable information from this book as they struggle with bringing new products to a competitive market.

In order to focus on best practices and techniques for the practitioner, there is very little introductory material presented, but pointers are given to reference books that cover basic software engineering concepts. Thus, users of this book typically would have at least an undergraduate degree in computer science, systems or software engineering and some experience developing systems.

Acknowledgments

Since requirements engineers work across the entire development life cycle, they must interface with engineers working on specialized project tasks. We're fortunate to have had the experience of working with many talented software and systems architects, testing experts, project managers, and requirements engineers. Some of these experts have also collaborated with us on this book project as contributing authors. We acknowledge the contributions of these authors here as well as in the chapters they have written: Sascha Konrad, Raghu Sangwan, Hans Ros, Xiping Song, Bea Hwong, Marlon Vieira, Bill Hasling, Gilberto Matos, Bob Schwanke, and Brad Wehrwein.

Like software system development, writing a book can be done using a very iterative process. Once the author puts the first words to paper, there is an iterative (seemingly endless) process of review and rewrite, until we either become comfortable with the work or run out of time. We'd like to acknowledge the contributions of our review team: Capers Jones, Manfred Broy, John Worl, John Nallon, Stephan Storck, and Mark Sampson.

We'd like to acknowledge the contributions of our cartoonist, Johnol Jones, who helped to insert some humor into a usually serious subject, and our intern, Lindsay Ivins, who developed the figures and helped keep us organized when the page counts started to grow.

Finally, we'd like to acknowledge the support of our editor, Wendy Rinaldi, and the staff at McGraw-Hill and International Typesetting and Composition. Sometimes, just knowing that someone has confidence in us to complete the project is enough motivation to keep us working toward a successful completion.

Brian Berenbach
Daniel J. Paulish
Juergen Kazmeier
Arnold Rudorfer
Princeton, NJ 08540 USA

CHAPTER 1

Introduction

by Brian Berenbach, Arnold Rudorfer

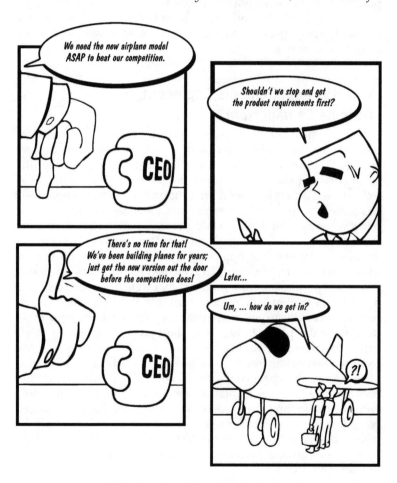

Studies such as the CHAOS report [Johnson 2000] indicate that about half of the factors associated with project or product success are requirements related. Recently, researchers have reported on studies showing that project success is directly tied to requirements quality [Kamata et al. 2007]. With such overwhelming evidence that requirements engineering is a cornerstone of software systems engineering, one could ask, why is it still a relatively neglected topic in university training? It is quite rare, for example, that a new Computer Science (CS) university graduate might be asked to participate in the development of a compiler or operating system, yet nearly every graduate working in the industry will, sooner or later, be asked to participate in creating the requirements specifications for a product or service.

1.1   Why Has Requirements Engineering Become So Important?

For years, many products were successfully created without the participation of professionals who specialized in requirements creation or management. So, why is requirements engineering (RE) so important today? The answer lies in the changing nature of industry and society in general. First, the pace of product development has picked up drastically. Whereas just a few decades ago, product improvements would be a slow process, today customers often demand new versions of a product in less than one year. For example, Siemens estimates that approximately 20 years ago, 55 percent of sales were from products that were less than 5 years old. Today, 75 percent of sales are from products that were developed less than 5 years ago (Figure 1.1). Second, turnover and technology change have impacted the experience levels of professionals engaged in the development of products. Just a few short years ago, engineers might expect to spend their entire careers with a single company, whereas today job change is more common. Finally, outsourcing and offshoring have dramatically changed the product life cycle. Specifications must now be created for implementation or manufacturing by organizations with potentially limited or no domain expertise. Imagine, for example, having to create a product specification for a washing machine, dishwasher, or luxury automobile to be built by staff who may have never even seen one! Under such circumstances specifications must be exact and detailed.

Software development is highly coupled to the domain; e.g., cell phone software and avionics software tend to be designed, built, and managed with processes that are heavily domain specific. Furthermore, industries have begun to use software as product differentiators. Product innovations can be more easily implemented in software than hardware because of the lower engineering

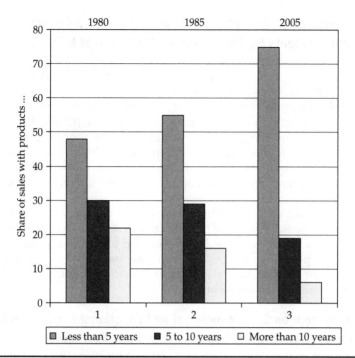

FIGURE 1.1   Acceleration of new product creation

investment and modification costs. This results in domain-specific, complex software for which high-quality requirements specifications are essential.

Requirements engineering is extremely important when a product, service, or industry is regulated. For example, the U.S. government's Food and Drug Administration (FDA) and Federal Aviation Administration (FAA) both mandate specific activities and work products (e.g., hazard analysis) where there is the potential for injury or death. Sarbanes-Oxley regulations mandate traceability for certain types of financial software used by companies doing business in the United States. The European Union and Japan have regulations for their respective businesses. Good requirements engineering practices are essential for companies that must comply with government regulations.

1.2   Misconceptions about Requirements Engineering

Misconceptions about requirements engineering can strongly influence a company's processes. Many companies and organizations have a solid understanding of requirements processes, but some do not. Some of the more common misconceptions are listed under the headings that follow.

Misconception 1: Any Subject Matter Expert Can Become a Requirements Engineer after a Week or Two of Training

Requirements engineers need strong communication and knowledge of engineering skills, the ability to organize and manage a data set of requirements, high-quality written and visual presentation skills, and the ability to extract and model business processes using both text and graphical (e.g., Integration DEFinition [IDEF], Unified Modeling Language [UML]) techniques. First and foremost, to elicit requirements from stakeholders requires the ability to interact with a variety of roles and skill levels, from subject matter experts (detailed product requirements) to corporate officers (elicitation of business goals).

Moreover, people have to be trained to write good specifications. High school and university training tends to teach a style of writing that is antithetical to the techniques needed to create unambiguous and complete documents. Requirements analysts typically need significant training, both classroom and on the job, before they can create high-quality specifications.

Misconception 2: Nonfunctional and Functional Requirements Can Be Elicited Using Separate Teams and Processes

The subject domains for nonfunctional and functional requirements are related, may impact each other, and may result in iterative changes as work progresses (see Chapter 5). Team isolation may do more harm than good.

Misconception 3: Processes That Work for a Small Number of Requirements Will Scale

Requirements engineering processes do not scale well unless crafted carefully. For example, a trace matrix is an $N \times N$ matrix, where N is the number of requirements of interest. In each cell, a mark or arrow indicates that there is a trace from requirement R_i (row i) to requirement R_j (column j). It is relatively easy to inspect, say, a 50-requirement matrix, but what happens when five to ten thousand requirements are needed to define a product? Filtering and prioritization become important in order to retrieve results that can be better understood, but the requirement annotations necessary to provide such filtering are often neglected up front because the database is initially small.

1.3   Industrial Challenges in Requirements Engineering

Over the last few years, the requirements engineering R&D focus program at Siemens Corporate Research has been involved with a substantial number of requirements engineering (RE) projects with Siemens development organizations. Many RE challenges have been identified as potentially impacting project performance. We have observed that problems tend to be exacerbated by three critical factors, the first being a decision to outsource the implementation, the second being a significant change in technology, and the third being the introduction of new products (e.g., entering a market where the company has minimal prior experience).

When a decision is made to outsource, changes must take place in all processes, especially in the area of requirements engineering. The implementation may be done by staff with minimal domain knowledge and, because of customs, logistics, time, or distance, with limited access to subject matter experts. Attempts to use the same processes and techniques used for in-house development for the development of specifications for subcontracting or outsourcing may lead to significant delays in delivery, sometimes even resulting in project cancellation.

When technology changes rapidly, domain experts may no longer be "experts." Techniques and solutions that worked for many years may become obsolete or irrelevant. Such technological discontinuities may require substantial new training, or the experts in the older technologies may make poor decisions for new product designs. A set of key success factors for identifying potential requirements engineering problems early has been developed at SCR and is described in the next section.

1.4 Key Success Factors in Requirements Engineering

This section contains a checklist describing key factors for success in requirements engineering. Most of the factors can be evaluated prior to project initiation. Although project success cannot be guaranteed, it is likely that if several of the success factors are not in place there may be significant project difficulties.

The Project Has a Full-Time, Qualified Chief Architect

On many large projects the only senior technical role that spans the requirements process through delivery is that of the chief architect. He provides technical continuity and vision, and is responsible for the management of the nonfunctional requirements (e.g., scalability, quality, performance, environmental, etc.) and for the implementation of the functional requirements. In our experience having an experienced, full-time architect on a project contributes significantly to its success [Hofmeister et al. 1999], [Paulish 2002].

A Qualified Full-Time Architect Manages Nonfunctional Requirements

The architect is responsible for managing nonfunctional requirements and the relationships among requirements analysis, development, and management.

An Effective Requirements Management Process Is in Place

The critical success factors in a requirements management process are well defined by the Capability Maturity Model Integration (CMMI), specifically those addressing change management and traceability. A *change control board (CCB)* performs an impact analysis and conducts cost/benefit studies when feature changes are requested. The CCB acts as a gatekeeper to prevent unwanted "scope creep" and ensures properly defined product releases.

Requirements Elicitation Starts with Marketing and Sales

The marketing and sales organizations and the project's requirements engineering staff must establish strong bonds to enable accurate definition of product and/or product line features. Incorrect features and requirements may be carried over into the requirements development activities and create downstream problems.

Requirements Reviews Are Conducted for All New or Changed Requirements or Features

Requirements must be reviewed, and the review must occur at the right level. Since it typically takes one hour to review four to ten requirements (e.g., for the first review—followup reviews may go faster), reviews must be conducted at a high enough level to avoid "analysis paralysis" and yet low enough to catch significant feature-level defects.

Requirements Engineers Are Trained and Experienced

Requirements engineering is like any other scientific or engineering endeavor in that the basic skills can be learned through training. But without experienced staff, the project may "stall" or "churn" in the requirements definition stage. If the staff is new, and the team has more than four members, RE mentors should be used to improve the skills of the team.

Requirements Processes Are Proven and Scalable

When processes are defined at the start of a project, they should be bootstrapped from prior successful efforts, not just based on "textbook" examples. As the size of a project increases, or the number or size of work products increases, the methodologies must be scaled to match.

Subject Matter Experts Are Available as Needed

Arrangements must be made early on to access the experts needed to assist in defining requirements. For example, during tax season, tax accountants and attorneys may be unavailable. Schedules cannot be defined unless the experts are available during requirements development.

All Stakeholders Are Identified

All the relevant stakeholders must be identified if requirements are to be properly defined and prioritized. The later key requirements are identified during the project, the greater the risk that major changes to the in-progress implementation will be necessary. Furthermore, the success of a product may be jeopardized by failure to validate key requirements.

The Customer Is Properly Managed

Customer management includes rapid feedback during prototyping, minimizing the number of points of contact between project staff and stakeholders, and maintaining strict control of feature change requests. It also includes using good techniques to elicit product features that are correct and unambiguous.

Progress and Quality Indicators Are Defined

The CMMI has a measurement and analysis practice area that overlaps with both requirements development and requirements management. Sometimes, a methodology (such as the Rational Unified Process [RUP] techniques for capturing text use cases) doesn't include progress or work product quality measures. These indicators must be defined in advance, or project management will find it difficult to gauge project progress and make appropriate corrections.

The RE Tools Increase Productivity and Quality

Any software tools used must enable a process (increasing productivity and CMMI compliance), rather than hinder it. Positive outcomes may require tool integration, customization, or, in rare cases where there is a justifiable cost benefit, creating a new tool from scratch.

The Core Project Team Is Full Time and Reports into a Single Chain of Command

Studies have shown that a full-time core team is essential to the success of a large project [Ebert 2005]. Without the continuity provided by a committed full-time core of people, issues may "fall through the cracks" or not show up until problems are revealed at integration testing time.

1.5   Definition of Requirements Engineering

"Requirements engineering [DoD 1991] involves all lifecycle activities devoted to identification of user requirements, analysis of the requirements to derive additional requirements, documentation of the requirements as a specification, and validation of the documented requirements against user needs, as well as processes that support these activities." Note that requirements engineering is a domain-neutral discipline; e.g., it can be used for software, hardware, and electromechanical systems. As an engineering discipline, it incorporates the use of quantitative methods, some of which will be described in later chapters of this book.

Whereas requirements analysis deals with the elicitation and examination of requirements, requirements engineering deals with all phases of a project or product life cycle from innovation to obsolescence. Because of the rapid product life cycle (i.e., innovation→development→ release→maintenance→obsolescence) that software has enabled, requirements engineering has further specializations for software. Thayer and Dorfman [Thayer et al. 1997], for example, define software requirements engineering as "the science and discipline concerned with establishing and documenting software requirements."

1.6   Requirements Engineering's Relationship to Traditional Business Processes

It is extremely important to tie requirements activities and artifacts to business goals. For example, two competing goals are "high quality" and "low cost." While these goals are not mutually exclusive, higher quality often means higher cost. Customers would generally accept the higher cost associated with a car, known for luxury and high quality, but would likely balk at paying luxury car prices for a car expected to compete in the low-cost automotive market.

Unfortunately, some organizations may tend to decouple business and requirements activities. For example, business goals may drive marketing activities that result in the definition of a new product and its features. However, the business goals may have no clearly defined relationship to the artifacts used and produced during requirements analysis and definition. RE activities start at the very beginning of product definition with business goals and innovation. Requirements engineering techniques can add an element of formality to product definition that can improve communication and reduce the downstream implementation effort.

1.7 Characteristics of a Good Requirement

Requirements characteristics are sometimes overlooked when defining requirements processes. They can be an excellent source of metrics for gauging project progress and quality. One question we typically ask organizations when discussing their quality processes is, "Given two requirements specifications, how would you quantitatively determine that one is better than the other?" This question may be answered by looking at the IEEE 830 Standard [IEEE 1998]. The characteristics of a good requirement, as defined by the IEEE, are listed next, with several additional useful ones.

It is important to distinguish between the characteristics of a requirement and the characteristics of a requirements specification (a set of related requirements). In some cases a characteristic can apply to a single requirement, in some cases to a requirements specification, and in other cases to the relationship of two or more requirements. Furthermore, the meaning may be slightly different when referring to a requirement or a specification. Care must be taken, therefore, when discussing the characteristics described here to define the context of the attributes.

Feasible

A requirement is *feasible* if an implementation of it on the planned platform is possible within the constraints of the program or project. For example, the requirement to handle 10,000 transactions per second might be feasible given current technologies, but it might not be feasible with the selected platform or database manager. So a requirement is feasible if and only if it can be accomplished given the resources, budget, skills, schedule, and technology available to the project team.

Valid

A requirement is *valid* if and only if the requirement is one that the system shall (must) meet. Determination of validity is normally accomplished by review with the stakeholders who will be directly responsible for the success or failure of the product in the marketplace. There can be a fine line between "must" and "nice to have." Because the staff of a development team may be mainly focused on technology, it is important to differentiate between stakeholder requests that are wishful thinking and those that are actually needed to make the project or product a success. The inclusion of requirements that are nice but not valid is called "gold plating." As the name implies, having requirements on a project that are not valid will almost certainly add cost without adding value, possibly delaying project completion.

The Use of the Terms "Valid" and "Correct"

The IEEE Standard 830 uses the term "correct." We use the term "valid" instead because "correct" can be misleading. Something that is "correct" is said to be "without error," or mathematically provable. However, in the context of a requirement, "valid" is more appropriate, as the requirement may be exactly what the customer wants, but it may still contain errors or be an inappropriate solution.

Unambiguous

A requirement is *unambiguous* if it has only one interpretation. Natural language tends toward ambiguity. When learning writing skills in school, ambiguity can be considered a plus. However, ambiguity is not appropriate for writing the requirements for a product, and care must be taken to ensure that there is no ambiguity in a requirements specification. For example, consider this statement:

"The data complex shall withstand a catastrophe (fire, flood)."

This statement is ambiguous because it could mean "The data complex shall withstand a catastrophe of type fire or flood," or it could mean "The data complex shall withstand any catastrophe, two examples being fire and flood." A person skilled in writing requirement specifications would rephrase as

"The data complex shall be capable of withstanding a severe fire. It shall also be capable of withstanding a flood."

An example of an ambiguous statement is "The watch shall be water resistant." An unambiguous restatement is "The watch shall be waterproof to an underwater depth of 12 meters."

A measure of the quality of a requirements specification is the percent of requirements that are unambiguous. A high level of ambiguity could mean that the authors of the specification likely need additional training. Ambiguity often causes a project to be late, over budget, or both, because ambiguity allows freedom of interpretation. It is sometimes necessary to take a holistic view of ambiguity; e.g., a requirement may be ambiguous, but when placed in the context of the background, domain, or other related requirements, it may be unambiguous. Product features found in marketing literature (e.g., shock resistant) are typically ambiguous. However, when placed in the context of the detailed specifications used by manufacturing, the ambiguity is no longer present. On the other hand, a requirement may be unambiguous, but when placed in the context of related requirements, there may be ambiguity.

When two requirements conflict with each other or create contextual ambiguity, they are said to be *inconsistent* (see the later section "Consistent").

Verifiable

A requirement is *verifiable* if the finished product or system can be tested to ensure that it meets the requirement. Product features are almost always abstract and thus not verifiable. Analysis must be done to create testable requirements from the product features. For example, the requirement "The car shall have power brakes" is not testable, because it does not have sufficient detail. However, the more detailed requirement "The car shall come to a full stop from 60 miles per hour within 5 seconds" is testable, as is the requirement "The power brake shall fully engage with 4 lbs. of pressure applied to the brake pedal." As we have noted, product features lack detail and tend to be somewhat vague and not verifiable. However, the analysis of those features and the derived requirements should result in a specification from which full coverage test cases can be created.

Modifiable

The characteristic *modifiable* refers to two or more interrelated requirements or a complete requirements specification. A requirements specification is *modifiable* if its structure and style are such that any changes to a requirement can be made easily, completely, and consistently while retaining the structure and style. Modifiability dictates that the requirements specification has a coherent, easy-to-follow organization and has no redundancy (e.g., the same text appearing more than once), and that it keeps requirements distinct rather than intermixed. A general rule is that information in a set of requirements should be in one and only one place so that a change to a requirement does not require cascading changes to other requirements.

A typical way of ensuring modifiability is to have a requirement either reference other requirements specifically or use a trace mechanism to connect interrelated requirements.

Consistent

In general, consistency is a relationship among at least two requirements. A requirement is *consistent* if it does not contradict or is not in conflict with any external corporate documents or standards or other product or project requirements. Contradiction occurs when the set of external documents, standards, and other requirements result in ambiguity or a product is no longer feasible to build. For example, a corporate standard might require that all user interface forms have a corporate logo in the upper-right corner of the screen, whereas a user interface requirement might specify that the logo be at the bottom center of the screen. There are now two conflicting requirements, and even though a requirements specification may be *internally* consistent, the specification would still be inconsistent because of conflict with corporate standards. Creating documentation that is both internally and externally consistent requires careful attention to detail during reviews.

Complete

A requirements specification is *complete* if it includes all relevant correct requirements, and sufficient information is available for the product to be built. When dealing with a high-level requirement, the completeness characteristic applies holistically to the complete set of lower-level requirements associated with the high-level feature or requirement. Completeness also dictates that

- Requirements be ranked for importance and stability.
- Requirements and test plans mirror each other.

A requirements specification is *complete* if it includes the following elements [IEEE 1998]:

1. Definition of the responses of the system or product to all realizable classes of input data in all realizable classes of situations. Note that it is important to specify the responses to both valid and invalid input values and to use them in test cases.

2. Full labels and references to all figures, tables, and diagrams in the specification and definitions of all terms and units of measure.

3. Quantification of the nonfunctional requirements. That is, testable, agreed-on criteria must be established for each nonfunctional requirement.

Nonfunctional requirements are usually managed by the project's chief architect. In order for the completed product to be *correct and complete*, it must include the testable requirements that have been derived from the high-level nonfunctional requirements.

It is difficult to create complete specifications, yet complete specifications are mandatory under certain circumstances; e.g., where the implementation team has no domain knowledge, or where communication between subject experts and developers will be problematic. We have seen projects where the requirements definition phase was shortened for schedule reasons. The general consensus was that "the developers will finish writing the requirements." But when doing a risk analysis, it was nearly always quite clear that having the developers complete the requirements was not an appropriate process, due to

- Limited access to subject matter experts
- Lack of experience or bias when defining product requirements

At the back end of the project, the failure to properly define the requirements almost always caused a greater delay than would have happened by allowing the requirements specification to be completed with the appropriate level of detail up front.

Traceable

Requirements *traceability* is the ability to describe and follow the life of a requirement, in both a forward and backward direction, i.e., from its origins, through its development and specification, to its subsequent deployment and use, and through periods of ongoing refinement and iteration in any of these phases" [Gotel et al. 1994]. Traceability is required for proper requirements management and project tracking.

A requirement is *traceable* if the source of the requirement can be identified, any product components that implement the requirement can easily be identified, and any test cases for checking that the requirement has been implemented can easily be identified.

Tracing is sometimes mandated by a regulatory body such as the Federal Aviation Administration (FAA) or Food and Drug Administration (FDA) for product safety. Furthermore, there are some rare situations where failure to create the appropriate traces between requirements can have legal repercussions. Traceability is discussed in more detail in Chapter 7.

Other Project- or Product-Specific Characteristics

Occasionally, the requirements for a specific project or product have characteristics that do not apply to all the projects or products. While it can be argued that an attribute that crosscuts all other requirements is just another requirement, when treated as a characteristic it is more likely that the requirement will be fulfilled. For example, if a new system is being built that must be downward compatible with an older system, it could be argued that the need for downward compatibility is just a nonfunctional requirement. However, we have found that having such all-encompassing requirements converted to characteristics makes it more likely that the completed system will be in compliance. A similar approach can be used for other "umbrella" requirements such as

- Compliance with Sarbanes-Oxley regulations
- Meeting all corporate security requirements
- Meeting electrical safety requirements

Characteristics of a Good Requirements Specification

As was stated in the definition of *consistency,* the definition of a characteristic may be different when applied to requirements and to a specification. A requirements specification is a filtered compendium of requirements. Having the requirements in a document rather than a database permits holistic views and allows the addition of history, a rationale, etc. There are certain characteristics that apply to specifications as opposed to individual requirements as listed here:

- A requirements specification is *feasible* if building the product specified is feasible given the state of technology, the budget, and the allotted time.

- A requirements specification is *unambiguous* if there is no pair-wise ambiguity in the specification.

- A requirements specification is *valid* if every requirement in it is valid.

- A requirements specification is *verifiable* if every requirement in it is verifiable.[1]

- A requirements specification is *modifiable* if there is no redundancy and changes to requirements are easily and consistently made; e.g., a change to one requirement does not require cascading changes to other requirements.

- A requirements specification is *consistent* if the requirement set is internally consistent.

- A requirements specification is *complete* if it provides sufficient information for complete coverage testing of the product or system.

- A requirements specification is *traceable* if every requirement in it can be traced back to its source and forward to test cases.

- A requirements specification is *concise* if the removal of any requirement changes the definition of the product or system.

---

[1] Product or business requirements specifications typically describe features, and as such there may be ambiguity and a lack of testability.

Requirements elicitation and analysis are typically done under project time constraints. Consequently, it is important to prioritize and identify risks when defining requirements. For example, "If this nonfunctional requirement is not completely analyzed, what are the risks to the project, the company, and/or the user?" By doing a risk analysis, the effort associated with fully defining a requirement set can usually be balanced against the needs of the project. Techniques for doing risk analysis of high-level requirements (e.g., balancing effort against need) will be discussed further in Chapter 5.

1.8   Requirements and Project Failure

It must be remembered that most systems under development are not new; i.e., only a fraction of the requirements in the product are new or unique [Jones 2007]. Yet issues of requirements maintenance and long-term support are often missing from project plans; e.g., the project plan is created as though the requirements will be discarded after project completion. When long-term requirements management is not planned, requirements creep can cause significant problems late in a project. Furthermore, Capers Jones reports that the defect rate increases significantly in requirements that are injected late over those that are created prior to the start of implementation, and the most egregious defects in requirements defined or modified late in a project can sometimes show up in litigation [Jones 2007].

1.9   Quality and Metrics in Requirements Engineering

As was mentioned in connection with the success factors for projects, project indicators need to be defined in order to have some measure of project transparency. It is important to be able to answer the questions "Am I making progress?" and "What is the quality of my work products?" How does one, for example, determine that a requirements specification is of high quality?

Requirement characteristics or quality indicators are extremely important for determining artifact quality. They can be measured by inspection (metrics), and the reported metrics can then be used to determine the quality of individual requirements and requirements specifications. Furthermore, metrics summaries tracked over time can be used to identify potential problems earlier to permit corrective actions, and provide guidance as to what type of corrective actions to take. For example, a high level of ambiguity in a requirement set might indicate that the analysts creating the requirements may need additional training in requirements writing. Some of the chapters in this book provide guidance on how to capture and use metrics to improve requirements processes.

Function Point Metrics as Leading Indicators

A function point is used to estimate the complexity and effort necessary to build a software product. Capers Jones has published extensively on this topic [Jones 2007, 2008]. Function point metrics are an excellent way of identifying potential problems with requirements prior to the implementation of a project. Furthermore, there is a clear correlation between function points and requirements; that is, function points can be used as an indicator of requirements creep and quality. Furthermore, it has been shown that function point analysis (FPA) can be effective in determining requirements completeness [Dekkers et al. 2001].

1.10   How to Read This Book

We suggest that you start by reading Chapters 1 and 2 before looking at any of the other chapters. They lay the groundwork for the remaining chapters by defining basic terminology that is used throughout the book.

Chapters 3 and 5 describe techniques for eliciting requirements. If you are interested in gathering requirements for software platforms or middleware, we also suggest that you read Chapter 6.

Chapter 4 describes modeling techniques that can be used for business or use case analysis. One specific method that has been used successfully at Siemens on several projects, the hierarchical decomposition of use cases, is described in detail.

Chapter 9 is devoted to rapid prototyping and describes a simple technique that has been found useful in the development of systems that are categorized by workflow and graphical user interfaces.

Chapter 7 describes techniques and best practices for requirements management. If you are interested in managing environments where the work may be distributed, then read Chapter 10 as well.

Chapter 8 describes advanced techniques for transforming requirements into test cases. It will be of interest to project and quality assurance staff. However, as Chapter 8 uses model-based methods, be sure to read Chapter 4 before reading Chapter 8.

Finally, Chapter 11 describes hazard and threat analysis and management in the context of a requirements engineering process. If you are an analyst working in a domain that is regulated or where there is the potential for physical or financial harm to an end user of a product, we recommend reading this chapter.

1.11   Summary

We've introduced some of the key challenges for requirements engineering and some of the success factors to achieve good RE. We've provided a definition of requirements engineering, and we've described the characteristics of a good requirement and a good requirements specification.

1.12   Discussion Questions

1. Why is good requirements engineering more important to product development than it was ten years ago?

2. What are the differences between good requirements and a good requirements specification?

3. What are some of the key full-time roles necessary for a project to be successful?

4. What is the role of the chief architect?

References

Dekkers, C. and Aguiar, M., "Applying Function Point Analysis to Requirements Completeness," *Crosstalk*, February 2001.

DoD 91, U.S. Department of Defense, *Software Technology Strategy*, December 1991.

Ebert, C., "Requirements BEFORE the Requirements: Understanding the Upstream Impact," *Proceedings of the 13th IEEE International Conference on Requirements Engineering (RE'05)*, 2005, pp. 117–124.

Gotel, O. and Finkelstein, A., "An Analysis of the Requirements Traceability Problem," *Proceedings of the First International Conference on Requirements Engineering*, Colorado Springs, CO, pp. 94–101, April 1994.

Hofmeister, C., Nord, R., and Soni, D., *Applied Software Architecture*, Addison-Wesley, Boston, MA, 1999.

IEEE Standard 830, *IEEE Recommended Practice for Software Requirements Specifications*, 1998.

Johnson, J., "Turning Chaos into Success," *Software Magazine*, Vol. 19, No. 3, December 1999/January 2000, pp. 30–39.

Jones, C., *Applied Software Measurement*, 3rd ed., McGraw-Hill, New York, 2008.

Jones, C., *Estimating Software Costs*, 2nd ed., McGraw-Hill, New York, 2007.

Kamata, M.I. and Tamai, T., "How Does Requirements Quality Relate to Project Success or Failure?" *Proceedings of the International Requirements Engineering Conference (RE'07)*, 2007.

Paulish, D., *Architecture-Centric Software Project Management*, Addison-Wesley, Boston, MA, 2002.

Standish Group Report, "CHAOS," http://www.projectsmart.co.uk/docs/chaos_report.pdf, 1995.

Thayer, R. and Dorfman, M., *Software Requirements Engineering*, 2nd ed., Los Alamitos, CA: IEEE Computer Society Press, 1997.

## CHAPTER 2

Requirements Engineering Artifact Modeling

by Brian Berenbach

*"Without goals, and plans to reach them, you are like a ship that
has set sail with no destination."*
—Fitzhugh Dodson

2.1   Introduction

In order to successfully reach a destination, travelers needs to know
where they are going. For most of the software and system
development life cycle, the work products are well understood, and
professionals generally have a reasonable understanding of how to
create them. Requirements engineering is somewhat different, since
it is a relatively new field in which fewer have worked; sometimes
the objectives can be a bit obscure or hard to define. A lack of well-
defined work products may result in ill-defined RE artifacts and
processes, with repercussions felt in the downstream phases of the
life cycle. This chapter discusses an important aspect of requirements
engineering work; that is, fully and accurately defining RE work
products and their relationships. While the examples shown here are
specific to RE, many of the techniques could (and in some cases
should) be extended to the entire project life cycle.

The purpose of requirements engineering artifact modeling is to

- Define a reference model for RE that provides the core set of
  RE artifacts (work products) and their interdependencies.

- Guide the establishment and maintenance of product- and
  project-specific RE processes [Geisberger 2006].

Thus, early requirements engineering activities include

- Analyzing marketing information, stakeholder, and user
  needs to derive the functional and nonfunctional requirements
  to be met by the system's design

- Understanding the effect of these requirements on the
  business that creates the product

- Consolidating these requirements into consistent and
  complete requirements and systems specifications as defined
  in the Requirements Engineering Artifact Model (REAM).

RE artifacts are used to support product design and project
management decisions throughout the entire product life cycle. The
quality and appropriateness of these artifacts is a key factor for
successful system development. Developing consistent and
comprehensive specifications of the "desired" system is an important
objective of RE.

Thus, the key components of requirements engineering artifact modeling are

- An RE artifact model as a measurable reference model that can be used to support interdisciplinary communication and specifications development
- A process tailoring approach that specializes the RE artifact model to specific organizational or project needs
- RE artifact-centered process guidelines that define *completion levels* of the RE artifact model. The specified completion levels form a baseline for measuring project progress and artifact quality.

2.2 RE Taxonomy[1]

It is important that all stakeholders and process participants in the development of products understand the meaning of each requirements engineering term to represent the same thing. If, for example, customers, product managers, and manufacturing understand the term "feature" to mean different things, there may be difficulty with quality assurance tasks and related productivity. While universal definitions exist for many terms in requirements engineering, there is still disagreement within the RE research community as to the meaning of some terms such as "nonfunctional requirement." Consequently, it may be necessary for an organization or project to create its own set of definitions wherever there is the potential for misunderstandings.

We recommend that a project or product team have a glossary of terms. An enterprise-wide dictionary is always preferable but may not be feasible; e.g., different parts of an organization may be working in different domains.

A *taxonomy* is a collection of controlled vocabulary terms organized into a hierarchical structure. Taxonomies are commonly used to *classify* things; e.g., a taxonomy of the insect world. An example of a taxonomy for requirements is given in Figure 2.1. In well-structured taxonomies, each term has only one parent. However, depending on need, it is possible to have poly-hierarchies where a term can have more than one parent. Figure 2.2 illustrates the difficulty of creating taxonomies; i.e., there may be multiple ways of representing concepts. Note that a term can appear in more than one place in a taxonomy.

---

[1] www.metamodel.com/article.php?story=20030115211223271

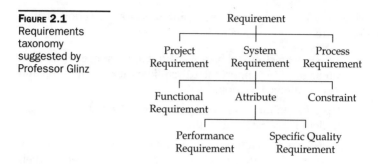

FIGURE 2.1
Requirements
taxonomy
suggested by
Professor Glinz

The difference between a *glossary* and a taxonomy is that in a glossary, terms are listed alphabetically and defined, whereas in a taxonomy, terms are grouped into classifications. To create a glossary, we recommend starting with a taxonomy of RE terms (e.g., Figure 2.1). The terms that would then go into the glossary are the leaves of the taxonomy tree plus any additional domain- or organization-specific terms.

A complete RE taxonomy would include the classification of all artifacts associated with a requirements engineering process, not just the categorization of requirement types. Since the artifacts can change from organization to organization or project to project, any such taxonomy would have to be extensible (see the later section "Using the Artifact Model").

Taxonomies can be quite extensive. As an example, see the fragment of the taxonomy for security requirements given in Figure 2.3 [Firesmith 2005].

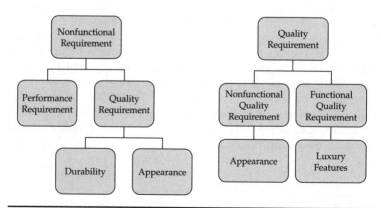

FIGURE 2.2   Two taxonomies illustrating differing representations of the same concepts

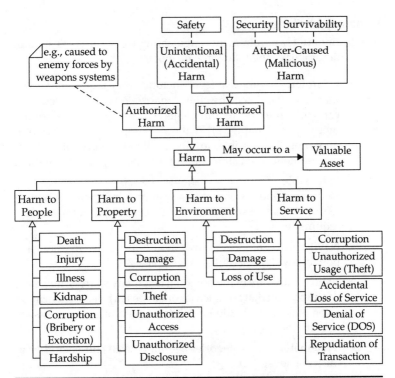

FIGURE 2.3 Sample taxonomy fragment for security requirements (Picture courtesy of Donald G. Firesmith, Software Engineering Institute, 2005)

A good starting point for creating a project- or product-specific taxonomy is the North American Industry Classification (NAICS) provided by the U.S. Government [NTIS 2007]. This classification system is a great starting point for creating a domain/project/product-specific taxonomy.

Getting Started with a Taxonomy

Capers Jones [Jones 2008] suggests the following approach as a starting point:

1. Start with the NAIC codes.

2. Using these codes, identify your industry or domain.

3. Then identify the scope (e.g., algorithm, prototype), class (e.g., internal product, external salable product), and type of application (e.g., batch, embedded software, mechanical panel).

Taxonomy Attributes

Any taxonomy for requirements engineering work products should, as a minimum, have the following attributes:

- **Complete** At the leaf level, include every requirement type that will be used by the organization or project. The categorization of requirements is critical when defining metrics (see Chapter 7). Without a proper categorization, it may not be possible to do a filtered query of a large requirements data store and return meaningful information.

- **Extensible** Companies should be able to take a core taxonomy and extend it. The sample fragment shown in Figure 2.3 is an example of a complex extension for security requirements.

- **Navigable** The taxonomy should be easy to navigate, possibly with hyperlinks on web pages.

- **Valid** There are many potential taxonomy sources; however, it is important that any such taxonomy used by an organization or on a product should be validated with other sources such as textbooks or experts.

- **Systematic** The categories should be well chosen and be at the same level.

Creation of an RE Taxonomy

There are many fine references and tools available to assist with the creation of taxonomies.[2] We recommend the following simple steps (see the starting point suggested by Capers Jones in the sidebar on the previous page):

- Identify the tooling that will be used and how the taxonomy will be presented to project staff, keeping in mind that the taxonomy may have to be updated periodically, and there may be links to other tools; e.g., the taxonomy and the artifact model that will be described in the next section are interrelated.

- Collect all the requirement types that are currently in use or planned. Group them together.

- If the project is an incremental development, mine the requirements for classes. Note that Capers Jones estimates that as many as 75 percent of all new projects are incremental changes to an existing product.

---

[2] www.loc.gov/flicc/wg/taxonomy.html

- Categorize by grouping and create a draft taxonomy. For example, network performance requirements, UI performance (response time), query response times, etc., might all be grouped under *Performance Requirements.*

- Make sure that complete, agreed-upon definitions are available for every term that will be in the requirements taxonomy, including parent terms.

- Create a draft taxonomy and circulate to stakeholders for comments.

- Revise and publish (usually to the web).

- Provide feedback and maintenance mechanisms (including processes and identified roles) for keeping the taxonomy up-to-date.

Other Types of Taxonomies Useful in RE

In addition to a "generic" RE taxonomy covering the classification of requirements, there are other artifact taxonomies that may be useful. For example, a *document classification taxonomy* can be used to identify common templates, assist with planning processes such as version control and baselining, and aid in the training of staff. The leaves of such a document classification taxonomy should all be real documents that are created by the organization or project staff. A partial requirements document classification taxonomy can be seen in Figure 2.4.

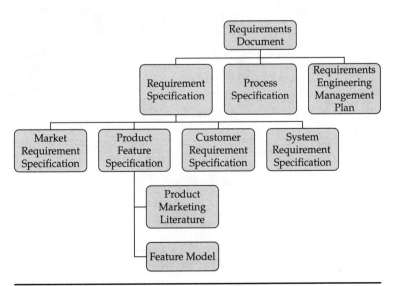

<small>**Figure 2.4**</small>   Sample partial taxonomy of requirement documents

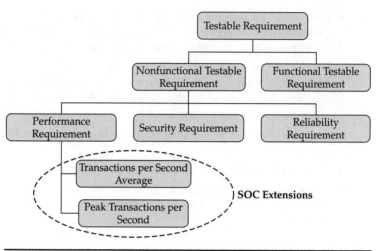

Figure 2.5   Sample extension of a taxonomy

Taxonomy Extension

To extend a taxonomy is a rather simple undertaking. The classification tree is extended with artifacts of the appropriate classification (see Figure 2.5). Figure 2.6 illustrates how detailed a taxonomy can become.

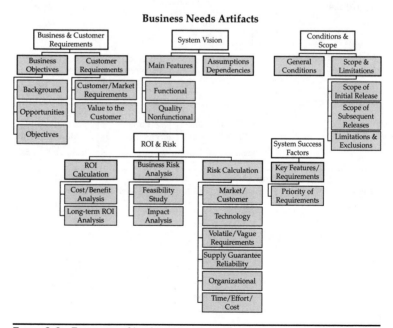

Figure 2.6   Taxonomy of business needs artifacts

If templates with the appropriate attributes are filled in for each artifact, process definition is much simpler (see the section "Extending an Artifact Model to Augment Process Definition").

2.3   RE Artifact Model

An RE artifact model (REAM) is a meta-model for the structuring of requirements engineering work products. A *meta-model* is an explicit model of the constructs and rules needed to build specific models within a domain of interest. An RE artifact model contains all the artifacts referenced, modified, or created during requirements engineering activities. The artifacts shown on REAM diagrams are those that are actually used in a project, and they each have a name and definition.

Upon first glance, the REAM diagram may appear similar to a software class diagram. However, there are some significant differences. A software class diagram may show many different types of relationships between objects, whereas an RE artifact model only shows simple associations (a single solid line). For example,

- Classes shown on a class diagram may have methods and attributes; an RE artifact only has a name and description.

- A class diagram may show abstract classes, or classes for which there is no physical representation; an artifact model only shows real objects that will be used or created during a requirements engineering activity.

An artifact model is different than a taxonomy in that it is a graph rather than a tree, has many more artifacts than what would be in a taxonomy, and typically contains many domain specific extensions.

Both a REAM and a taxonomy can be multitiered, so that selecting an object can open onto a different diagram. However, care must be taken in that while a taxonomy lends itself well to a hierarchical approach, artifact models tend to be flatter. For example, an object on one REAM diagram might have a relationship with an object on a different diagram.

Elements of an Artifact Model

A fragment of an artifact model is shown in Figure 2.7. It consists of the following elements:

FIGURE 2.7   Simple artifact model

- **Artifact**   A rectangular box with the name of the artifact. The definition of each artifact should be in a glossary or taxonomy accompanying the model.

- **Association**   A line connecting two artifacts. The line indicates that there is a relationship between the artifacts. Every association must be labeled to indicate the relationship between the artifacts.

- **Cardinality**   The cardinality indicates quantities. Any numbering convention can be used if appropriately defined; however, the Unified Modeling Language (UML) notation[3] is typically used. If the cardinality is not specified on an association, then unity is implied.

Figure 2.7, showing a sample model fragment, can be read as follows: "One or more actors participate in one or more use cases, and an actor can initiate one or more use cases."

Creation of a Requirements Engineering Artifact Model

The actual creation of an artifact model is not difficult. What is important is to have a holistic understanding of the business processes used from product creation through maintenance. It may be necessary to identify an individual within an organization who can interact with stakeholders across the different organizational units. Across the entire organization and product life cycle, then, these questions must be asked:

- What are the artifacts that the roles use?
- How are the artifacts related?
- Who creates them?
- Who modifies them?
- How do they become obsolete?

Consider, as an example, a small company creating a software product. They may have the following artifacts:

- Business plan
- Business goals
- Marketing brochure(s)
- Product features
- Customers
- Product definition
- Test plan

---

[3] The UML specification can be found at www.omg.org.

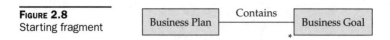

FIGURE 2.8
Starting fragment

- Test cases
- System requirements
- Customer requirements
- Product design
- ...

For creating the REAM, we first want to see how the products are related. We expect, for example, that a business plan will contain business goals (Figure 2.8). We can then model the artifacts and the relationships between them. We know that the business goals will be used as inputs to define the products. The products will be described in a marketing brochure (Figure 2.9).

Various techniques are used to define the features that the product needs to have in the marketplace to meet the business goals. At this point, product features have to be tied to business goals. Since the model is a simple construct, any drawing tool can be used to create one. UML modeling tools work quite well, as do general-purpose drawing tools such as Visio. However, it may be necessary to trace between different artifacts. Furthermore, it is important to have clear definitions of all the artifacts. This, in turn, may require stakeholder involvement. Also, if there is a taxonomy, all the leaves in the taxonomy should be in the artifact model. Since artifact models can be quite comprehensive, we may start with a subset. Let's say, for example, that, given the artifacts described, we wind up with an initial draft REAM as shown in Figure 2.10.

There are some things missing from this draft REAM that would have to be added, including metrics, artifact reviews, project plans, standards and procedures, and so forth. Here are some other important things to consider that tend to be neglected until well into the project:

- Internal training standards and procedures
- Maintenance requirements (e.g., how will the product be maintained, what are the artifacts that will be needed to properly maintain the product after deployment?)
- Product documentation, including training manuals, marketing literature, internal maintenance manuals, and so on
- Holistic tool support that works across organizational boundaries (e.g., from the help desk to design)

FIGURE 2.9
Next model
fragment

Marketing Brochure — Describes — Product
1..*

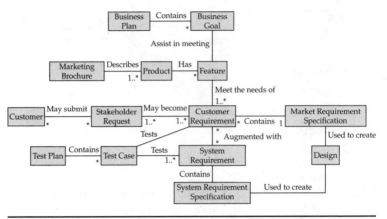

Figure 2.10   Example requirements engineering artifact model

2.4   Using the Artifact Model

The artifact model that is created prior to the start of a project is like looking at the X-ray of a patient prior to starting surgery. The model is used by most stakeholders (except possibly customers). Examples of the RE artifacts that will be used by the various roles of a development project are given in Table 2.1.

Extending an Artifact Model to Augment Process Definition

Artifact models can be extended to support process definition. For example, we may add artifacts such as completion status, decision gates, checklists, etc. (Figure 2.11). At the beginning of a project, a draft artifact model is created. The model is then used to define the product life cycle processes. After review, the artifact model and the defined processes are continually updated. While the upfront costs of creating a model may appear high, in our experience it is a very fast and cost-effective activity. Furthermore, just having project staff think about downstream artifacts, quality gates, and approval checklists can result in significant efficiencies.

2.5   Using Templates for Requirement Artifacts

A suggested way to get started creating a REAM is to use a template to fill in the information about each artifact in the model. A sample template is shown in Figure 2.12.

The template is filled out for each artifact and then maintained with the same tool used to create the drawings. As mentioned previously, commercial tools are available; however, for a staff with

Role (Cluster)	Objective	Functional Area	RE Artifacts
Product Management (ProdM)	Delivery of cost-effective products and solutions that meet customer needs	Planning and managing the entire life cycle of a product, including identifying customer needs, system vision, and scope	Business objectives, customer/user requirements, system vision, conditions and scope, product portfolio, return on investment (ROI), risks, system success factors
Requirements Engineering (RE)	Qualified and comprehensible/reusable product decisions	Refinement and analysis of business objectives, reasonable and consolidated modeling of customer/user and business processes (functional, domain, quality goals, constraints)	Analysis models of customer and business needs (functional, domain, quality goals, constraints), user interface and system specification, acceptance conditions
Systems Architecture (SA)	High-quality and cost-effective system design that meets business requirements	Specifying system architecture according to quality and business requirements, defining the system structure, decomposing the system into functional interface specifications	Comprehensible functional system specification, system integration and interface specification, release planning, system test criteria
Project Management (ProjM)	Delivering the product solution within project constraints	Planning and managing the product development, process definition, measurement and control	System specification, design constraints, risk analysis, process requirements and constraints
Development (Dev)	Build to specifications	Implementation of product solution, including (hardware) design, coding, integration, testing	System/interface specification, design constraints, integration plan, system test criteria
Quality Assurance (QA)	Ensure verified product quality	Review and measurement of all specifications according to domain-specific quality standards	Measurable specifications, system integration, and (acceptance) test specification
Release Management (RelM)	Incremental release of product features	Release planning and execution according to market strategy, system structure, development sequence, and integration	Release strategy, system specifications, release planning, corresponding system interface, integration and test specification

TABLE 2.1   Use of an Artifact Model by Project Roles

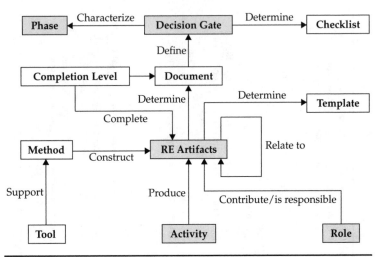

FIGURE 2.11   Process artifacts

developers it would be a relatively simple matter to extend a tool such as PowerPoint or Visio using the macro language. Once published to the web, the model and definitions are available to all the roles involved in the definition and creation of a product. A sample filled-in template for business and customer requirements is shown in Figure 2.13.

If the template is for an artifact that will be created by the staff associated with the product, we recommend creating a checklist

Artifact group		
Artifact X		Mandatory
Responsible:	*Contributing*:	
Description:		
Content item		Mandatory
Content item		Recommended
Content item		Optional
Purpose:		
References:		
Artifact Y		
Responsible:	*Contributing*:	

FIGURE 2.12   Sample artifact information template

or set of quality indicators (see Figure 2.11) that can be used to determine:

- What is the quality of the artifact? Does it need rework?
- Has the artifact been completed? What are the criteria for completion?
- What is the status of the artifact; e.g., suggested, draft, completed, sunset?

Business and Customer Requirements	Mandatory
Responsible: Prod M	*Contributing*: RE, SA

Description: The Business Objectives and Customer Requirements identify the primary benefits that the new system will provide to the customer and to the organization that is developing the system.

Business Objectives	Mandatory

Summarize the important business benefits the system will provide, preferably in a way that is quantitative and measurable. The background and business opportunities of the future system are described. This includes a description of business problems that are being solved, and a comparative evaluation of existing systems and potential solutions. The rationale for the system development is described, and how the system aligns with market trends or corporate strategic decisions is defined.

Customer Requirements	Mandatory

Summarize the needs of typical customers or users. Customer needs are defined at a high level for any known critical conditions, interface, or quality requirements. They provide examples of how the customer will use the system and identify the components (hardware and software) of the environment in which the system will operate. Explicitly define the value the customer/user will receive from the future system and how it will lead to improved customer satisfaction.

Purpose: Business and customer requirements serve as entry points to context analysis and the specification of the required features and characteristics of the *System Vision* and the definition of the general *Conditions & Scope* of the development.

By identifying the business objectives, the situation, and the critical conditions, collect business risks associated with the developing (or not developing) this system systematically as input to risk and cost/benefit analysis (*ROI & Risk*).

References: [Wie 1999] gives an overview of business requirements and provides a list of possible customer values.

Figure 2.13   Filled-in artifact template for business requirements

2.6   Dynamic Tailoring of an Artifact Model

Software projects come in different sizes and use different methodologies. Large plan-driven projects can take years to implement and have staffs of well over 100 developers. Small, agile projects might have just two or three developers, and the project duration could be as short as a week or two. When creating a REAM for a project, clearly one size does not fit all. If an organization has a range of projects on an ongoing basis, it is a good practice to provide some built-in tailoring facilities. An artifact, for example, could be mandatory on a "large" project, optional on a "medium-sized" project, and not used at all on a "small" project. If the project artifacts are tagged during the creation of the artifact model, it then becomes possible to filter and present the required information, or to couple it to a workflow used to reinforce the process. Tailoring techniques range from simple manual selection of artifacts to very sophisticated approaches such as the use of neural nets [Park et al. 2006]. Regardless of the tailoring approach, it will not work unless the artifacts in the model have attributes that permit them to be evaluated based on type, size, and duration of the project. An example of a small model used to define the artifacts for a prototyping effort can be seen in Figure 2.14. An example table fragment for defining tailoring rules is shown in Figure 2.15.

2.7   Organizational Artifact Model Tailoring

In addition to the tailoring of an artifact model for a specific project, high-level organizational models can be used as the starting point for the creation of project-specific models. An example is given in Figure 2.16. The starting point was a corporate-level model defining the core artifacts needed on any project. That model is then modified for the specific organization within the company, and finally the model is completed on a per-project basis.

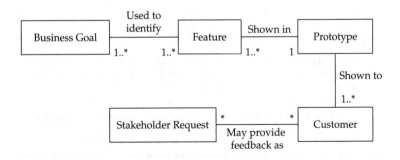

Figure 2.14   Artifact model for small prototyping project

Project Artifact	Prototyping	Small Agile	Medium Agile	Large Agile	Small Plan Driven	Medium Plan Driven	Large Plan Driven	Government Contract
Stakeholder Requests in Database	X	X	X	X	X	X	X	X
Requirements in Database			X	X		X	X	X
Customer Requirement Specification			X			X	X	X
Decision Gates			X			X	X	X
Business Goals		X	X	X	X	X	X	X
Feature Model			X	X			X	X

FIGURE 2.15   Sample table for tailoring RE processes

2.8   Creating a System Life Cycle Process

As was mentioned earlier, both a taxonomy and an artifact model are useful in the creation of system life cycle processes. By adding attributes to the artifacts that specify when they are needed (based on the type and size of the project), a query will result in the production of a list of all the appropriate artifacts. Project management can then use this list for planning, including the definition of decision and review points, work products needed, and quality artifacts needed to measure project quality and efficiency. An example process creation approach is illustrated in Figure 2.17.

Process creation to some extent can be automated, depending on how much of an investment the organization is willing to make in tooling. Automation of process creation can include

- Generation of selected project templates
- Assembly of standards and procedures from a library

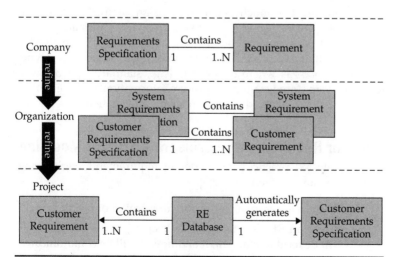

FIGURE 2.16   Organizational tailoring of an artifact model

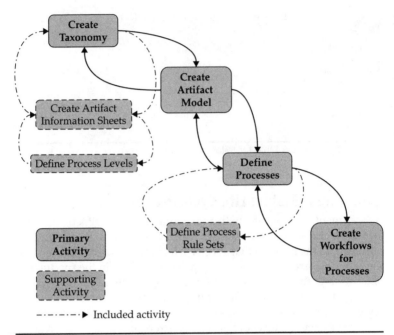

FIGURE 2.17 RE activities for process creation

- Drawing of a filtered, domain, and project-specific artifact model
- Population of a rule set for a workflow engine

In general, it is much better to have an "active" rather than a "passive" process. An *active process* is one where rules are used to prompt and inform staff about activities and provide templates for documents that have already been tailored based on the project type. A *passive process* is where documents (e.g., standards, procedures, templates) are stored containing process information, and the project staff has to download and read the relevant information.

2.9 Tips for Requirements Engineering Artifact Modeling

Some suggested practices for modeling requirements engineering artifacts are summarized below:

- Define a Glossary of Terms for your project or product.
- Create an RE Taxonomy while keeping in mind what tools will be used to maintain it and how it will be communicated to the project team (e.g., publish to a project web site).
- Develop an RE Artifact Model specific to your project.

- Communicate project roles to all team members and the artifacts they are responsible for as defined in the RE Artifact Model.

- Use templates to define RE artifacts.

- For scaling projects, provide tailoring information in the RE Artifact Model; e.g., a specific artifact may be mandatory, optional, or not used, depending on the project size.

- Tailor the RE Artifact Model for a specific project from any corporate-level models, if they exist.

- Create a system life cycle process by adding needed timing to the defined artifacts.

2.10   Summary

We have seen in this chapter how taxonomies are used to define and classify work products that are referenced, created, or modified during the requirements engineering process. A taxonomy is typically the starting point for the creation of a project glossary and a Requirements Engineering Artifact Model. An artifact model for an organization is essential for the definition of requirements engineering processes; however, the same techniques can be extended to defining the entire life cycle model. Organizations that have different types of projects need to be flexible in their approach to process definition, so that small projects will not be burdened with excessive bureaucracy and paperwork, while larger projects will have the infrastructure and tools necessary to succeed.

2.11   Discussion Questions

1. Where are taxonomies used outside of requirements engineering?

2. What are the differences between a taxonomy and a glossary?

3. What are some project roles, and which artifacts do they use?

4. Must each project create its own artifact model? Are there tailoring techniques to help select artifacts for different projects?

References

Berenbach, B., "The Evaluation of Large, Complex UML Analysis and Design Models," *Proceedings of the 26th International Conference on Software Engineering,* ICSE 2004, Edinburgh.

Firesmith, D., "A Taxonomy of Security Related Requirements," SEI, *International Workshop on High Assurance Systems (RHAS'05* – Paris), August 29–30, 2005, www.sei.cmu.edu/programs/acquisition-support/publications/taxonomy.pdf.

Geisberger, E., "Requirements Engineering Reference Model (REM)," Technical University of Munich Report, October 31, 2006.

Glinz, M., "A Risk-Based, Value-Oriented Approach to Quality Requirements," *IEEE Software*, March–April 2008.

Jones, C., *Applied Software Measurement*, 3rd ed., McGraw-Hill, New York, 2008.

National Technical Information Service (NTIS), *North American Industry Classification System (NAICS)*, U.S. Department of Commerce, 2007.

Park, S., Naa, H., Parka, S., and Sugumarun, V., "A Semi-Automated Filtering Technique for Software Process Tailoring Using Neural Networks," *Expert Systems with Applications*, Vol. 30, NO. 2, February 2006, pp. 179–189.

Wiegers, K., *Software Requirements*, Microsoft Press, 1999.

CHAPTER 3

Eliciting
Requirements

by Brian Berenbach

"The hardest single part of building a system is deciding what to build…
No other part of the work so cripples the resulting system if done wrong.
No other part is more difficult to rectify later."
—Dr. Fredrick P. Brooks, Jr.

3.1   Introduction

Elicitation is the process of identifying the needs and bridging the disparities among involved communities for the purpose of defining and distilling requirements to meet the needs of an organization or project while staying within imposed constraints. It involves all aspects of meeting with stakeholders, recording their needs, and classifying them into a manageable set of stakeholder requests that will later, through an analysis process, become requirements. There are many different elicitation techniques that can be used, and many of these techniques (brainstorming, for example) have been rigorously described in several texts [Clegg et al. 2007], [Conway Correll 2004], [Souter 2007]. We differentiate between elicitation and analysis as follows:

- *Elicitation* is the interaction with stakeholders to capture their needs.

- *Analysis* is the refinement of stakeholder needs into formal product specifications.

In this chapter, we will describe some of the more well-known techniques of elicitation from the perspective of what works, what is important, and how to drive a successful elicitation effort. Rather than describe any single elicitation technique in detail, we will review some commonly used techniques, suggest some best practices, and identify problems that can arise during elicitation and how to address them.

As Dr. Brooks points out in the opening quotation [Brooks 1995], one of the most difficult parts of the development life cycle is the identification of key requirements. Analysts can sometimes begin working on a project with a predisposition or bias that may impact their work. For example, if software developers are given the task of defining product requirements, they may start with solutions with which they are most comfortable, e.g., "Sentence first—verdict afterwards."[1] Analysts must be trained to separate solutions from requirements when transcribing client needs and creating requirements specifications.

We start by discussing some of the difficulties in successfully eliciting the requirements for a product or service, including the different types of situations that can affect the approach used for collecting requirements. We then discuss key issues. Finally, we discuss approaches that can be used to elicit customer needs along with some metrics that can be used to measure progress.

---

[1] As stated by the red queen in *Alice's Adventures in Wonderland* by Lewis Carroll.

3.2   Issues and Problems in Requirements Elicitation

Eliciting requirements from stakeholders can sometimes become a painful, drawn-out, and thankless task. Collecting requirements may be viewed as an afterthought or assigned to junior staff. There may even be situations where there are no documented requirements until the project is nearing completion and the staff realizes that requirements are necessary to create test cases, or even worse, a requirements review is necessary for client acceptance or payment. A difficult task may then begin to reverse-engineer requirements for a system that is already in system test or nearing completion. When requirements are reverse-engineered from a product under construction purely for contractual reasons, the finished system may not meet the client's needs or be accepted. If the definition of nonfunctional requirements is delayed until the end of the project, the system may turn out to be inadequate for the intended purpose; e.g., it may not meet the needed performance, reliability, or security goals. Typical situations that may impede or otherwise affect the requirements elicitation process are described in the sections that follow, along with suggestions for handling them.

The Missing Ignoramus

Elicitation should be led by senior staff members with experience and training in requirements elicitation techniques. An elicitation team composed of a mixture of experienced staff and not-so-experienced staff enables the mentoring and training of less-experienced members of the team. Furthermore, it is usually advisable to have someone involved with the elicitation process who has no domain knowledge, e.g., someone who is not afraid to ask "what does that mean?" Professor Dan Berry of the University of Waterloo refers to such an analyst as a "smart ignoramus" [Berry 1995]. Without such people present, situations can arise where insufficient information is collected, or worse, the same term is used to mean different things. On one occasion one of the authors was the facilitator in a brainstorming session to gather requirements for a payroll system for automobile dealerships. During a discussion of contractual issues he asked the simple question "what is a contract?" Several managers were dumbfounded that he should ask such a question—after all, it was perfectly obvious what a contract was. Yet it still took three days for the participants to agree on a viable definition of contract.

It is beneficial to have the elicitation team ask the question "why?" When a need is identified, by asking why, you may find legitimate reasons for the need, or you might find out it is "feature folklore." Folklore is something that has been done on every project, but such features have no value to the customer and nobody knows why they are there. This can result in the elimination of an unnecessary need that turns into a requirement that you implement and the customer does not want.

The Wrong Stakeholders

A stakeholder or subject matter expert may not speak for an entire organization. It is important during elicitation that the team capturing the data understands the relationship of the expert to the organization and project; i.e.:

- Is the expert speaking for the entire organization?

- Are there differences of opinion regarding functionality or issues that have not been resolved?

- Are the stakeholders knowledgeable about the domain under discussion?

Untrained Analysts

An untrained analyst may be a very senior, skilled, or business-savvy person. However, the job of the analyst is to capture organization, project, or product needs, and not to engage in wishful thinking or make solution decisions.

On occasion, we have used software developers or database staff to assist in capturing stakeholder requests (note: requests are not requirements until they have gone through a review process and been accepted). It can be very difficult for an untrained person to separate need from solution. For example, database analysts might think of database configurations as they conduct interviews and place their thoughts in with the stakeholder requests. For example: "There shall be a table for storing customer names and addresses" rather than "The new system shall store customer names and addresses." Similarly, developers will naturally try to design as they capture needs or define requirements: "The customer names shall be cached to ensure rapid retrieval" as opposed to "The new system shall be able to rapidly retrieve customer names and addresses."

Not Identifying Requirements Level

Requirements are often captured at different levels of detail (see Figure 3.1). For example, "The car shall have power steering" recorded alongside "The power steering coupling shall use metric

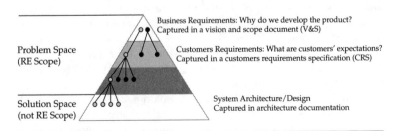

Figure 3.1   Requirements pyramid

hex head screws." Meetings to elicit requirements can be sometimes chaotic, with customers rambling or not necessarily focusing on one specific topic. While it is important to have stakeholders' focus, it is also important not to lose any worthwhile information. Therefore, when stakeholder requests are captured, it is important to tag the information recorded with one or more attributes describing the level of the captured information, along with which stakeholder is requesting it. For example,

"We want to have the safest car on the market. So we plan to have an interlock system between the brake and the transmission. The interlock will decouple the transmission when the brake is pressed. We should use ½-inch stainless steel for the decoupling rod for safety purposes, and to prevent corrosion in climates where salt is used on the roads from eroding the coupling."

In this example there are requirements at several levels, along with some design decisions mixed in with the requirements. When captured and placed in a requirements database, the tagging might look as shown in Table 3.1.

Note that the selection of stainless steel was removed because it was a proposed solution, not a requirement.

Failure to Accurately Identify Stakeholders

Imagine being at a meeting with ten or fifteen stakeholders representing hospitals and health care networks. One stakeholder suggests a product feature that would allow patients or doctors to schedule appointments for medical services over the web. Another stakeholder feels that it is a good idea, but not as urgent as having doctors schedule appointments and services from their PDAs. During prioritization meetings it is determined that both requests cannot be satisfied in the first release of the hospital scheduling system. One of the requests came from a ten-thousand-bed health care network, and the other request came from a small, one-hundred-bed hospital.

Request	Request Type (or Level)	Stakeholder
Safest Car on the Highway	Business Goal	Sales VP Smith
Interlock Between Brake and Transmission	Customer Requirement	Rental Car VP Jones
Corrosion-Resistant Coupling Mechanism	System Requirement	Engineering Mgr. Carlson

TABLE **3.1**   Level of Requirements

Unfortunately, while the meeting information is available, the names of the customers requesting the features were never recorded. Thus, the information needed for prioritization and release scheduling is missing. So, it is very important to record stakeholder information when collecting product requests.

Problems Separating Context from Requirement

Eliciting stakeholder requests to create requirements can be a difficult task when stakeholders ramble. Sometimes, stakeholders will confuse background with need. For example,

> "We need to have cars stop at the intersection when the light changes in order to avoid accidents. Drivers should therefore be able to see the signal from at least 50 feet away in the rain, and then apply their brakes if the light is red. We do not want drivers going through red lights."

In the preceding paragraph there is only one real potential requirement, that the drivers should be able to see the signal from at least 50 feet away. Everything else is either wishful thinking or out of scope for requirements for a signaling system. It is possible that a township might insist on a contract clause that states "after installation of the signaling system there will be no more accidents caused by cars running red lights." However, it is not physically possible for any commercial traffic signal system to guarantee that there will not be any accidents, since drivers and their cars are not controlled by the system and furthermore, even if they were, no system can have perfect reliability.

One way to prevent the intermixing of requests and requirements with need is to carefully separate context and background from stakeholder requests. Requests are something that the system *shall* do. Context might include information about the way the environment *will* be impacted by the system after installation. Context might also include background information about the reason the system is being purchased or created; it might include background information describing the environment. We recommend that background information be kept in separate documents or, at the least, in separate sections of a document, e.g., sections on what the customer would like to accomplish, and the customer's environment before and after the system being proposed is operational. Under no circumstances should the *"will"* statements appear in a requirements specification. Specifications may become part of binding contracts, and it is important to avoid having wishful thinking or expected external behavior contractually guaranteed by a supplier.

Failure to Collect Enough Information

Some stakeholders or domain experts can be difficult to track down and meet with. Problems of elicitation can be exacerbated if a key subject matter expert is available for only limited periods of time. On a taxation system project that we worked on, for example, the requirements engineers were informed that the tax accountants and attorneys were very busy (during tax return preparation season) and could meet with the analysts only one hour a week.

Once an elicitation cycle is completed, it can be difficult in some cases to revisit open issues with stakeholders. Therefore, it is important to collect as much information as possible during elicitation sessions. One way to do this is to have representatives of development, manufacturing, and testing present their requirements wishes during elicitation sessions. We also recommend that access to subject matter experts be part of the initial planning for a project. Very often the people who know the most about a topic are those a company may rely most heavily on, and consequently, their availability may be very limited.

Requirements Are Too Volatile

Capers Jones and Walker Royce have estimated that for most projects there is a 1–3 percent change per month in the meaning or interpretation of requirements [Jones 2008], [Royce 1998]. If needs are changing rapidly, defining a stable set of product requirements may not be feasible. It may be necessary to wait until there is some level of stability before attempting to finalize a baseline requirement set for a product (Figure 3.2).

System Boundaries Are Not Identified

Several years ago one of the authors worked on the requirements for an insurance underwriting system. As underwriting systems are used by

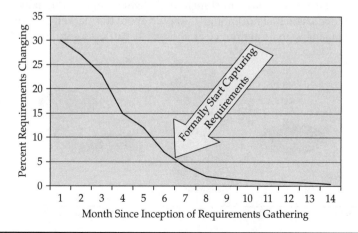

Figure 3.2   Requirements volatility vs. time

many functions within the insurance industry, there were interactions with sales, marketing, policy writing, accounting, and independent insurance agents. The requirements gathering was being done in a distributed fashion, so it was important to ensure that there was no duplication of work, and that time was not spent on topics that were out of scope (e.g., how marketing uses underwriting information). High-level, color-coded models were used to indicate the distribution of work and identify out-of-scope topics (see Figure 3.3).

Understanding of Product Needs Is Incomplete

Analysts are often asked to help define requirements for products where the stakeholders are uncertain of their needs. Sometimes they are even uncertain as to what the business goals are. There are several techniques that can be used to assist in clarifying customer needs. One method, prototyping, is discussed in detail in Chapter 9. Sometimes, just the act of eliciting requirements with several stakeholders present will stimulate discussion and help to clarify customers' needs. Another technique that we recommend is to start by creating marketing literature, a user manual, or lightweight specification sheets for the product. For example, create a simple, two-page marketing brochure or fictional product advertisement that might be given to customers:

- Is it what the customers want and need?
- Is it feasible to build (with the available technology, time, and budget)?
- Does it adequately describe, at a high level, the proposed product features?
- Does it indicate why customers should buy it (e.g., over the competitive products)?

Such a mock marketing brochure development task might lead to the conclusion that not enough is known about the market, or perhaps the business goals are not clear enough. If work does go forward to

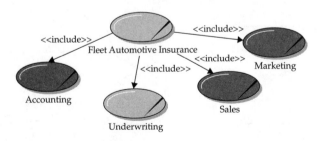

FIGURE 3.3   Using color to identify subjects that are out of scope

create a full requirements specification and to design and build the product, then, at the very least, the product vision will be described in an internal document.

Users Misunderstand What Computers Can Do

Stakeholders may ascribe virtues to computer systems that are futuristic, wishful thinking, or simply impractical. For example,

> "We would like the new payroll system to automatically detect the employee's marital status from public records."

It is important for analysts to adjust the phrasing of stakeholder requests so that a reasonable discussion can be held on whether to make the requests requirements or not, e.g., feasibility, legality, and practicality. However, it is a good idea to record cutting-edge requests, as they may go from cutting-edge to commonplace in short order. For example, in 1992, we saw the following statement in a requirements specification:

> "As there will never be a need for computers to have more than one processor, there is no need for a requirement for the new system to support multiple processors."

The Requirements Engineer Has Deep Domain Knowledge

If a requirements analyst has strong domain knowledge, there may be a tendency to minimize communication with stakeholders. That is, the analyst may try to do it all himself or herself without seeking outside validation or views. Failure to communicate with external stakeholders can be especially dangerous in a domain where technology is changing rapidly (e.g., cell phones).

Stakeholders Speak Different Natural and Technical Languages

When stakeholders are from different domains or speak different languages, communication can be even more difficult. Problems may arise in several areas, such as

- Ensuring efficient quality reviews of requirements
- Smoothly running elicitation sessions
- Domain experts understanding the impact of stakeholder requests made in one area on their area
- Understanding complex needs, processes, or algorithms

Because of the difficulty in getting stakeholders and analysts to understand and review each other's work, we recommend wherever possible using visual techniques, including models, diagrams, and tables, to communicate important concepts.

Stakeholders Omit Important, Well-Understood, Tacit Information

On occasion, a stakeholder or domain expert may be "too close" to the material he or she is describing and forget to include salient points, assuming that the material is so basic that it does not need to be communicated. You may have been in a situation where you were reading the instructions for doing something, could not get it to work, and then found out that steps were missing from the instructions. For example,

> "To drive a stick-shift car, start the engine, put the car in gear, and go!"

Of course, there are a few missing steps such as putting the key in the ignition and making sure that the clutch is pressed in order to start the engine. But a driver who uses such a car every day might take for granted putting the key in the ignition and pressing down on the clutch, while someone who has never driven before might realize that some steps had been left out. The "smart ignoramus" (see the earlier section "The Missing Ignoramus") can help, but a trained analyst or facilitator is really necessary during elicitation sessions to ensure that every last detail needed to define a product is captured. There is also a crossover point between elicitation and analysis; sometimes the boundary between the two activities is clearly defined, and sometimes it is not.

Stakeholders Have Conflicting Views

When stakeholders have conflicting views, a heated discussion (possibly started by the "smart ignoramus" asking a question) may ensue. The conflict must be resolved, but not during the elicitation session (unless it is just a matter of a minute or two). Conducting an elicitation session requires the same skill at moderation or facilitation as any other professional meeting, and complex or lengthy discussions need to take place elsewhere to avoid a loss of productivity. Facilitation of brainstorming sessions is described in more detail in the next section.

3.3   Requirements Elicitation Methods

As mentioned early in this chapter, requirements elicitation is the interaction with stakeholders to capture their needs. No decisions have been made at this point about which of the needs will become requirements, and which of the requirements will be included in a release of the product that is yet to be built. Furthermore, in many cases the same techniques can be used for both elicitation and analysis (Figure 3.4). As there are so many different ways to capture stakeholder needs, we only mention a few here. The reader is encouraged to seek out techniques that are appropriate to their situation.

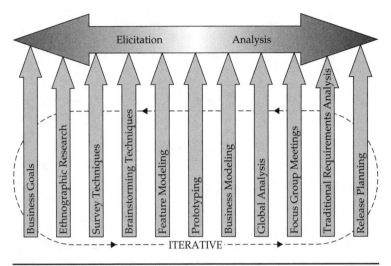

Figure 3.4   Example elicitation and analysis methods

Eliciting Business Goals

A sometimes overlooked aspect of requirements elicitation is the determination of business goals. These goals are associated with the needs of the manufacturing or development organization rather than the needs of the customer or purchaser. For example, sample business goals might be

- Increase profitability by 5 percent the next fiscal year.
- Customers should associate our product with high quality.
- Customers should associate our product with best value.
- Our next product should take advantage of emerging technologies.

One way of visualizing and capturing business goals is a simple graphical technique known as goal modeling. Two of the more popular techniques are KAOS [Dardenne et al. 1993] and I* [Yu 1993]. A nice survey of different goal modeling techniques can be found in the article by van Lamsweerde [van Lamsweerde 2001].

Goal modeling is a nice way to crystallize ideas, to present corporate goals in a simple-to-understand and unambiguous way, and to identify and balance difficult choices. In Figure 3.5, we see a simple goal model fragment, where a plus sign indicates that the lower-level goal contributes to the higher-level goal, and a minus sign indicates that the lower-level goal detracts from the higher-level goal. If the additions and detractions can be quantified, then the selection of

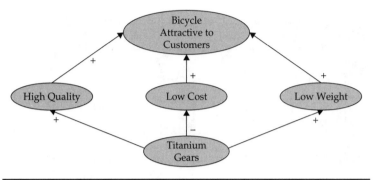

FIGURE **3.5**   Simple goal model fragment

the optimal goal set can be calculated. However, the reality is that the contribution of many high-level requirements cannot be calculated for a variety of reasons, including changing demographics, rapid shifts in technology, etc. Sometimes, difficulties associated with conflicting goals are not recognized until the requirements have gone through a complete review cycle. The refinement of nonfunctional requirements can bring to light issues that may otherwise remain hidden. The importance and impact that nonfunctional requirements can have warrant their consideration and elicitation as early as possible in the product development cycle.

Goal models can be as simple or as complex as necessary. Figure 3.6 shows some of the goals for a nuclear power plant simulator. Such simulators, mandated by regulation, are used to train the operators of nuclear power plants and must have high fidelity and reliability. The figure shown identifies quality assessment methods, or QAMs, that are used to determine how well the business goals meet the desired quality [Cleland-Huang 2005]. For example, QAM 5 states that when any action is taken, the simulator indicator light response shall be within 200 milliseconds of the response in the real plant. That is, if a button is pressed in the power plant closing a valve and an indicator light comes on in three tenths of a second, then in the simulator, that light must come on within three to five tenths of a second. The actual QAM was evaluated by randomly connecting an oscilloscope to button/light pairs (there were thousands of such pairs) in the simulator and determining that the response was within specification by measuring the step wave on the oscilloscope. Goal models with QAMs can be used as checklists to ensure that important nonfunctional requirements have not been overlooked. If a QAM cannot be defined for a nonfunctional requirement, then it may not be possible to test that the requirement has been met, and the requirement should then not be part of a contract or requirements specification, as it may not be feasible to implement.

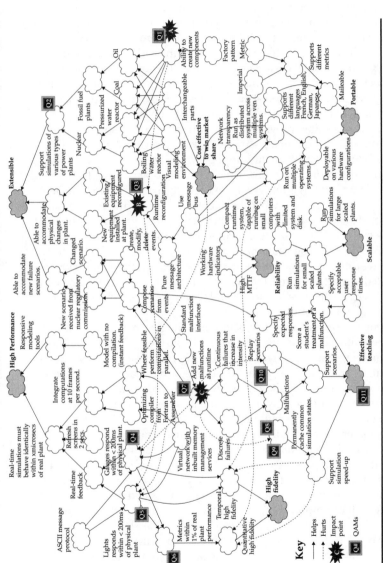

Figure 3.6 Partial goal model for a nuclear power plant simulator (Picture courtesy of Professor Jane Cleland-Huang, DePaul University, 2005)

Ethnographic Techniques

Ethnographic research tends to focus on a particular community or culture [Agar 1996]. Typical collection methods are interviews and surveys. These are techniques not normally thought of as being a part of requirements engineering, yet some survey methods are heavily used to evaluate market demands, possible interest in a product, and even emotional content. Furthermore, where there is a large customer base to draw on, it is possible to perform statistical analyses on surveys to measure customer interest or the emotional appeal of product features. One of the most common survey methods for analyzing customer interest in features is Kano modeling, named after its inventor, Professor Noriaki Kano [Kano 1984].

Kano modeling provides three variables to measure customer interest: one-dimensional, expected, and attractive quality. One-dimensional, or linear quality, applies where the potential value of a product feature increases linearly with some aspect of the feature. A good example of this is refrigerator energy efficiency. The more efficient the refrigerator is, the greater the likelihood it will attract purchasers. Expected quality is a feature that is mandatory for a product to succeed in the marketplace. Attractive quality is a feature that is not expected but would add to the emotional appeal of a product. Product features can have different types of Kano quality variables, depending on locale, targeted market, and time. For example, a camera in a cell phone would have been an attractive quality several years ago but is now an expected quality in most markets.

One interesting aspect of Kano modeling is that measurements can be culturally sensitive. For example, in the United States most automobile customers would expect to purchase a car with an automatic transmission, while in Europe, a manual transmission is the norm. Kano modeling is widely accepted; some commercial requirements engineering management software tools come with Kano analysis facilities built in.

Another interesting use of survey and interview techniques is the measure of the emotional appeal of a product feature. Engineers and software developers are often not aware of or interested in the emotional appeal of their products, yet such factors can have important consequences for product sales. One extreme example of failing to take emotional appeal into consideration is the case of the Ford Edsel. The *Washington Post* called it the "The Flop Heard Round the World" [Carlson 2007]. After the car was introduced, customer response was extremely negative, including comments such as "an Oldsmobile sucking a lemon" and "a Pontiac pushing a toilet seat."

Prioritization and Ranking of Requirements

While prioritization and ranking of requirements typically occur after analysis (or even later), the topic is worth mentioning here, as customer priorities are best captured during elicitation.

First, we should mention the difference between the two, as there tends to be some confusion regarding the use of the two terms. Prioritization is the assignment of importance to a requirement using a tag or label. For example,

- "The base engine sold with the car shall be a 1.8 liter turbocharged engine"—priority *high*.
- "18 inch wheels shall be offered as an option with the car"—priority *medium*.

Priorities are usually defined at the start of a project, using either a numerical or verbal ranking; e.g., 1 means most important and 5 means least important (a numerical ranking has the advantage of being sortable).

When priorities are assigned to requests and requirements by stakeholders, only one of the defined values is acceptable.

Ranking is the assignment of a unique order to each requirement in a group, such that no two requirements have the same rank. For example,

Under $100 street price	1	(the lower number is more important)
Built-in camera	2	
Operable with one hand	3	
LCD panel can be seen in daylight	4	

When deciding which features will be in a product release, a ranking technique is normally used, whereas prioritization is used more for initial scoping. When questionnaires or surveys are sent out to customers, they will typically be asked to assign a priority to a feature (e.g., more likely to buy the product, no difference, less likely to buy the product).

A common problem can occur when customers label their stakeholder requests as being of "high," "medium," or "low" priority, since to some customers, every request will be of "high" priority.

An effective approach when scoping a product or planning schedules or releases is to use pairwise ranking [Karlsson 1996], [Sobczaka et al. 2007]. Pairwise ranking, sometimes called the

"Analytic Hierarchy Process" (AHP), is where the stakeholder or analyst ranking the requirements looks at only two requirements, compares them, and ranks them; e.g., the more important of the two is placed higher in a list. This process is done iteratively until all the requirements have been ranked. While the approach may work well for small requirements sets, as the number of requirements N increases, the number of rankings that must be done increases quadratically ($N(N - 1)/2$) [Sheehan et al. 2000]. Since different stakeholders may rank the same requirements set differently, an approach must be formulated to merge the different sets of ranked requirements. We therefore recommend that a pairwise ranking prioritization be restricted to stakeholder requests or product features (near the top of the pyramid), to reduce the ranking effort.

Another technique used to prioritize requirements is the "planning game," or PG, approach, popularized with extreme programming [Beck 1999]. In the PG approach, stakeholder requests, features, or requirements (depending on when prioritization takes place) are partitioned into three sets that align with Kano qualities: "needed for the system to function," "add real value," and "nice to have but not necessary." An informal risk analysis is done to determine the ease of implementation effort, and a final decision is made as to which features or requirements to implement.

Ranking cannot take place in a vacuum; e.g., the cost and risk associated with implementation must be known. Furthermore, in some industries additional factors such as hazards (to the consumer) and technology shifts must be considered. For example, a novel technique for opening and closing car windows is evaluated that uses a light sensor; i.e., no physical contact with the switch is required. The cost to implement is low, customers evaluate the feature very highly, and it seems to have high positive emotional value. However, the hazard analysis (see Chapter 11) indicates the potential for an unsafe condition, as a child can be hurt or injured when the window rises accidentally. As a result, the feature is not included in the next year's car model.

In summary, initial prioritization of stakeholder requests should take place as early in a product life cycle as possible. Several prioritization activities may be needed, one just for the stakeholders, another when the architect or designers evaluate the cost and risk of implementation, and possibly additional sessions prior to the build/ no build decision. Prioritization should be accomplished as far up the requirements pyramid as is feasible, with ranking taking place once the requirements are sufficiently finalized such that the cost and resource impact of implementation is understood. Furthermore, some techniques such as pairwise ranking may not be feasible with a large number of requirements, e.g., rank at the feature level and not at the system level. Prioritization (and the ranking of small sets of requests) can be combined with the stakeholder review process where the determination is made as to whether a request is "in" or "out"; i.e., will or will not become part of the approved requirements set.

Quality Function Deployment (QFD) Method

QFD was developed by Drs. Shigeru Mizuno and Yoji Akao in an effort to integrate customer needs into product designs [Akao 1990]. According to the QFD Institute,[2] the QFD method:

1. Seeks out spoken *and* unspoken customer needs from the fuzzy voice of the customer verbatim.

2. Uncovers "positive" qualities that wow the customer.

3. Translates these into design characteristics and deliverable actions.

4. Builds and delivers a quality product or service by focusing the various business functions toward achieving a common goal—customer satisfaction.

As QFD is well documented, it will not be described here. QFD is often part of a Six Sigma program [Mikel et al. 1999]. The "house of quality" matrix (so named because the matrix shape resembles a house) is a widely used technique for capturing unspoken customer needs and then correlating them with requirements.

Brainstorming Sessions

Brainstorming sessions are widely used to elicit initial stakeholder requests for products. They tend to take place with multiple stakeholders or customers, and the sessions are usually managed by experienced facilitators in one session over one or two days maximum. The objective of a brainstorming session is to come up with new and innovative ideas or product features in a very rapid period of time. A brainstorming session tends to have a set of discrete, well-defined activities. A capable facilitator is essential to the success of the session. When defining ideas, it is important to avoid conflicts: e.g., one participant disparaging the ideas of another. Since very senior people can be in the session, it is important that they not intimidate the other, less senior-level participants.

An interesting story was told to one author during his military service. Military schools for senior officers often teach brainstorming techniques. At one such class, an Air Force captain, who was a friend of the author, engaged in a heated discussion with one of the other participants. After the session was over, the captain went over to the other participant to review their in-class discussion, only to find out to his dismay that the other officer was a lieutenant general.

---

[2] www.qfdi.org/

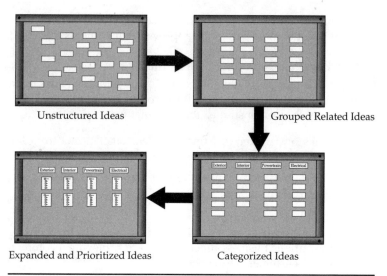

Unstructured Ideas

Grouped Related Ideas

Expanded and Prioritized Ideas

Categorized Ideas

Figure 3.7   Stages of a brainstorming session

The general explained to the captain that when he went in to class, he always hid his rank as best he could to avoid intimidating the other students, as he wanted their unbiased opinions. In business, it is the role of the facilitator to prevent intimidation or speech making from occurring, and to keep the session moving smoothly.

The objective and duration of the brainstorming session must be agreed upon by all the participants. This should ideally be determined prior to the start of the session. The session starts with a free flow of ideas, creating an unsorted set of product suggestions. Often "sticky notes" are used to record the ideas, and they are placed on a board (see Figure 3.7). Some general brainstorming protocols include allowing duplicates or similar ideas to be recorded, and discouraging filtering or censorship; e.g., allow "extreme" ideas.

The next activity in brainstorming is the condensation of the ideas to group related concepts and eliminate redundancy. The third activity is to formally assign the ideas to categories. Next, the group breaks up into small teams that assess the ideas and expand upon them.

Within each group, the ideas are then ranked (pairwise ranking). Finally, the brainstorming session is concluded with action items where appropriate for participants in the session. If the session was attended by customers not involved in analysis, then the post-session activities are usually done internally by project team members and company stakeholders.

Tabular Elicitation Techniques

The use of tables can provide a compact, unambiguous method for capturing stakeholder requests. Two types of widely used tabular techniques are decision tables and state tables. Decision tables are most often used where there are discrete sets of conditions that can be determined with a "yes" or "no," actions to take if the conditions are met, and a set of rules, where each unique set of conditions and the action to take is one rule.

Most of us have seen or used decision tables at one time or another. A very common form of decision table is the tax table shown in Figure 3.8.[3] Each row represents a condition, in this case the taxpayer's income. Each column represents a rule; i.e,. a condition (single, married filing jointly, etc.) and a set of actions, where the actions in this case determine what tax should be paid. When eliciting draft requirements from stakeholders, a decision table can be an efficient, compact, and unambiguous technique for capturing business rules.

State tables are different than decision tables in that they are used where the object under consideration can be in various states at different times, and well-defined, simple events trigger the change from one state to another. An object that transitions only on discrete events and has a predefined number of known states is called a state *machine*. In the case of a taxpayer, a state table would not be appropriate, as there is only one state: "about to pay taxes."

State tables, which show the behavior of a state machine, usually have a single start state, and then a set of states that an object transitions to, and finally either a successful exit state or one or more "error" states where activity stops because an error of some kind has occurred. Each state change is associated with one or more events

If line 43 (taxable income) is—		*rule*	And you are—		
At least	But less than	Single	Married filing jointly	Married filing separately	Head of a household
			Your tax is—		
1,300	1,325	131	131	131	131
1,325	1,350	134	134	134	134
1,350	1,375	136	136	136	136
1,375	1,400	139	139	139	139
1,400	1,425	141	141	141	141
1,425	1,450	144	144	144	144
1,450	1,475	146	146	146	146
1,475	1,500	149	149	149	149

FIGURE 3.8   Example decision table

---

[3] www.irs.gov/pub/irs-pdf/i1040tt.pdf

that cause the change, and one or more actions that take place as the object transitions from one state to another.

A summary of the different kinds of state tables can be found in the March 2008 *Crosstalk* article by Herrmannsdörfer et al. [Herrmannsdörfer et al. 2008]. As an example, consider the design of a simple CD player with three buttons (Figure 3.9). The only states that the player can be in (assuming the power is on) are open, closed and loaded, closed and empty, and playing (which is only possible if the player is closed and loaded). There are also well-defined events that determine what state the player is in, and clear actions to take for any given event. On an event (in this case pressing a button), one or more actions are taken, and the player transitions to a different state or stays in the same state. The particular state table shown is *nondeterministic* because if the state is "Open" and the "Open/Close" button is pressed, there are two possible transitions. If there is a CD in the tray, the player will transition to state 2 (closed and loaded), whereas if the tray is empty, the player will transition to state 3 (closed and empty), depending on whether a CD is detected in the tray. In general, *deterministic* state machines, where an event can have only at most one transition from a given state, are preferred because design and testing is simplified. However, it is sometimes possible to make a nondeterministic machine deterministic by adding intermediate states.

Process Modeling Techniques

A variety of process modeling techniques are suitable for the elicitation of requirements. Just a few of them are listed here, and model-driven techniques that are suitable for both elicitation and analysis are described in more detail in Chapter 4.

State Number	State	Open/Close	Play	Stop
1	Open	Close Tray {if No Disc Display "No Disc" go to 3 else Display "Ready" go to 2}	No action	No action
2	Closed Loaded	Open Tray {Display "Open"} Go to 1	Start Playing {Display "Playing"} Go to 4	No action
3	Closed Empty	Open Tray {Display "Open"} Go to 2	{Display "No Disc"} No action	No action
4	Playing	Stop Playing Open Tray {Display "Open"} Go to 1	{Display "Playing"} No action	Stop Playing {Display "Stop"} Go to 2

FIGURE 3.9   Simple CD player

Data flow diagrams (DFDs) have been around for a long time. There are several similar methodologies, such as those defined by [Gane et al. 1997] and [Yourdon 1988]. A sample data flow diagram is shown in Figure 3.10. The vertical lines on the data stores indicate the number of times that the store is shown on the diagram. While DFDs appear to have fallen out of favor and viable tools can be hard to find, they still have their proponents. DFDs can be very effective diagramming techniques for analyzing business needs. The primary difference between the data flow and newer (object-oriented) techniques is the focus on data flows and data structures rather than services. With data flow techniques, a customer's data and the flow of that data are analyzed. Stores needed to hold the data and processes needed to manipulate the data are added. The results of the analysis are then captured in data flow diagrams for review with the stakeholders.

Use case analysis [Jacobson et al. 1992] (use case = business process) involves either defining a customer process (business modeling) or showing the relationship of a system or product to the outside world. The analysis can be done using natural languages and tables or visual techniques such as those described in Chapter 4. A use case consists of the following:

- **Actors**   People or things interacting with the use case
- **Events**   Things that cause the use case to happen
- **Preconditions**   Things that must be true for the use case to happen
- **Postconditions**   Things that must be true if the use case has successfully completed
- **Activities**   The processes that occur in the use case
- **Included use cases**   Other processes used by this use case
- **Extending use cases**   Other processes that may optionally take place during the occurrence of this use case

When using natural language, activities are normally described using a table similar to the one shown in Table 3.2. In addition to the "sunny day" scenario, tables are normally created for alternate scenarios. For the "cash a check" example shown in Table 3.2, alternate scenarios might include how to handle insufficient funds or an ID that is not acceptable.

One problem with using natural language is that the set of use cases describing viable business processes makes up a graphical structure that is not well represented by text documents. For example, two different use cases might use or include the same use case (Figure 3.11). Furthermore, as we interact with the customers or stakeholders, the number of use cases can grow rapidly. If the use cases are kept in text files, document management issues can arise.

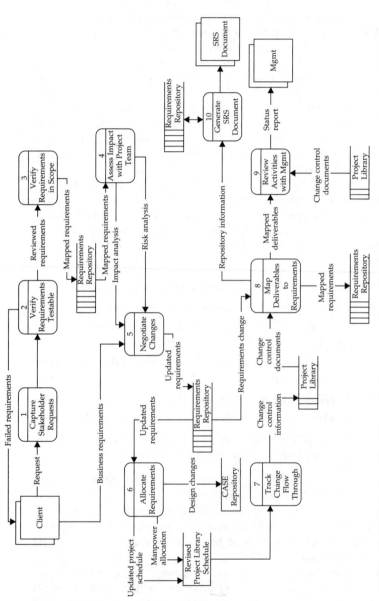

Figure 3.10 Data flow diagram for a requirements management process

Step	Actor	System Response (Bank Teller)	Output
1	Give check to teller	Can I see your ID?	
2	Give ID to teller	ID is okay	
3	Put ID away	Return ID	
4		Check account for enough money	Hold on account to cover check amount
5	Take money	Cash check	

TABLE 3.2 Sample Use Case Activity

Another problem with textual use cases is the occurrence of crosscutting issues that require use case modifications. With graphical models, it is a relatively simple matter to make changes, since the CASE tool handles the updating of other diagrams. Scenario diagrams take the place of tabular descriptions of activities (see Figure 3.12). With text, a crosscutting change can involve heavy manual effort to keep primary and alternate use cases across all relevant documents up-to-date, especially going into the activity tables and changing steps and responses.

More information about model-driven requirements engineering and the effective use of graphical modeling techniques can be found in the next chapter.

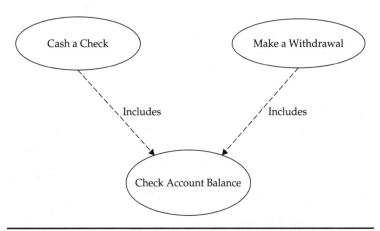

FIGURE 3.11 Graphical nature of use cases

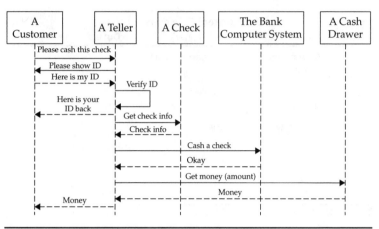

Figure 3.12   Detailing a use case with a scenario diagram

3.4   Customer-Specific Business Rules

Business rules are a special category of customer requirements. They are different in that rather than defining a fixed customer need, they describe the implementation of a customer policy that may be changed by the customer after delivery of a product or system. Hence they describe a special category of user-implemented extensibility.

A business can enact, revise, and discontinue the business rules that govern and guide it. A business policy is an element of governance that is not *directly enforceable*, whose purpose is to guide an enterprise. Compared to a business rule, a business policy tends to be less structured; i.e., less carefully expressed in terms of a standard vocabulary and not directly enforceable. For example, a banking business policy might be: "Bank customers should not be able to make too many bank withdrawals in a single day or withdraw more than a certain amount of money in a fixed period of time; the maximum amount being based on their total account value and history."

Why Are Customer-Specific Business Rules Important?

Customer-specific business rules must be kept separate from regular requirements (at least logically, using database tags or attributes), since they are not requirements. However, customer requirements can be derived from the business rules; the requirements may look different than the rules that they derive from.

What Are Their Characteristics?

Customer-specific business rules are implementations of the customer's company policies, where the business rules may change after system or product delivery. It is mandatory that the customer have the ability to alter the rules without system or product modification.

Example Customer-Specific Business Rules

A sample business policy, rules, and some derived requirements are shown here:

- **Policy** The hospital shall be able to define the difference between adult and child patients for check-in and medical records purposes.

- **Rule** Any patient under the age of 14 checking in shall be considered a child.

  When a child checks into the hospital, depending on the hospital's business policy, a parent or guardian may have to accompany the child and sign all the admission forms. Detailed rules explain under what circumstances (e.g., an accident, emergency, or life-threatening situation) a child may be checked in without a parent's or guardian's consent.

- **Requirement** A facility shall be provided with the system such that the hospital check-in process for adults and children can be changed by hospital administrators without the need for system or software modifications.

Note in the preceding example, the hospital may, at any time, change the age at which a patient is considered a child, as well as the rules governing the emergency check-in of a child without parental consent. The relationships among business policies, rules, and requirements are illustrated in Figure 3.13.

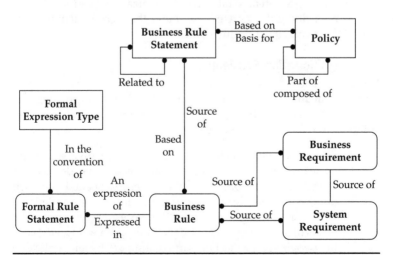

Figure 3.13 Business policies, rules, and derived requirements

3.5   Managing the Customer Relationship

Managing the customer relationship is important during the entire project or product life cycle, and it is crucial during the elicitation process. Both the consumer and the supplier need to have an ongoing understanding of the product. It may be necessary to continually interact with the customer to maintain good relations and keep the customer informed; e.g., bring them bad news early rather than later. Project management should never go into denial over issues such as delivery dates. Rather, open and frequent communication with the client can usually prevent more severe difficulties from occurring later.

Furthermore, it may be necessary to secure customer cooperation in order to get access to domain expertise. If, for example, a project is on a fixed schedule and relations with the client are not managed properly, access to the client's domain experts may be restricted, resulting in late delivery.

It is our experience that constant communication with the customer is essential for a positive outcome. There may be a tendency on some projects to elicit the requirements and then forget about the customer until the factory acceptance test. Doing so is a mistake, as the potential for misunderstandings widens significantly as a project progresses. Keeping the customer up-to-date on progress, demonstrating features (e.g., for prototypes, see Chapter 9), and eliciting comments or suggestions are both ethically correct and good business.

3.6   Managing Requirements Elicitation

Requirements elicitation is like any other project activity. It must be planned, it must be managed properly, and speedy follow-up on open issues is essential. While every organization or group has its own way of doing things, we have found that certain activities are essential to achieving a positive outcome.

Planning Elicitation Sessions

In order for elicitation sessions to be successful, they must be planned. Planning includes setting up the framework for conducting the sessions, managing the output of the sessions, and defining completion. We offer these suggestions:

1. Set up a schedule of elicitation sessions. Since diverse domain expertise may be needed, sessions need to be defined for capturing needs based on the expertise needed for each domain that is in scope. For example, in sessions to define a new insurance system, it might be necessary to capture the needs of marketing, sales, underwriting, accounting, etc. Since the people who would be participating are usually critical to the operation of an organization and access to them may be limited, the schedule may need to be carefully defined.

2. Define the venue and the media. This includes where the sessions will be held, as well as any audiovisual techniques used (e.g., whiteboard, stickies, RGB projector). The format for capturing the results of each elicitation session needs to be defined. Capture mechanisms may include a requirements database (viewed using a browser or the database screens), Excel spreadsheets, modeling tools, or other electronic capture mechanisms.

3. Define standards, schemas, and processes prior to the start of the elicitation sessions. When capturing stakeholder requests, they may be at very different levels (see the earlier section "Not Identifying Requirements Level"). It is important that any information captured be properly identified (including the stakeholder), partitioned (level), and identified as to type or other project characteristics, at the time of capture. Once the requests start to be added, it will be very difficult to go back and revisit the tagging of requirements. In order to have an electronic system set up to properly capture the relevant request or requirement attributes (e.g., priority, stakeholder, level, type), the database schema or model attributes need to have already been planned and defined in the toolset being used. Furthermore, having guidelines for conducting elicitation sessions will help in soliciting the cooperation of stakeholders or domain experts to provide the needed information at the time of elicitation.

4. Provide a clearly defined agenda for each elicitation session, with the role of each attendee clearly understood. The agenda should be feasible and reasonable given the duration and the people present. Finally, action items should be recorded and assigned with short due dates and careful follow-up.

5. Arrange for a senior manager (on the customer side) to participate in the elicitation sessions. While it may be difficult to convince clients or customers to have one of their senior stakeholders participate, it may be the only way to ensure that customer-provided domain experts actually show up at the meetings and cooperate. Not that they will be unwilling to participate, but the priorities of the manager of a domain expert may be quite different than those of the project manager for the product under design; they may be in different organizations or companies. Consequently, when pulling in domain experts, their presence may not be guaranteed without the participation of a senior manager in *their* organization.

6. If necessary, arrange for someone on the customer side (the senior manager mentioned above may suffice) to set up the schedule and manage it. The analyst in charge of requirements elicitation may not have access to the scheduling system of

the domain experts or may not have the authority to request their presence at elicitation sessions.

7. Hold sessions in the morning, if feasible, and schedule them to last half a day. People tend to tire a bit over time, and about four hours or less is best for sustaining high productivity. In addition, work will be generated outside of the elicitation session (see the next item), and it is recommended that assigned work be completed the same day that the session was held.

8. If heavy writing is assigned during an elicitation session, have it done offline, preferably the afternoon that the session was completed. This includes definitions, descriptions of processes, and so on. Text can then be reviewed the following morning or offline at a later date.

9. Preferably, find a venue where everyone can see the same thing at the same time. Whether looking at text or graphics, all the attendees should be seeing the same information. If you are able to have the relevant stakeholders in the room during the elicitation session, the requirements review process can be shortened, since the reviewers were present during the elicitation session.

10. Chunk reviews of work. Imagine being sent an e-mail containing the following request: "Please review this paragraph [or page] and send your comments by tomorrow." Contrast that with "Please review this 200-page requirements specification and send your comments within the next two days." Clearly the former is likely to happen, and the latter may result in the reader hitting the Delete button. Reviews are best done online, with everyone reviewing a reasonably small amount of material together. When that is not feasible, the review of material should be partitioned, so that only the relevant stakeholders see the material they need to review, and the amount of material to be reviewed is kept small.

11. Keep reviews of elicitation sessions short and immediate. When reviewing the output of an elicitation session, we normally conduct the reviews the same afternoon, not later than one or two days after the session (before the domain experts vanish back into their environments).

12. Keep attendance at an elicitation session (as contrasted with a brainstorming session, where everyone possible is in the room) small, no more than six to eight people. A typical session might consist of: a facilitator or lead analyst, one or two other analysts (including the designated "smart ignoramus"), participating stakeholders at the management level, and one or two domain experts. It is always better to have two domain experts than one. Two experts can check each other's work as the session progresses, minimizing the

need for post-session reviews. Three subject matter experts in the same session may or may not be effective, depending on their interpersonal dynamics.

To summarize, conducting elicitation sessions may require a significant planning effort, depending on the scope of the project. Furthermore, if any needed standards, procedures, and tools are in place prior to the start of the elicitation sessions, rework will be minimized and the sessions will proceed more smoothly.

3.7 Requirements and Cost Estimation

A strong correlation has been found between function point counts and requirements [Jones 2008]. With proper planning, it is possible to generate function point counts from sets of requirements or an analysis model. For example, if use cases are annotated with the appropriate information, a function point count estimate can be generated by walking the directed graph of the underlying model. Software requirements automation can play an important role in software requirements estimation. The Bachman Analyst Workbench developed in 1991 and the Texas Instruments Information Engineering Facility (IEF) developed in the early 1990s both provided automatic derivation of function point metrics from software requirements.

3.8 Requirements Elicitation for Incremental Product Development

It was mentioned in Chapter 1 that Capers Jones reported that less than 25 percent of the requirements for typical applications are new or unique [Jones 2007]. For projects that are not new, two situations typically exist:

- A well-defined RE process was used to define the initial requirements. In this situation, elicitation and analysis can be a continuation of previous efforts, with new requests and requirements recorded using the appropriate database attributes to permit partitioning of the requirement sets.

- An enhancement to a legacy system is to be built, with prior requirement set(s) either incomplete or missing completely.

The latter situation tends to be quite common; e.g., enhancements to systems are often done with no prior requirement specifications or documentation to refer to. When this occurs, it may not be feasible to reverse-engineer a full requirement set, but rather, only the new requirements can be captured. In this case the old system and its functions may have to be treated as a set of legacy requirements;

e.g., review the new requirements primarily for compatibility with the prior system. Depending on the project type, advanced techniques such as dynamic tracing [Cleland-Huang 2005] can be used to assist with impact analysis. Some general suggestions when defining the requirements for incremental improvement to a system for which requirements do not exist are:

1. Where cost effective, reverse-engineer a set of high-level requirements and use it as a starting point. User guides and help files are an excellent source of such requirements.

2. Identify any programmatic interfaces, document them, and treat them as new requirements.

3. Be sure to review all new requirements, considering downward compatibility and the sensitivities of users. A very common complaint for new releases is "I liked the old system better."

3.9   Tips for Gathering Requirements

The following set of tips was learned through trial and error and was based on input from SCR staff members and some of our academic colleagues. It is not intended to be inclusive, but rather to provide a starting point.

- Add a "smart ignoramus" to your requirements analysis team.
- Include stakeholders in requirements elicitation sessions who can speak with authority for the organization, and be sure to differentiate the "user" from the "customer" when describing stakeholders.
- Record the level of information and the stakeholder source of requirements during elicitation sessions.
- Separate context and background from stakeholder requests.
- Plan a project such that access to subject matter experts is scheduled.
- Where appropriate, start a project by creating marketing literature, a user manual, or lightweight specification sheets for the product to help clarify incomplete or undefined customer needs.
- Force requirements engineers with deep domain expertise to communicate with external stakeholders, especially for a domain where technology is changing.
- Wherever possible, use visual techniques, including models, diagrams, and tables, to communicate important requirements concepts.

- Prioritize stakeholder requests as early in a product life cycle as possible. Several prioritization activities may be needed, one just for the stakeholders, another when the architect or designers evaluate the cost and risk of implementation, and possibly additional sessions prior to the build/no build decision. If possible, have key stakeholders participate in any ranking activity.

- Keep the customer up-to-date on RE progress, demonstrate features, and elicit comments or suggestions.

- Plan elicitation sessions to include the schedule, session agenda, equipment, and tools needed; the types of information to be captured; and the stakeholders who should be present.

- Include a senior manager from the customer's organization in requirements elicitation sessions.

- Schedule elicitation sessions in the morning, and then use the afternoon for miscellaneous activities such as writing definitions and descriptions and correcting diagrams and documents.

- Whether looking at text or graphics, assure that all the participants in a requirements elicitation session see the same information.

- Organize requirements reviews into small chunks with small amounts of material together. When that is not feasible, the review of material should be partitioned, so that only the relevant stakeholders see the material they need to review, and the amount of material to be reviewed is kept small, short, and immediate.

- Keep elicitation sessions small, no more than six to eight people. Three subject matter experts in the same session may or may not be effective, depending on their interpersonal dynamics.

3.10   Summary

There are many different techniques for eliciting customer needs and business goals. Whatever methods are used, the analysts eliciting the needs, goals, or requirements should be trained in the techniques they will be using. Furthermore, the elicitation process will be more productive and execute more smoothly if process, methods, and capture mechanisms are well defined, documented, and communicated to the participating stakeholders prior to the start of the elicitation sessions.

Those responsible for the elicitation of requirements should be cognizant of the techniques needed, as well as of the issues and

FIGURE 3.14
Facilitation skills
are important.

problems described in this chapter. Furthermore, being a project lead analyst or facilitator is an art in itself, requiring the ability to get diverse stakeholders to follow an agenda without deviation, and drive the elicitation process smoothly to completion in the allotted time (Figure 3.14).

3.11   Discussion Questions

1. When and how should stakeholder requests be reviewed?
2. How large should a requirements elicitation session meeting be?
3. What are some of the differences between a brainstorming session and a requirements elicitation session?

References

Agar, M., *Professional Stranger: An Informal Introduction to Ethnography*, 2nd ed., Academic Press, 1996.

Akao, Y., *Quality Function Deployment: Integrating Customer Requirements into Product Design*, Productivity Press, 1990.

Beck, K., *Extreme Programming Explained*, Addison-Wesley, 1999.

Berry, D., "The Importance of Ignorance in Requirements Engineering," *Journal of Systems and Software*, Vol. 28, No. 2, February 1995, pp. 179–184.

Brooks, F.P., Jr., *The Mythical Man-Month: Essays on Software Engineering, Anniversary Edition*, Addison Wesley, 1995.

Carlson, P., "The Flop Heard Round the World," *Washington Post*, September 4, 2007.

Clegg, B., and Birch, P., *Instant Creativity: Simple Techniques to Ignite Innovation & Problem Solving*, Kogan Page, 2007.

Cleland-Huang, J., "Toward Improved Traceability of Non-Functional Requirements," *International Workshop on Traceability in Emerging Forms of Software Engineering*, Long Beach, CA, November 2005. (In conjunction with ASE'05.)

Conway Correll, L., *Brainstorming Reinvented: A Corporate Communications Guide to Ideation*, Response Books, 2004.

Dardenne, A., van Lamsweerde, A., and Fickas, S., "Goal-Directed Requirements Acquisition," in IWSSD: *Selected Papers of the Sixth International Workshop on Software Specification and Design*, 1993, pp. 3–50.

Gane, C., and Sarson, T., *Structured Systems Analysis: Tools and Techniques*, McDonnell Douglas Information, June 1977.

Herrmannsdörfer, M., Konrad, S., and Berenbach, B., "Tabular Notations for State Machine–Based Specifications," *Crosstalk Magazine*, March 2008.

Jacobson, I., Jonnson, P., Christerson, M., and Overgaard, G., *Object-Oriented Software Engineering: A Use Case Driven Approach*, Addison-Wesley, 1992.

Jones, C., *Applied Software Measurement*, 3rd ed., McGraw-Hill, New York, 2008.

Jones, C., *Estimating Software Costs*, 2nd ed., McGraw-Hill, New York, 2007.

Kano, N., "Attractive Quality and Must-Be Quality," *The Journal of the Japanese Society for Quality Control*, April 1984, pp. 39–48.

Karlsson, J., "Software Requirements Prioritizing," *Proceedings of the ICRE*, 1996, pp. 110–116.

Mikel, H., and Schroeder, R., *Six Sigma: The Breakthrough Management Strategy Revolutionizing the World's Top Corporations*, Doubleday, 1999.

Royce, W., *Software Project Management*, Addison-Wesley, 1998.

Sheehan, M., Brace, C., Williams, S., and Sullivan, L., "Optimal Allocation of Resources to Distribution Investments Using the Analytic Hierarchy Process to Balance the Impacts of Investments on Safety, Customer Interruption Costs, Levelized Annual Revenue Requirement, Contribution to Margin, and Other Considerations," *Proc. IEEE Power Society Summer Meeting*, Vol. 3, Seattle, WA, 2000, pp. 1311–1316.

Sobczaka, A., and Berry, D., "Distributed Priority Ranking of Strategic Preliminary Requirements for Management Information Systems in Economic Organizations," *Information and Software Technology*, Vol. 49, Nos. 9–10, September 2007, pp. 960–984.

Souter, N., *Creative Business Solutions: Breakthrough Thinking: Brainstorming for Inspiration and Ideas*, Sterling, 2007.

van Lamsweerde, A., "Goal-Oriented Requirements Engineering: A Guided Tour," *Proceedings RE'01, 5th IEEE International Symposium on Requirements Engineering*, Toronto, August 2001, pp. 249–263.

Yourdon, E., *Modern Structured Analysis*, Prentice-Hall, 1988.

Yu, E.S.K., "Modelling Organizations for Information Systems Requirements Engineering," *Proc. REP3 – 1st International Symposium on Requirements Engineering*, IEEE, 1993, pp. 34–41.

## CHAPTER 4

Requirements Modeling

by Brian Berenbach, Sascha Konrad, Juergen Kazmeier

> *"'What is the use of a book,' thought Alice,*
> *'without pictures or conversations?'"*
> —Lewis Carroll, *Alice's Adventures in Wonderland,* 1865

> *"A picture shows me at a glance what it takes*
> *dozens of pages of a book to expound."*
> —Ivan Turgenev, *Fathers and Sons,* 1862

4.1 Introduction

As products become more complex with increasing functionality, it becomes harder to describe and understand their requirements. Furthermore, some product concepts that may be easily represented by a picture can become extraordinarily difficult to comprehend when transcribed to text. A good example of this is a bicycle. Its design is easily understood when viewed as a picture, but incredibly complex and difficult to describe textually. Pictures may be used in different ways; for instance, they may precisely describe something, or they may describe an *abstraction* of something. An abstraction is defined as "a mental representation or concept that isolates and generalizes an aspect of an object or group of objects from which relationships may be perceived" [White et al. 2002]. When a set of related pictures are combined such that the objects contained in the pictures are stored along with their relationships, a model is created. The associated pictures are then views into the model.

In Chapter 2, we discussed the basics of requirements engineering artifact models to help define the product development life cycle, or processes used to build a product. In this chapter, we discuss models that help describe the product itself.

Models require work and skill to produce. Consequently, there is always a rationale for creation of a model. For example, a *fault tree* is a model that graphically represents the interactions of failures and other events within a system. A fault tree may be mandated when there are hazards associated with a system, and an analysis is necessary to determine that there is no danger to the users of the system or the environment. Sometimes the use of such a model is mandated by regulation (e.g., medical devices).

Models can be created at different levels of abstraction for different purposes. In software, a *business model* can describe why a product is needed. A *feature model* then describes the features of a product being created to enable the business model. A *requirements analysis model* then explains the features in sufficient detail to define product specifications. A *design model* illustrates the architecture for the product. An *implementation model* describes the construction of the product (for software, the actual source code is the implementation model). Finally, a *test model* would describe how the product would be tested (see Chapter 8 for more information on test models). All these models must be interconnected for a variety of reasons (see the section on traceability in Chapter 7).

Models may have varying degrees of formality, depending on their use. Models for safety-critical systems (see Chapter 11) tend to be very formal. A *formal model* is one where the semantics for model construction are defined (e.g., a set of rules for creating the model), and where criteria for determining the correctness of the model are established. Most models are not formal. For example, software developers creating designs in the Unified Modeling Language (UML) or systems engineers creating designs with the Systems Modeling Language (SysML) are usually not creating formal models because there are no rules for model creation, and there is no way to determine if the model is correct (determining correctness requires validation against the rule set). The degree of formality and the way the models are described vary depending on the domain and experience of the team. For example, for many of the domains we have worked in, models have been described in UML because of specific applications and customers, but for embedded systems state charts are often used.

Moreover, it is even possible to create a formal model by describing objects and their relationships in a database without any diagrams or pictures [Rugaber et al. 2001]. It is common, for example, to reverse-engineer or create UML models (www.uml.org) by loading and analyzing software source code. The model is contained in the objects and their relationships.

Figure 4.1 illustrates the use of a conceptual diagram to show abstraction. In it we see a boiler with water feeds, outlets, and valves. This diagram alone is sufficient to understand how to install the Parker boiler. Note that

- Minimal expertise is required to read the schematic.

- It conveys a great deal of useful information.

- It is simple enough that a viewer can easily comprehend the content.

- It is coherent; that is, everything in the schematic is related in a visible, understandable way.

When using models as part of an engineering process, one of the objectives is to convey as much information as possible as succinctly as possible. This is relatively easy to do in domains where each object in a model represents something tangible such as a door, window, capacitor, etc. However, how can the relationships among requirements, hazards, product features, and business goals be readily understood for a complex product with thousands of requirements? Furthermore, unlike the boiler shown in Figure 4.1, electromechanical and software components may have relatively

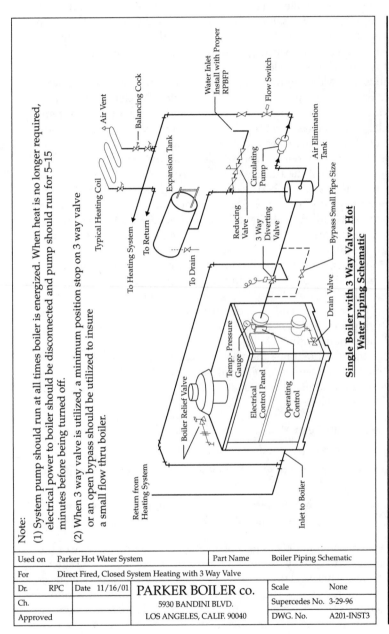

FIGURE 4.1 Conceptual diagram in mechanical engineering (Picture courtesy of Parker Boiler Company, Los Angeles, CA)

complex processes that can be difficult to understand, even for a subject matter expert. Some very simple modeling needs can be inferred from the need for abstraction:

- Process models should, in general, be understandable by viewers who are not experts in the domain being described (there are, of course, exceptions, such as views of complex, domain-specific information).

- Models should be coherent. That is, there should be no holes or discontinuities. For example, when describing how a bank customer cashes a check, the reader should be able to traverse views easily from the point where the customer enters the bank until the customer is handed money.

- Tools used to create and view models should be easy to use and should enable processes, not cause difficulties.

Modeling tools and techniques must work in the context of the organization and project where they are being used. For example, if requirements are being elicited in a distributed fashion, then the tools should support distributed requirements elicitation.

For our purposes, a *model* can be defined as "A representation of a system that allows for investigation of the properties of the system and, in some cases, prediction of future outcomes." We can infer then that requirements models can be used to

- Provide views that allow us to understand product requirements precisely.

- Provide views that show generalizations or simplify complex relationships between requirements.

- Describe the context or background in which a product will be used.

In systems and software engineering, modeling for analysis has very different goals than modeling for design. Martin Fowler has stated about software design: "The fundamental driver behind [graphical modeling languages] is that programming languages are not at a high enough level of abstraction to facilitate discussions about design" [Fowler 2004]. This chapter concerns itself with the use of models for elicitation and analysis. In requirements engineering, elicitation and analysis models are specifically used to

- Provide aids for the elicitation of customer needs.

- Clearly define customer processes and the context for any products being developed.

- Provide a vision for how a product might be used after completion and deployment.

- Aid in identifying potential hazards (to users of a product).

- Identify all possible users of a product and external systems, and how each of them interacts with the system or product under consideration.

Each engineering discipline and domain has its own standards for design or modeling. In civil and mechanical engineering, for example, blueprints are often used. More generally, the term "blueprint" has come to be used to refer to any detailed plan. In electrical engineering, there is the traditional circuit diagram. This has been augmented in electronics design with standards for circuit board design. In the software world, it is recognized that working in the problem domain results in higher productivity and better quality products than working at a low level (www.darpa.mil/ipto/programs/hpcs/). When modeling for elicitation and analysis, depending on where you are in the product development life cycle, there are many different approaches to modeling (see Figure 3.4 in the preceding chapter).

Goal modeling is used to define business goals and relate them to needs and features (see "Eliciting Business Goals" under Section 3.3 in the preceding chapter). Goal modeling can be done at any time, but it is usually correlated with the definition of product features, to ensure that the features are synchronized with business needs or goals. Goal modeling is sometimes used to show nonfunctional requirements and their relation to goals and functional requirements.

Feature modeling is a modeling approach normally associated with defining product lines. The model shows all possible features in all products in the product line, their dependencies, and their mutual incompatibilities. Since an unconstrained feature model is generally too broad in scope to be useful, the models are normally coupled with product maps that identify which features are associated with identified products. Feature models can also be used to identify potential variations within a single product; e.g., user configurations.

Process modeling is typically used to show user workflows either before or after a product is delivered (or sometimes at both times). Some modeling techniques, such as the UML, are also used for software design, as the diagrams that are used to show customer processes can also be used to illustrate software processes. Unlike Goal and Feature Models, which tend to be static representations of structure, process models can show both static structures (e.g., the structure of an organization) and temporal behavior (steps in activities, changes in the state of an object over time, etc.). There are many types of process models, including Integrated Definition (IDEF) methods developed for military contractors [IEEE 1320.2-1998]. Other techniques such as those of [Gane 1979] and [Yourdon 1988] enjoyed some early success but were limited by the quality of the tools available and the limited functionality of early desktop computers and workstations. More recently, simplified modeling techniques such as SysML have emerged to support systems engineering efforts (www.sysml.org).

Video-based requirements engineering couples workflow models with video streams. It is a relatively new field, enabled by advances in video capture and editing techniques [Creighton et al. 2006].

The remainder of this chapter will focus on our experience with process modeling techniques that have been successfully used on Siemens projects to support requirements elicitation and analysis, specifically model-driven requirements engineering. Sometimes the two activities are confused because the same tool and physical model (or files) are used; however, they take place at different points in the life cycle. *Elicitation* is an activity accomplished with stakeholders to determine what their needs are. In order to better understand the context, a business model may be created that describes business activities where a new product or set of services will be used. A prototypical product may then be defined and refined, so that the customer's needs are better understood. Once a set of product features is known, analysis modeling may take place to define in detail how the product will be used. The Model-Driven Requirements Engineering (MDRE) methodology described in the next section covers *both* business modeling and analysis modeling activities, starting with business activities and ending with the detailed interaction of users and the proposed product or system in the same integrated physical model.

4.2   Model-Driven Requirements Engineering (MDRE)

We have used MDRE on Siemens projects because we have found that, under certain circumstances, it is often a good way to effectively manage the requirements for large and complex systems. On one project, for example, there were over eight hundred use cases. Most of those use cases described product functionality to be developed. Consequently, tasks had to be placed in a project plan. Creating the plan manually would have taken at least two weeks, with the risk of human error (e.g., leaving out tasks). Using the MDRE tool set, the draft project plan was created directly from the model for use by the project manager in a matter of minutes, with associated hyperlinks between the model use cases and the plan tasks.

MDRE uses models as an enabler for all requirements activities and includes the use of modeling techniques for elicitation (business modeling and use cases) and analysis (detailed descriptions of the use cases). Initially, processes are modeled to better understand how a product might support potential customer activities. For example, when building a new underwriting system for an insurance company, we would want to know what systems and roles the new system would interact with; what kind of data was used, modified, and created; how the underwriting information was managed; and what constraints the underwriting staff operated under (e.g., time, quality, organizational). The output of early modeling efforts would be a business model that described either the customer's "as is" or "to be defined" processes. From that business modeling effort, a product or set of IT services would be derived to support the underwriting process as a set of product features. As product features tend to be high level, they then need to be analyzed by expanding all the features to show how they are used. This is typically done in an analysis model, where each feature is a starting point for analysis (note: features typically are shown as abstract use cases). The analysis of each feature then results in a coherent use case model (typically, in the same modeling tool). As the use cases are decomposed during analysis, testable functionality is described in concrete use cases. The full, hierarchical set of use cases then become the requirements for product construction.

The following activities are from a project to develop an underwriting system for a major insurance company, and they illustrate the approach used for a typical MDRE effort.

- A business model of the organization was created, showing how underwriting works in an insurance company. This was accomplished by conducting requirements elicitation meetings with corporate officers and underwriters, and building the model in their presence with their inputs.

- When reviewing the business model, we observed that certain operations were being done inefficiently. For example, letters would be sent to various parties containing forms that had to be filled out and returned (e-mail was not acceptable, as many of the forms required signatures or notarization). There was no tracking of when the letters were sent, and when (or if) they came back.

- A feature was added to the new, planned underwriting system called a "Diary" that would track all sent and returned mail, and would automatically notify officials if responses were not received in a timely manner.

- During analysis, the Diary feature was expanded through use cases to define the interaction of the new underwriting system with users, including data, form, and function. Each of the low-level functions supported by the Diary feature, after careful review, became a customer requirement. Finally, during triage, the requirements were prioritized by the stakeholders and then allocated to product releases by the project staff.

- The business model and use case model were seamlessly integrated in that the use case (or analysis) model was an extension of the business model. The requirements were generated from the use case model and loaded into a requirements database for tracking.

FIGURE 4.2
Example types of
models

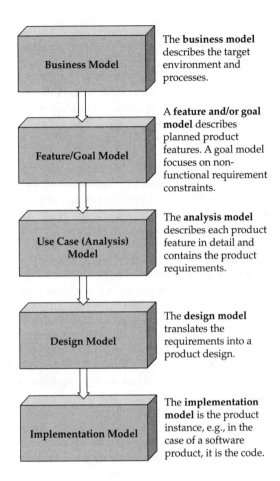

The **business model** describes the target environment and processes.

A **feature and/or goal model** describes planned product features. A goal model focuses on non-functional requirement constraints.

The **analysis model** describes each product feature in detail and contains the product requirements.

The **design model** translates the requirements into a product design.

The **implementation model** is the product instance, e.g., in the case of a software product, it is the code.

A design model can be created, using the analysis model as a starting point or guide. Finally the product is implemented, where, in the case of software, the implementation model is the actual software or code (see Figure 4.2).

Project plans, test plans, traces, and requirements can be generated from a model, depending on the modeling objectives and effort put into creating it. We want models to be sufficiently formal that we can check for correctness. That means we need semantics for model construction. A useful by-product of increased formality is the use of metrics to determine work product quality and project progress. Finally, if the end product is software, an analysis model can be the starting point for the generation of a software design. Parts of the design can be derived semiautomatically or manually from the model. As most, if not all, MDRE activities take place prior to design decisions, they are appropriate for both systems and software engineering. We have used MDRE techniques on mechatronic projects such as mail sorting systems, where it was impossible to tell, from the model and the requirements derived from the model, whether the resultant components would be hardware, software, or firmware [Bradley et al. 1991].

The use of MDRE processes requires a significant amount of up-front planning, skilled staff, and viable tool sets. The creation and use of an MDRE process will be described in the following sections, with a suggested set of modeling heuristics and best practices. Results of the use of MDRE techniques are reported in [Berenbach and Borotto 2006].

With MDRE, instead of using text as the framework for the requirements in a project, models are used. In Chapter 2, we saw how artifact models can improve the quality and productivity of RE processes. When using MDRE, as many artifacts as possible are generated from or stored in the requirements artifact model. For third-party artifacts or objects that cannot be stored in or generated from the model, traces are used to create hyperlinks (see Figure 4.3 and Table 4.1, later in this chapter).

All MDRE artifacts either are stored in a model or have a placeholder in the model to represent them. Ideally, the textual description for an artifact will be stored with the artifact. On demand, the text can be extracted to a specification or transformed as needed. External documentation such as standards and government regulations are usually referenced via hyperlinks, which are object links in the model. However, hyperlinks should be used with discretion, as they can only point to a whole "something." That is, a requirement in a model referencing an external document via a hyperlink can only reference the entire document. In order for the links to be effective, they should ideally have a tighter granularity; e.g., they should reference a paragraph or sentence.

The most commonly used tools tend to be disjoint. That is, information is kept in different databases, with synchronization requiring manual effort of custom programming. Keeping a model

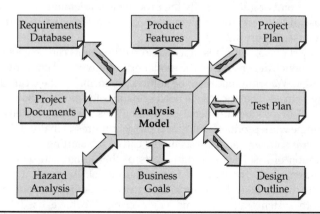

Figure 4.3   The analysis model as a nexus for project activities

and a requirements database synchronized can be a problem. It is a straightforward process to create a first draft of a requirements database from a model. However, there is the open issue of keeping the model and the database synchronized, as they are now in two separate databases, and changes made to one might not be reflected in the other. We feel that tools that will combine requirements management and process modeling facilities are still several years away; consequently, special attention should be paid to tool integration and automatic updates.

At Siemens, several pilot projects were conducted to determine the effectiveness of MDRE with currently available tool sets on large projects [Berenbach and Borotto 2006]. Additional projects used MDRE effectively, where the requirements were generated automatically from an analysis model and transferred to a requirements database. The combination of programmatic quality assurance checks (using our internal DesignAdvisor tool) and automated requirement generation worked well; the only open issue being the need to manually synchronize the model and the generated requirements as part of the requirements management process.

An MDRE process or set of processes can span the entire product development life cycle from innovation through maintenance. It is therefore important to determine the objectives of the process, and what the process stakeholders will expect (Figure 4.4). Typical questions

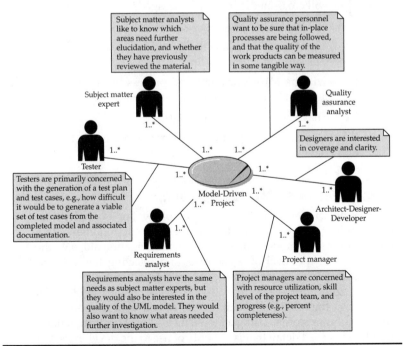

FIGURE 4.4 Sample shareholder needs within an RE process

that must be answered when defining a process and an integrated tool set to support that process include:

- How will business goals and stakeholder requests (business requirements) be captured and traced to product features and/or requirements?
- How will product features be captured?
- How will requirements be traced to features?
- What will test cases be traced to?
- How will the project plan be synchronized with the MDRE processes?
- How will requirements be elicited and analyzed using an MDRE process?
- How will quality and productivity be measured?
- How will artifact completeness be determined?
- What is the most effective way to execute the various processes?
- What are the best tools to use given the scope of the project?
- How will tools be integrated, e.g., how will they be synchronized?
- How will cross-media traces be managed?
- How will the MDRE processes scale?
- Do we have a product line? If so, will any proposed MDRE processes support a product line?
- How will the MDRE artifacts and process be supported or maintained once the product is in maintenance?
- Do we have adequately trained staff?
- What standards, procedures, and samples are needed? If we don't have them, how do we get them?

4.3 Advantages of an MDRE Approach

MDRE is not an "all or nothing" methodology. For example, if an organization wishes to focus on textual use cases and requirements, a high-level use case model makes a very nice navigation aid; e.g., the model stops at the level of a use case, and selecting the use case symbol launches an editor with the use case document.

With agile approaches to software development, lightweight models (e.g., the models are incomplete) can be used to represent a collection of user stories. Using a model instead of short textual notes provides increased detail that is not only of use to the developers, but also to testers and reviewers.

Use case modeling has also been found to work well when discovering requirements for service-oriented architecture (SOA) systems [Lau 2004], and the use of modeling for SOA products seems to have become the de facto approach for identifying SOA requirements.

Models used for navigation work especially well when the models are published to the Web, giving stakeholders unfamiliar with the project a simple navigation guide for finding documentation. Each organization, and each project within that organization, needs to do a cost, benefit, and risk analysis to determine what aspects of MDRE are desirable. Often, when evaluating methodologies, organizations will focus on "the easy stuff"—such as "how do we write use case documents?"—while ignoring the details that can cause problems later during development. For example, a cross-cutting requirement is a requirement that may impact several areas (or use cases). A security requirement, for instance, may impact reports, user interfaces, logon, etc. As the work products of MDRE are artifacts that can be queried or mined, MDRE techniques tend to be better than traditional natural language approaches for managing such cross-cutting requirements.

MDRE can have significant advantages over other approaches on large projects. Some of these are listed in the sections that follow.

Using MDRE to Estimate Project Size and Cost

Karner provides guidelines for creating function point estimates from analysis models [Karner 1993]. His approach involves ranking actors and use cases as simple or complex using a weighting system. A high-level use case model is a good fit with function point counting. When modeling, actors and use cases can be assigned weights based on Karner's guidelines. As the directed graph underlying the model is traversed, "use case points" are summed up and converted to function points for estimating cost. Note that this approach is not as simple as it sounds; high-level models should be used, and the numbering scheme for ranking use case and actor complexity needs to be applied judiciously. That having been said, it is an excellent way to estimate the cost of completing very large projects when the first project phase includes an analysis model.

Improved Management of Cross-Cutting Requirements

Cross-cutting requirements are those that trace to or impact other requirements in different areas. With traditional approaches, it can be very difficult to manage change control with nonfunctional requirements. It can, for example, be difficult to see how a new or changed requirement impacts other parts of a system. With MDRE, however, it is relatively easy, as the traces are visual, and since the views are into a homogeneous model, it is easy to query for changes and make modifications; e.g., changing, adding, or deleting artifacts and their relationships will automatically be reflected everywhere the related objects are shown.

Navigation of Complex System Requirement Sets

Navigating through volumes of text can be very difficult. Even when items are traced to each other in databases, as projects get larger, trace matrices increase in size as the square of the number of requirements and it can become a daunting task to find information for an impact or coverage analysis. Moreover, for someone not familiar with the domain, navigation can be a time-consuming, trial-and-error process. Navigation with a well-crafted model is no more difficult than finding a route with a map. Touch, zoom, touch, zoom, etc., and you are there. Finding related objects is as easy as doing an ad hoc query (remember, everything is in a database). As models scale well, ease of navigation remains the same regardless of model size, although it might take a few more mouse clicks to find the material of interest.

Rapid Review of Business Processes and Requirements Relationships

Reviewing diagrams is significantly faster and more thorough than reviewing similar material in text. We have found that model reviews tend to be more culture and language neutral than reviewing text documents. Furthermore, if the models are extended to support the Unified Requirements Modeling Language (URML) concepts (see later Section 4.5), then the relationships between hazards, threats, processes, product features, business goals, and functional and nonfunctional requirements can all be viewed at the same time by distributed teams [Berenbach and Gall 2006]. Pictures tend to be less ambiguous than text, and relationships (or the lack thereof) are immediately apparent.

Metrics for Quality and Progress

Unlike text, models are mathematical structures (directed graphs). It is therefore possible to define metrics for quality and progress, and then semiautomatically extract the metrics at periodic intervals [Berenbach and Borotto 2006]. The rapid extraction and analysis of metrics improves transparency and product quality.

Semiautomatic Generation of Project Plans and Requirements Database Content

With a properly crafted model, where one of the goals of the modeling effort is the automatic generation of downstream artifacts such as project plans and the population of requirements databases, the manual transcription of information can be avoided, along with the potential for transcription errors [Berenbach 2003].

4.4   Prerequisites for Using MDRE

There are some organizational prerequisites for effective use of MDRE. These prerequisites are described in the sections that follow.

Modeling Skills Not Readily Available

Our experience with RE projects is that, after training, it takes about a month of apprenticeship before an analyst can effectively use MDRE techniques. For an analyst to be a facilitator or lead an RE team, it will likely take at least six months working with MDRE under an experienced team leader. These training times are rough rules of thumb; the actual times depend on the experience and skills of the staff and the complexity of the domain.

In an ideal situation, at least one of the team members, preferably the team leader, should have been completely through an MDRE cycle, that is, through the end product going into maintenance. We have all had the experience of the "do-it-yourselfer" fixing a washing machine or a bicycle, and we know that after we are done, we think to ourselves, "Now why didn't I do that in the beginning, it would have made my life so much easier?" The same is true with systems engineering; often, going through a complete product development life cycle can significantly change one's perspective on what is important.

Inadequate Tooling

Tools for requirements engineering are viewed by some to be in their infancy. Vendors would have practitioners believe that their requirements databases will solve all of our RE process problems, but this is not usually the case. We cannot always do everything with one tool; for example, consider maintaining cross-database or cross-document traces. Furthermore, some tools do not scale well; as the number of artifacts in use increases, the performance and ease of use of the tool degrades. Also, with the current business turmoil in the requirements and development tools area, there is always the concern that a vendor will stop manufacturing a tool being used on an important project, leaving the user with limited support.

Organization Not Ready for MDRE

When tools are being discussed and an organization frequently asks "how much does it cost?" that may be an indicator that the organization may not be ready for MDRE. Tools can be expensive, but the real question is, "What is the cost/benefit impact of MDRE on the product life cycle?" Furthermore, the organizational structure may not lend itself to MDRE techniques. For example, if there are impediments to cooperation across organizational units, then MDRE may not be feasible, since business goals need to trace to product features, and product features need to trace to test cases. If organizational barriers prevent the creation of those traces, then an organization may not be mature enough to support MDRE. MDRE does require skilled staff, and that means training, mentoring, and broad experience across the life cycle. We have also seen situations where business analysts who have been using text-based elicitation and analysis techniques were very apprehensive about trying new methods, especially techniques with which they would be working at a novice skill level.

Another organizational issue is that of finding the right first project. As MDRE techniques might not work as well as desired the first time they are used, a small, noncritical first-time project would be best. Sometimes organizations are in constant "fire-fighting" mode and cannot spare staff to try something new.

> *"Begin at the beginning", the King said, gravely,*
> *"and go till you come to the end; then stop."*

—Lewis Carroll, Alice's Adventures in Wonderland, 1865

4.5   MDRE Processes

MDRE processes include requirements gathering activities up to but not including design, where the focus of the elicitation and analysis activities is model creation and utilization. That includes, for example, goal and feature modeling activities, hazard analysis, threat modeling, and requirements elicitation and analysis using models. Depending on the sophistication of the modeling tools used, a full implementation of the URML would permit an organization to do most of its RE activities with a URML, generating artifacts such as documents or requirement specifications as needed on an ad hoc basis. If less sophisticated tooling is used, or more traditional tools are used for storing requirements, a traditional process modeling tool (e.g., IDEF, UML, etc.) can be used for process modeling. In this section, we will start with a holistic view of MDRE processes, and then later in the chapter, we will provide step-by-step guidance for model creation during elicitation and analysis. We use the UML as a starting point because of its acceptance and available tool sets. It must be noted that limitations of MDRE are often imposed by the tools used. Since the focus of the MDRE effort is the creation of models from which high-level requirements can be extracted, tools must enable whatever techniques are used. Where tools cannot provide the needed functionality, then customization or the additional use of other tools may be necessary.

Initial Understanding

In the beginning of a project, we would like to know why a system or product is being built. There are, of course, conflicting points of view as to why products are created. However, in software and systems engineering, the view that counts the most is that of the stakeholder paying for the system (or the requirements elicitation effort, if the decision to build has not yet been reached). If it is at all possible, we want to capture the early business goals so that when an impact analysis is performed later in the project or design tradeoffs are made, the rationale as to why a feature is in the delivered system is readily understood. Looking ahead to Figure 4.14 we can see the context diagram for a sporting event management system. Several of the diagrams in this chapter use this system as a modeling example. Look at Figure 4.14 first, then look at Figure 4.5. In Figure 4.5 we see a goal model fragment showing some of the goals we hope to achieve in creating a sporting event system (commercially desirable; e.g., make a profit). The model shows that some business goals are in conflict, that is, the goal of high reliability may conflict with the goal for a low-cost system; those goals will need to be resolved. If a documented goal cannot be in the model (e.g., the goal is part of a strategic vision document), then at least a symbol in the model can trace to or reference the original goal. Ideally, when viewing goals in the modeling tool or a published web model, it should be possible to hyperlink to the goal details.

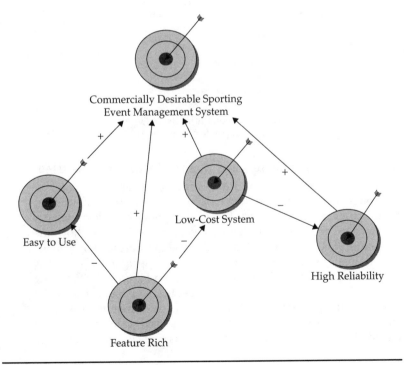

Figure 4.5   Goal model fragment

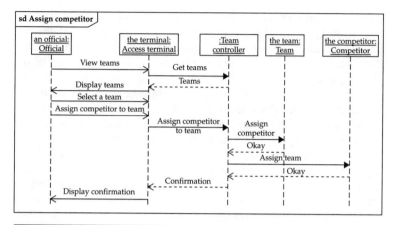

FIGURE 4.6   Sample scenario illustrating assignment of a competitor to a team

FIGURE 4.7
Terminal use case
as a testable
requirement

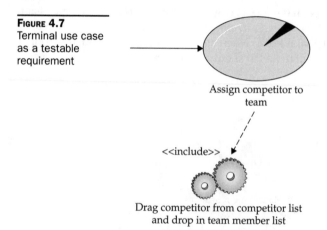

Understanding the Context and How the Product Will Be Used

Product vision and scope documents may provide insight into the
environment where the product will be used as well as information
about the users of the product. These descriptions include contextual
information, as well as sufficient details to understand how the
product will be used by customers. For the example shown here we
provide use cases, although other techniques such as IDEF models
could also be used. In the scenario shown[1] in Figure 4.6, a sporting
event official wants to assign a competitor to a team. Figure 4.7
illustrates the process by which the official uses menus to assign a
competitor to a team. A special symbol is used to indicate that an
included use case is "terminal"; that is, it has no included or extending

---

[1] See any reference on the UML for a description of how such diagrams are created
and read.

use cases and is an endpoint of the analysis (see the next section for more information). The figure illustrates only one possible scenario; there may be many. For example, there may be scenarios where the official enters the wrong competitor (e.g., by assigning a U.S. citizen to the Albanian ski team) or tries to enter a competitor who does not exist. All of these scenarios will have to be defined.

A very common mistake at this point in the elicitation process is not to define error scenarios. The oversight may very well be hidden until it is time to start testing the system, at which point the elicitation of error scenarios may become the responsibility of testers. When testers have to complete scenarios, the elicitation process becomes inefficient to say the least. Not only are testers less likely to have access to the stakeholders to elicit error scenarios, but some of the system may have been designed and built at this point without taking into consideration the need to handle the "to be discovered" error conditions.

While creating the scenario just described, we find that some person or thing must have information about teams and provide information about them (arbitrarily called the "team controller" in Figure 4.6). So we have identified, while creating a scenario, what is typically called a *business object*. A business object is an object that is part of the system (it could be a person, it could be a group of people, it could be a computer system or systems) that performs a needed function or set of related functions. If we can't find a business object that does what we need early in the elicitation process, we create one. Later, we will be collecting requirements by looking at the services that these business objects have to provide in order for the scenarios to work. During this effort we identify needed product features, including the ability to store and retrieve information about teams, store and retrieve information about individual competitors, and so on. As these product features are identified, we can create a *feature tree* that shows the relationship of all these features (see Figure 4.8).

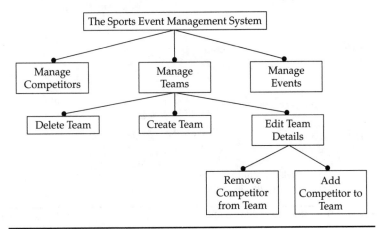

FIGURE 4.8   High-level feature tree

Ideally, the feature tree would be supported in the modeling tool being used. If not, any graphical media could be used to illustrate the full scope of features in the idealized product. Of course, not all the features identified would make it into the final product; they would need to be prioritized. After an analysis effort to expand the product features into well-defined, testable requirements, a product release would then be specified with the desired features. During initial product definition, a feature model is kept relatively "lightweight." However, the same model can be extended to fully support a product line. It can also be used to define product variations or customization that may be made by the user after delivery. Feature models are especially useful in identifying test cases where the system can be configured by the user after delivery.

Analyzing Product Features and Creating a Use Case Model

Once we have a draft set of features, we are able to start creating a model from which we will derive all our customer requirements (all of them, before ranking). Product features become high-level abstract use cases, from which we start the decomposition process to elicit details that will become requirements (Figure 4.9). As we go through each of the features, scenarios are created describing the feature in action; the scenario diagrams describe the usage details (Figure 4.10), and the use case diagrams provide structural information; e.g., which other use cases (or processes) are included or sometimes included (called *extending use cases*).

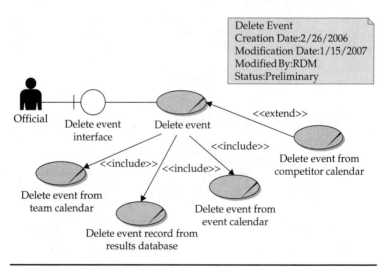

FIGURE **4.9**   Use case decomposition

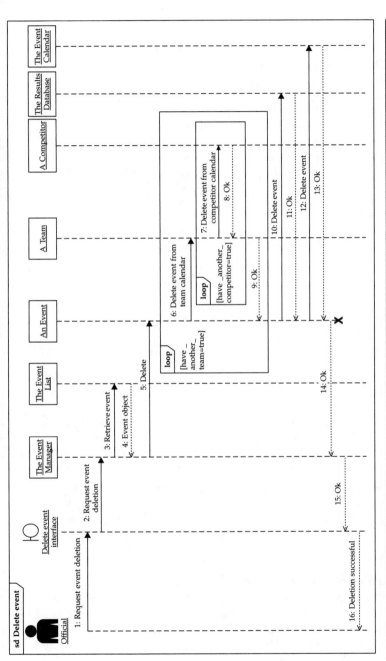

Figure 4.10 Scenario defining the Delete Event use case

As previously mentioned, depending on the starting point, several different types of models (e.g., business, feature, goal, analysis, design, implementation) may be used. As we descend to lower and lower levels within a business, feature, goal, or analysis model, we include more detail.

The lowest level in an analysis model consists of testable use cases, as described with scenarios, flowcharts, and state diagrams. The lower-level use cases and requirements are the same except for phrasing. For example, the use case might be "schedule a patient for a followup visit"; with the corresponding requirement being "It shall be possible to schedule a patient for a followup visit using the scheduling system." It is important to define the lowest use case level from the perspectives of both semantics and mechanics in order to determine when a model is complete. For example, a definition of use case completeness might include these considerations:

- An individual use case shall be considered terminal (e.g., no further decomposition) when it has no included or extending use cases.

- It has been defined with state or activity diagrams describing both successful and unsuccessful outcomes.

- It provides sufficient information for the creation of test cases.

- Its documentation is suitable for use as a requirement definition.

- It has been given a special stereotype of terminal use case (see Figure 4.7).

- A nonterminal concrete use case shall be considered complete when it meets all the quality assurance checks for a nonterminal use case, and all of the leaf use cases that are included or extend it have been defined and are complete.

- A nonterminal abstract use case shall be considered complete when all of the concrete use cases reachable from it are complete. By reachable we mean by traversing the graph consisting of nodes (use cases) and edges (dependencies, e.g., "includes," "extends").

Extracting Requirements from the Model

Prior to starting elicitation and analysis, it is necessary to understand how model(s) will be used on a project. If models are only to be used for background context and to provide information for testers, less formality is required. However, if models are to be mined for requirements and metrics, or if various artifacts are to be semiautomatically generated from the model, then a more formal approach is needed. Since a properly crafted model is an acyclic

```
3.0 Event Management
    3.1 Create Event
    3.2 Delete Event
        3.2.1 Delete Event from Team Calendar
        3.2.2 Delete Event Record from Results Database
        3.2.3 Delete Event from Event Calendar
        3.2.4 Delete Event from Competitor Calendar
    3.3 Edit Event
    3.4 View Events
4.0 Competitor Management
    4.1 Register Competitor
    4.2 Disqualify Competitor
```

Figure 4.11   High-level requirements extracted from model

directed graph, it is possible to extract requirements from models programmatically to populate a requirements database [Berenbach 2003]. An alternative is to keep the requirements in the model, generating tabular views for review or a Systems Requirements Specification (SRS) directly from the model (Figure 4.11).

The UML provides the ability to create profiles with specialized icons and object types. In addition, extensions to the UML exist specifically for business modeling. We recommend improving the clarity and simplicity of business and analysis models by augmenting traditional flowchart or use case symbols with symbols unique to business modeling or the domain wherever possible, and then defining semantics, such as those that we have proposed [Berenbach 2004]. For example, one business rule that has been found to be effective is to require that actors (users of a product) be required to communicate with concrete (testable) use cases through a boundary, except on the context diagram. By enforcing this rule, every point where an interface or form must exist is captured and can be viewed in an inventory report.

In Figure 4.12 we see the nonfunctional requirement that operations must complete within one second impacting the software user interface used by spectators. As mentioned previously, we have

Figure 4.12
Adding
requirements to
diagrams

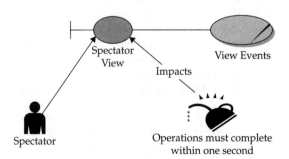

found that using markers to place nonfunctional requirements on a model improve their visibility and reduce the risk that an important nonfunctional requirement will be overlooked during design.

Once the model is complete, a properly constructed tabular set of detailed requirements can be extracted and used as a starting point for the creation of both project task lists and test plans. In addition, it should be possible to generate an interface (user and software) inventory.

Starting an MDRE Effort

When starting an MDRE effort for elicitation or analysis, it is important to

- Define model completion.

- Understand how the model will be used and maintained after completion—this defines what tools are needed and how they are to be integrated.

- Have the appropriate standards and procedures available. Modeling style is important. Without guidelines or directions, analysts might create models that cannot be used effectively for requirements generation, metrics extraction, or data mining.

- Have at least one person on the team to act as a facilitator who has been through a complete MDRE cycle.

- Have the desired tool set in place and ready to use.

Organization of a model is key to performing programmatic verification and requirements extraction. It is important to have the goal of a coherent verifiable model in mind throughout the analysis effort and model construction process. The knowledge contained in an analysis model is valuable to an organization and can be disseminated by publishing to the web. The heuristics described in the following sections will make a model more understandable by making navigation intuitive.

Managing Elicitation and Analysis Sessions

With MDRE, the management of elicitation and analysis sessions is done using the same process, although the participants may be different. Initially, subject matter experts, the team lead, and analysts will participate. At the initial kickoff meeting, the team lead should describe to the core team how the sessions will be run, and provide examples of MDRE artifacts. Thus, the team lead will

- Review guidelines and procedures such as style guides for content and revise (offline) as necessary.

- Describe the modeling techniques and tools to be used.

- Show sample "idealized" models.
- Explain how QA will be performed.
- Define completion criteria.
- Review the draft schedule and expected participants.

The modeling sessions start with a skilled facilitator or team lead modeling across and then down the model (see the heuristic for breadth first modeling in the later section "The Early Modeling Effort Should Cover the Entire Breadth of the Domain"). Once other analysts have gained some experience with modeling sessions, they can take over the lead and get experience as facilitators.

Sessions are usually run in the mornings, three or four times a week. At each session, the subject area to be modeled is known in advance and the appropriate subject matter experts or customers are scheduled into the meeting (see Figure 4.13).

The first order of business in the modeling session is the analysis of metrics from any automated analysis tools that were used on the model. Also, any descriptions that were created offline are reverse-engineered into the model. Assignments to make repairs (offline) are done, and the elicitation sessions continue.

As modeling activities continue, no more than 5–8 people should be present. A projector is used so that participants can see the model under construction or review. Sessions should last no more than half a day. At the conclusion of each modeling session, the facilitator exports a spreadsheet from the model with artifacts and their descriptions.

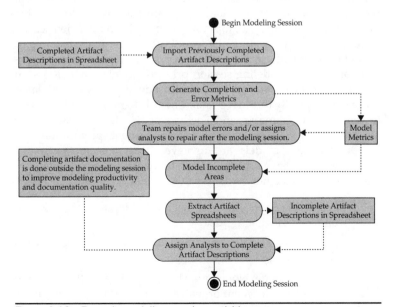

FIGURE **4.13** Example modeling session activities

Missing descriptions are then added to the spreadsheet by the assigned subject matter experts or analysts offline and imported back into the model before the next modeling session.

Wherever possible, the entering of textual descriptions should be avoided during modeling sessions, as it significantly reduces productivity. On the other hand, detailed artifact descriptions (e.g., use cases, requirements, actors, objects) are needed in the model in order to create high-quality documentation. Thus, a facility for "round-tripping" descriptions in and out of the model is essential, and quality assurance reviews of the artifact descriptions should be part of the modeling process.

Improved Productivity Through Distributed Modeling

Once a routine is established and some initial modeling has taken place, all the team members should understand how to use some tools; they will start to model in a consistent style. In addition, after a short period of time, different subject areas that are to be elicited or analyzed will have been identified in the model. At this point, the team can split into groups; each group can then model in their identified domains, bringing in the relevant subject matter experts or stakeholders as necessary.

Conducting Model Reviews

Model reviews are conducted at periodic intervals. During the reviews, everyone on the team and the relevant stakeholders and experts are present. If the team has split into groups, each group will present their work. The facilitator or team lead walks through the model using a hierarchical, top-down approach, and deficiencies are recorded. After the meeting, the team lead assigns analysts to repair the deficiencies in the model, and the repairs are reviewed by the core team at the next modeling session prior to modeling new areas. In addition, spreadsheets of artifacts and their descriptions are circulated for review, typically through e-mail. Careful attention should be paid to the content, grammar, and spelling of the descriptions, as the narrative text will become part of any requirement specifications.

On occasion, models are reviewed with customers. In our experience, we have observed the following positive outcomes resulting from customer model reviews:

- Customers gain confidence that the development organization understands their needs.

- The customer is relieved of the necessity of reviewing massive amounts of text-based documentation.

- The material developed may be reused by both the customer and the development organization (depending on the terms of the contract).

4.6   Elicitation and Analysis Model Heuristics

This section describes a set of heuristics and guidelines for requirements elicitation and analysis sessions when using the UML. These heuristics have been successfully used on several of our larger projects. Note that as heuristics and style guides for the UML have been widely described elsewhere [Riel 1996], [Ambler 2005], the topic will not be covered here. Rather, we have concentrated on heuristics that are necessary for the construction of verifiable models and the programmatic extraction of requirements.

The Model Should Have a Single Entry Point

In order to force a navigable structure, the starting or context diagram should have only a single entry point in the form of an abstract use case or product feature (see Figure 4.14). Giving the diagram a special name, such as "context," will help to identify it. The context diagram is also important because it has all the external entities that the system or product being investigated will have. As we are using use case notation here, we will refer to these entities as actors. They can be people (e.g., team captain), organizations (e.g., sales department), or systems (e.g., police department computer system). Getting the list right is critical, as we will see later that important quality assurance checks are based on the list of actors derived from the context diagram. Hence, we have the related heuristics described in the sections that follow.

All Actors Associated with the System Being Analyzed Should Appear on the Context Diagram

The model should be built as an acyclic directed graph [Crochemore et al. 1997], and the single product feature or use case symbol on the context diagram is the starting node for the graph. Use cases, actors,

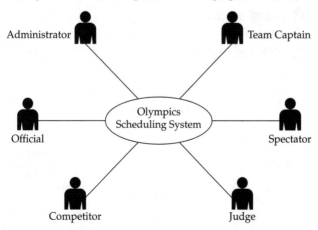

Figure 4.14   Example context diagram

objects, and boundaries or interfaces are the nodes, and the relationships between them are the vertices. However, in order to keep the model simple enough to analyze programmatically, the core of the graph will be the relationship between the use cases and product features. This heuristic, along with the heuristics that describe the use of factors and boundaries, provides one of the semantics for model completion.

The Early Modeling Effort Should Cover the Entire Breadth of the Domain

"Drilling down" too soon risks missing interfaces and subject areas that need to be modeled. By modeling across the entire domain, identifying major areas to be modeled and those that are out of scope, missing interfaces will become readily apparent. For example, in the event management system for the Olympics, rather than the context diagram showing just event management, the first one or two high-level diagrams should include information on team management, competitor management, etc. Once the interfaces between these functions have been identified, then modeling of the event scheduling domain can proceed with confidence that all interfaces to outside organizations, people, and systems have been identified (see Figure 4.15).

Identify "Out-of-Scope" Use Cases as Early as Possible

Define scope and identify "out-of-scope" domains as quickly as possible. We suggest color-coding high-level use cases that are out of scope (see Figure 4.16). When working with distributed teams, it is most important to identify out-of-scope subject areas, to avoid wasting time on material not relevant to the project.

Every Diagram Should Have an Associated Description and Status

Ideally the status will be in a legend on the diagram (see the engineering drawing example shown in Figure 4.1). Real-world models tend to

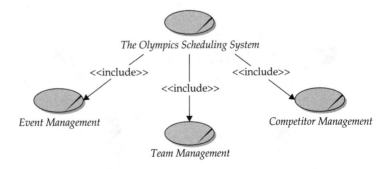

FIGURE 4.15   Initial modeling effort is cross-domain

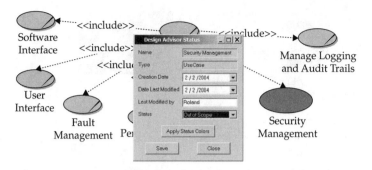

Figure 4.16   Marking an area as out of scope

have a large number of diagrams. When viewing the diagrams in a document, web document, or presentation, it is easy to get lost without a legend. If the legend includes the diagram status, incomplete work is much easier to find (especially if the legend information can be queried programmatically).

Avoid the Early Use of Packages

Packages are used for partitioning work and as virtual folders to store related artifacts. It may not be possible to discern a correct partitioning of the model and work effort until some significant amount of use case modeling has been completed. We have found that the premature use of packaging may result in frequent model reorganizations. If packaging does not follow the logical organization of the subject matter, flaws in construction may surface at a very late date (e.g., components that are tightly coupled).

Do Not Substitute Packages for Abstract Use Cases

As stated previously, the model is a single unbroken directed graph. Directed graphs or digraphs can be traversed using breadth- or depth-first searching techniques. Substituting packages for abstract use cases or product features breaks the graph and creates semantic ambiguity because packages are just storage mechanisms or placeholders; i.e., they have no meaning in the context of process (Figure 4.17).

Every Artifact in a Model Should Be Visible on a Diagram

A model stores artifacts and their relationships. It is possible to remove objects from diagrams without removing them from the model. The hidden artifacts may only show up during reviews of printed material generated from the model. In order to be able to conduct visual inspections of the model, every artifact in it should be visible on at least one of the appropriate types of diagram.

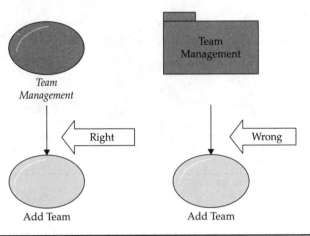

FIGURE 4.17   Incorrect use of packages

Every Symbol Should Have a Bidirectional Hyperlink to the Diagrams That Define It

The ability to create a link from a symbol on a diagram to another diagram is tool specific. However, when navigating large models, the ability is mandatory. This makes navigation intuitive and enables programmatic model traversal. Table 4.1 highlights the kinds of links that would be expected when using a UML CASE tool to do MDRE.

Package Dependencies Should Be Based on Content

If any artifact in package A has a dependency on an artifact in package B, then on a class diagram a dependency should be shown between package A and package B. If, however, none of the artifacts belonging to package A have any dependencies with artifacts in package B, then there should not be a dependency relationship between package A and package B. Since in complex models it may be difficult to determine dependencies by inspection, an automated mechanism is recommended.

Every Concrete Use Case Must Be Defined

A use case diagram identifies business processes and their static relationships with actors, entities, and other use cases (see Figure 4.18). Without temporal information, the use case description is incomplete. Consequently, every concrete use case must be defined using one or more sequence, collaboration, activity, or state diagrams that provide temporal information. Note also that one diagram is usually not sufficient, as there may be many different outcomes, depending on the starting conditions and preconditions.

Symbol	Hyperlink To	Rationale
Abstract use case representing a set of functions	Use case diagram	An abstract use case is a placeholder for a product feature or concept and does not have logic. It is the included use cases that would have concrete logic.
Abstract use case representing a product feature	Use case diagram	Abstract use cases and product features may need to be decomposed several levels before concrete, testable features or use cases are reached. In order to keep the diagrams simple, it is necessary to be able to hyperlink use case diagrams that continue the hierarchy.
Concrete use case	Use case diagram	Use cases with many ancillary processes may need to be decomposed several levels. The ability to put only one level of decomposition on a diagram reduces clutter and makes the model more manageable.
Concrete use case	Activity diagram	When a use case is concrete (e.g., testable), there may be many possible paths. While scenario diagrams are good for showing one path, the best way to see all the possible outcomes or variations is to use an activity diagram as an overview, showing, in simplified fashion, all possible paths that the process may take.
Concrete use case	Sequence diagram	A use case is a process. One specific thread (e.g., a success mode or a failure mode) is best shown on one diagram for clarity.
Concrete use case	Activity diagram	When a process is primarily sequential logic (e.g., an algorithm or computation) activity diagrams do a much better job of presenting the logic than sequence diagrams, showing activities, inputs, and outputs.

TABLE **4.1**   Example Hyperlinks

Symbol	Hyperlink To	Rationale
Concrete use case	State diagram	Event-driven logic (e.g., the process behaves as a state machine) is best described with a state diagram.
Message	Activity or state diagram	A message on a sequence diagram represents a single service that is usually described with an activity or state diagram.
Activity	Activity or state diagram	An activity may be relatively complex. One property of activity and state diagrams is that each activity (activity diagram) or transition (state diagram) can be exploded to another activity or state diagram to reveal increasing levels of detail.
Hazard	Hazard analysis diagram or document	When extending the UML or other modeling language (e.g., the URML) a hazard symbol may be shown on a use case diagram. If hazard models are built into the tool, the hyperlink may be to a hazard model-specific diagram; otherwise, it may link to a complete hazard analysis document.
Threat	Threat model diagram or document	In a similar fashion to hazards, threats shown on use case diagrams can hyperlink to either threat model diagrams or threat analysis documents.
Requirements	Requirements may be shown on use case or other diagrams as either stereotyped use cases or custom artifacts	Requirements can hyperlink to their corresponding entry in requirements databases, or to other documentation that contains more details. Where feasible, a bidirectional link is best, e.g., requirement on diagram hyperlinks to requirement in database, requirement in database hyperlinks to requirement on diagram.

TABLE 4.1   Example Hyperlinks (*continued*)

Add Competitor
to Team

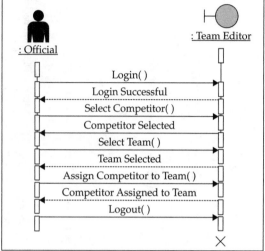

FIGURE 4.18   Example of defining a use case with a scenario

Use an Activity Diagram to Show All Possible Scenarios Associated with a Use Case

Sequence and collaboration diagrams are typically used to show a single thread of execution per diagram. It is possible to put more than one thread on a collaboration diagram, but it makes the diagram cluttered and hard to read. Using an activity diagram as an overview (e.g., "all paths") of the process makes it easier to identify important logic threads that need to be defined. Where possible, create hyperlinks on the "all paths" diagrams to create an intrinsic trace to the associated threads. For example, an item can be either scheduled or back-ordered. Both possibilities are shown in Figure 4.19.

Use Sequence Rather Than Collaboration Diagrams to Define One Thread/Path for a Process

The UML is flexible (sometimes too flexible) regarding the choice of diagrams for defining a process. Sequence, collaboration, activity, and state diagrams can all be used. However, we have found that sequence and activity diagrams are the easiest for nontechnical reviewers to read. As sequence and activity diagrams have a timeline, they force subject matter experts to be methodical when eliciting process information.

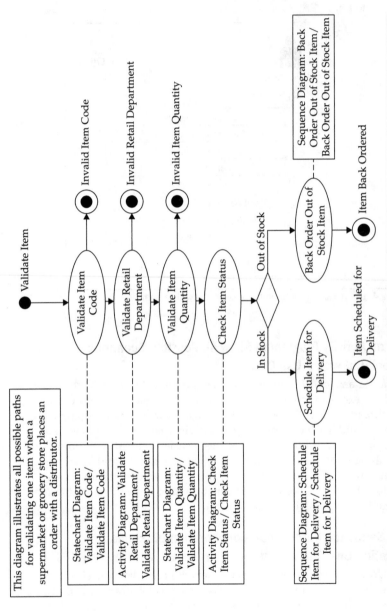

Figure 4.19 Sample "All paths" activity diagram for the "validate item" use case

Since the MDRE process starts with product features that become use cases, when explaining them with sequence diagrams the objects that communicate are initially not known (with the exception of actors). During sequence diagram creation, objects necessary to provide services are "discovered." The objects are then placed as classes on class diagrams and later organized by combining similar classes or splitting classes that provide too many services or have disjoint or unrelated services. Sequence diagrams force the early discovery of objects, along with their associated classes and business services. We have found that sequence diagrams are better for elicitation services and sequence features, while activity diagrams do a better job of illustrating complex logic.

Abstract Use Cases Must Be Realized with Included or Inherited Concrete Use Cases

Abstract use cases represent product features that are at a very high level (e.g., "power steering") or can be a placeholder for sets of processes (e.g., "manage teams"). They must be decomposed to sets of features or processes that are testable.

The definition of a use case must be consistent across all diagrams defining the use case. A use case shown on a use case diagram can *include* other use cases and can optionally be *extended* by other use cases. Included and extending use cases will appear on sequence diagrams as messages to objects that will perform the requested service. Consistency can be defined as follows (see Figure 4.20):

- There will be at least one message on a defining sequence diagram with the same name as each included use case; that is, how a use case fits into a process must be explained. Otherwise, the use case is ambiguous; e.g., it uses other processes but does not explain how they are used.

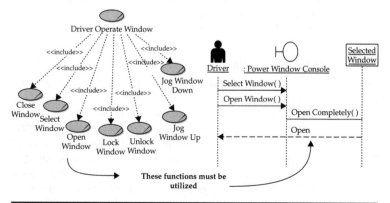

Figure 4.20   Semantic correctness requires that every concrete use case must be used in a scenario.

- There will be at least one message on a defining sequence diagram with the same name as each extending use case.
- Every actor interface or boundary communication will appear on at least one sequence diagram.
- Any entities shown attached to a use case will appear as an item being passed (message argument) on at least one sequence diagram or as an object on an activity diagram.

Extending Use Case Relationships Can Only Exist Between Like Use Cases

The extending relationship is a specialized extension to a well-defined process. As such, both the extending and extended use cases must be of the same type. Using the extending relationship where one of the use cases is abstract and the other is concrete leads to ambiguity. For example, extending "manage documents" with "place document under configuration management" is ambiguous, as we don't know whether a new or existing document is being placed under configuration management.

A Concrete Use Case Cannot Include an Abstract Use Case

The rationale is the same as for the extending relationship. A concrete use case that includes an abstract use case is ambiguous; e.g., it cannot be defined.

Avoid Realization Relationships and Artifacts in the Analysis Model

Realization relationships have different meanings, depending on the context in which they are used. This can lead to ambiguity and confusion. A realization relationship between two use cases means that one of the use cases "implements" the other use case. Realization of a use case by a sequence diagram indicates that the sequence diagram explains the use case process.

Business Object Modeling

Business object modeling is the process of describing behavior in a domain. By describing the behavior of the subject areas associated with feature-level requirements, we expose details of the subject area, and by doing so we elicit requirements and business rules. During the analysis modeling effort, classes are sometimes referred to as "business objects," not to be confused with the objects on sequence and collaboration diagrams that are class instances. Defining classes for objects as they are discovered will keep the effort focused on the domain processes (as opposed to data).

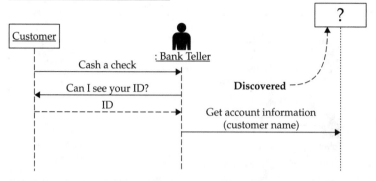

In this "Cash Check" scenario, we discover that a business object is needed that can retrieve a customer's account information.

FIGURE **4.21**   Using scenarios to discover needed business objects

Discover Business Objects and Their Services Through Use Case Definition with Sequence Diagrams

Modelers with a development background sometimes start building a model by defining classes and then drawing class diagrams. This skews the model and makes it data-centric. Sequence diagrams consist of objects and messages. When objects are placed on diagrams, they initially will not belong to a class. The objects needed are discovered by identifying services that have to be provided, and then identifying who will provide them (see Figure 4.21).

Every Service in a Business Object Should Have Defined Pre- and Post-Conditions

In an analysis model, services are discovered using sequence diagrams, usually as messages. The messages are then incorporated into the servicing object as services or methods. Pre- and post-conditions are then attached. In order to distinguish "none" from an oversight, an entry can be made indicating that there are no pre-post-conditions.

A Boundary or Interface Should Only Communicate with a Concrete Use Case

An abstract use case is an arbitrary container for a set of features, some of which may not require an interface. Consequently interfaces or boundaries permitting communication between an actor and a use case should only be associated with concrete use cases (Figure 4.22).

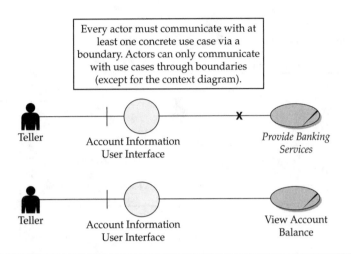

> Every actor must communicate with at least one concrete use case via a boundary. Actors can only communicate with use cases through boundaries (except for the context diagram).

Teller   Account Information User Interface   *Provide Banking Services*

Teller   Account Information User Interface   View Account Balance

FIGURE 4.22 Illustrating the correct and incorrect way for an actor to communicate with a use case

We prefer the use of boundaries in the analysis model to distinguish them from interfaces in the design model. A boundary symbol and an interface symbol are different, and, depending on the modeling tool, can be selected by choosing the artifact stereotype. Actors should be shown communicating with concrete use cases through actors at the lowest possible level. For example, instead of having a boundary "Bank_Computer_Boundary," there would be "Find_Customer_ Boundary," "View_Customer_Account_Boundary," "Cash_Customer_ Check_Boundary," and so on. While this may appear to be a lot of extra work, in reality it saves a significant amount of time in that when the analysis model is complete, the architect will have a complete inventory of every form, partial form, or other interface type needed for each function (see Figure 4.23).

Report

Interface	Actors	Diagrams
Account for Cost Interface		Account for Cost [Use Case]
Add Location Interface	IS Worker	Add Location [Use Case]
Allocate Payment Interface	Cashier	Allocate Payment [Use Case]
Approve Adjustment Interface	Collection Supervisor	Approve Adjustment [Use Case]
Archive Encounter Interface	IS Worker	Archive Encounter [Use Case]
...	...	...

Generates

FIGURE 4.23 Creating a boundary report

A Concrete Class Must Be Instantiated

If a concrete class is not instantiated, it means that the class is not used in any processes; e.g., it does not appear on a sequence, activity or collaboration diagram. The question then arises, if it is not used, why is it in the model?

A Boundary or Interface Class Is Properly Defined If and Only If It Has Public Methods, and Each of These Methods Is Shown on a Sequence or Collaboration Diagram

This heuristic is self-explanatory. Missing public methods (services) in a boundary or interface are typically an oversight.

Every Business Object Service (i.e., Class Method) Should Be Defined

Class methods are typically defined using a state or activity diagram. A state diagram is used when the logic is "event driven," and an activity diagram is often used when the logic is procedural.

Every Actor in the Model Should Communicate with Use Cases Through Boundaries

At the context level we identify all the actors associated with the domain being modeled. However, in order to adequately explain the nature of the communication, at some point every actor–use case interaction must take place through a boundary.

Using Boundaries as Proxies for External Objects

During a project to create a medical billing system for a hospital, we observed that the scheduling function was out of scope, yet scheduling services were needed. A "scheduling system" boundary was created as a catchall, and in any scenario where scheduling was needed, a message would be sent to the scheduling system requesting a service, along with the supplied and returned information. As the modeling effort neared completion, the project manager for the scheduling system development effort approached our team and inquired about what scheduling services the billing system would need. She was shocked when within five minutes we were able to generate a complete report showing all scheduling services needed by medical billing, which billing system actors used the service, and what scenarios (context) they were used in. Even though the model had over eight hundred use cases and several thousand diagrams, such complex queries were a relatively simple matter as the model had been designed with scale in mind.

Avoid Passive Objects

A *passive object* is one that receives messages but never sends any (including replies). Broadcasting messages where there is no mechanism for determining whether the message was received may cause instabilities or unreliable behavior and is not recommended.

Avoid Loquacious Objects

Loquacious objects are those that send many messages to other objects without receiving any. Although sometimes necessary, they can lead to instability and poor performance.

Coherent Low-Level Processes Should Be Defined with State or Activity Diagrams

As previously mentioned, a concrete use case is defined by showing temporal behavior with sequence, state chart, or activity diagrams. If the use case does not include and is not extended by use cases, then it is a "leaf" or terminal use case and should be defined with a state or activity diagram or perhaps with just a paragraph of text. If there are many possible scenarios associated with the use case, then an overview activity diagram should be used and each individual scenario can hyperlink from the "all paths" activity diagram associated with the use case.

Elicit Requirements and Processes by Starting at Boundaries and Modeling Inward

The static relationships between processes and their associated requirements are defined first using use case diagrams. As concrete use cases are exposed, their communication with actors is discovered and boundaries (e.g., a class with a boundary stereotype) are defined.

Hide Complexity by Using Compound Business Objects

On a high-level sequence diagram a compound object such as a "Master Schedule" will hide complexity. On a lower-level diagram, "Master Schedule" will be decomposed into the objects that contribute to processes (such as an inventory object that could determine if an item is in stock and, if so, which warehouse it is in).

Initiate Prototyping Efforts Quickly

Prototyping is an extremely valuable way of eliciting requirements from subject matter experts. There are normally two types of prototypes. The marketing prototype is a "throwaway" tool to elicit customer interest and define potential product features. It is treated as a background reference when modeling. The requirements prototype may be reusable; prototype development and model development are synchronized such that each provides information that assists in defining the other (see Chapter 9).

Ideally, the requirements prototype will be reusable for construction of the actual product. This will only happen if the target language, coding standards, and architecture are known prior to the start of model construction. Unfortunately, those facts being known, the model might wind up being "skewed" toward development.

4.7 Determining Model Completeness

Models are reviewed for completeness by looking at three areas: diagram quality, content correctness (reviewed with subject matter experts), and model faults. The criteria for completeness should have been defined prior to the start of modeling.

Diagram Quality

Diagrams should be reviewed for clarity and completeness. Upon acceptance of a diagram, its status can be changed from draft to accepted. In order for a model to be accepted, every diagram in the model should have a status of accepted. Depending on the organization's specific quality assurance procedures, an MDRE model could pass conditionally if diagrams have minor changes to be made and those changes

- Are well understood.
- Are quickly accomplished.
- Do not change the semantics of the model.
- Do not impact other parts of the model.

Content Correctness

Content correctness is accomplished by having subject matter experts and analysts review reports and documents generated from the model. The following criteria are applied:

- Every use case, whether abstract or concrete, must have a text definition that is meaningful and correct.
- Every concrete use case with extending or included use cases must have at least one activity or sequence diagram describing its logic.
- Every boundary (user interface or software interface) must be shown on at least one diagram explaining how it is used, and that explanation must be correct.

Model Faults That Should Be Corrected
Before a Model Is Completed

Some MDRE model faults are serious and, if not corrected, can lead to problems during development. Where possible, the fault checks should be performed programmatically, as performing them manually could be prone to errors and time consuming. Some of the checks that can be performed are shown in Table 4.2.

Error	Indicates That
Circular Dependency	There is the possibility of deadlock, e.g., a depends on b, which depends on c, which depends on a. This can result in confusing or incomplete requirements.
Class Not Instanced	A concrete class has been defined to the model; however, an instance of the class cannot be found on any sequence or activity diagram. This means nowhere is it shown how this business object is used.
Concrete Use Case Not Defined	A process has not been adequately described. It does not have enough information provided to extract requirements.
Dangling Abstract Use Case	A subject area has not yet been modeled, the model is incomplete.
Hidden Artifact	Something in the model is not shown on any diagram. It appears to have been forgotten or overlooked.
Illegal Extending Association	An extending relationship has an abstract use case at least on one end, causing ambiguity.
Illegal Interface Association	A boundary or interface has an association with an abstract use case. This association will result in ambiguous requirements being generated.
Interface Not Used	An interface or boundary (a class with a stereotype of boundary) has been shown on a use case diagram, but nowhere is it explained how it is used.
Missing Boundary	The interaction of an actor with the product, either via software (a software interface) or visually (a user interface, panel, etc.), is missing.
Mixed Use Case Relationships	A use case with mixed abstract/concrete included/ extending use cases is ambiguous, and as a result any requirements derived from it may also be ambiguous.
Unused Concrete Actor	It probably means that the model is incomplete, or the actor does not communicate with the system. An actor can only access a process through a boundary.
Use Case Completeness	Parts of the definition of the use case are missing. This may result in incorrect or incomplete requirements.

TABLE 4.2 Serious Model Faults

4.8　Transitioning from Analysis to Design

At some point, we may be interested in taking an analysis model, and creating a design model from it. We must ensure that traceability is maintained from analysis to design, where the development effort is relatively straightforward, with the target hardware and/or software platform known in advance. A good starting point for design heuristics can be found in the *Design Patterns* text by Gamma et al. [Gamma et al. 1994], and the text on *Design Heuristics* by Arthur Riel [Riel 1996]. Note that the heuristics described here are primarily for software components.

4.9　Suggested Model Conversion Heuristics

We will start with some important low-level heuristics and then describe some high-level heuristics/guidelines.

Design Model Package Structure

The design package structure will resemble, but not be exactly the same as, the analysis structure. This is because the analysis views mirror the problem, whereas the logical views show the design of the solution to the problem.

Use Case Tracing

Use case tracing can be done with "off the shelf" CASE tool techniques. A concrete use case in the analysis model MUST be realized[2] by one or more use case realizations in the design model. The use case realization then becomes a subsystem, set of components, etc., further down in the model (see Figure 4.24).

Interface Tracing

Interface tracing is illustrated in Figure 4.25. In general, a boundary in the analysis model will be realized by one or more interfaces in the design model.

Artifact Tracing

Tracing between the analysis and design model elements can be done using the "<<realize>>" stereotyped association. Table 4.3 lists the most important elements and their relationships.

---

[2] "Realized" is UML terminology meaning "implemented by." In the UML the arrows are drawn from the solution back to the problem definition (requirements) and the stereotype of the line is "<<realize>>."

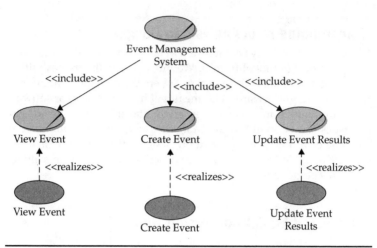

FIGURE 4.24   Tracing use case realizations to use cases

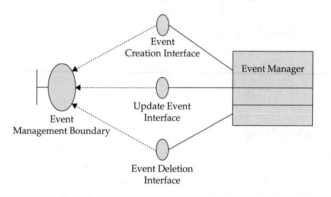

FIGURE 4.25   Boundary-to-interface tracing

Design Model Element	Analysis Model Element	Comment
Use Case Realization	Business Use Case	The use case realization represents a physical implementation of a process or set of processes, as an executable program, a subsystem, etc.
Interface	Boundary	Analysis Model concrete classes with a stereotype of boundary are realized by one or more design model classes with a stereotype of interface.
Software Classes	Business Objects	Business Objects represented as analysis model classes are realized in the design model by "plain" software classes.

TABLE 4.3   Analysis to Design Tracing Relationships

4.10   Design Model Structure

The design model structure is flexible and dependent upon

- Granularity of model for parallel development.
- How close the design model (solution) matches the analysis model.

Tracing Requirements Through the Design Model

Tracing of requirements through the design model (see Figure 4.26) can be accomplished as follows:

- Ensure that all requirements in the requirements database (if used) trace to one or more use cases in the analysis model. For "child" requirements, it is acceptable for the parent requirement to trace to a use case.
- Every concrete use case or requirement as shown in the analysis model must be realized by one or more use case realizations in the design model.
- All software classes or components in the design model are associated with one or more use case realizations. Association means that they are shown on class diagrams that are owned by the respective use case realization or one of its derivatives.
- Wherever possible, have the package structure in the design model mirror that in the analysis model.

Intermodel Quality Assurance Checks

Some quality assurance checks can be performed to ensure that the analysis and design models are synchronized.

1. Can every requirement be traced to a component, either directly or indirectly?
2. Can every component be traced to a use case?
3. Can every concrete use case trace to a component?
4. Are there test cases for each component?

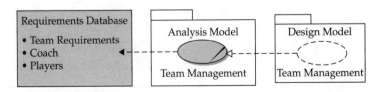

FIGURE 4.26   Tracing from design to requirements

5. Do the test cases match (are appropriate) for the related requirements?

6. Do system-level requirements derive from the components; e.g., a component must perform the following functions...?

Design Model Initial Construction

When a design model is derived from the analysis model, the following steps are normally taken:

1. Naming conventions and design standards are identified and applied.

2. For each major use case in the analysis model, packages are created in the design model.

3. Use case realizations provide tracing from the requirements to the design. These realizations are inserted at whatever level is deemed necessary by the lead architect and quality assurance. Reports can then be generated showing the analysis model use case, associated requirements, and associated components (by tracing from the use case realization to its associated components).

4. Boundaries transform to one or more user interface forms or other (software or hardware) interfaces (see Figure 4.27).

Impact analysis can then be performed on an ad hoc basis, by simply pointing to a requirement, tracing through the use cases associated with that requirement to the use case realizations, and from the realizations to the components associated with those realizations (e.g., the realizations are the trace points that join the analysis and design models).

Figure 4.28, for example, shows an artifact model with the relationships between an analysis model created using the MDRE and a design created from the analysis model using the UML.

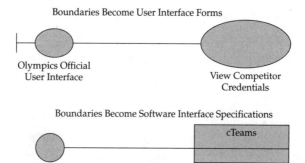

Boundaries Become User Interface Forms

Olympics Official
User Interface

View Competitor
Credentials

Boundaries Become Software Interface Specifications

cTeams

ITeams

Figure 4.27 Boundaries become forms or interface specifications.

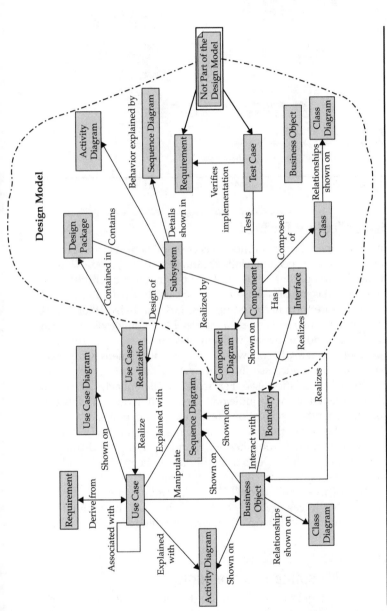

FIGURE 4.28   Relationship of elements in the analysis and design models

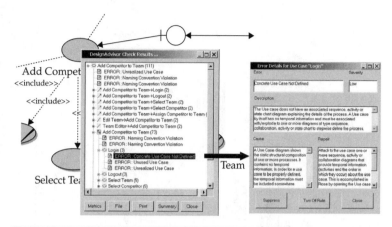

FIGURE 4.29   Using the tool DesignAdvisor to find errors

4.11   Use of Tooling for MDRE

When a large model or set of models is created, there is just too much material for visual inspection. Unlike natural languages, models have a mathematical grounding that enables programmatic checks. For example, analysis models are usually acyclic directed graphs, and feature models are normally tree structures. Such graphs lend themselves to programmatic traversal and data mining. Ideally, any tools used can be customized and simplified with profiles and semantics (rules). A plug-in tool, DesignAdvisor, was developed at Siemens Corporate Research and used successfully to provide automated checking of critical model heuristics (see Figure 4.29) [Berenbach 2003]. As mentioned previously, with judicious use, instrumented models can be made to generate specifications, tests, and project plans.

If a model is not in the final requirements repository, a first set of requirements is mined from the model and then imported into the requirements repository. Decisions will have to be made about how the two different data stores will be kept synchronized. We suggest the creation of an artifact model (Chapter 2) and the identification of all the possible traces or links, and how they will be maintained (during and after project completion) when defining a tool integration strategy.

4.12   Tips for Modeling Requirements

The tips shown below are "food for thought". Holistically, they suggest an engineered rather than an ad hoc or artistic approach to model creation.

- Develop models at different levels of abstraction for different purposes.

- Develop process models that are understandable by viewers who are not experts in the domain being described.

- Develop models that are coherent, with no holes or discontinuities.

- For creating and viewing models, select tools that are easy to use and enable processes, not cause difficulties.

- As MDRE techniques might not work as well as desired the first time they are used, select a small, noncritical project as the first pilot for MDRE.

- Understand how the model will be used and maintained after completion—this defines what tools are needed and how they are to be integrated.

- Have at least one person on the team to act as a facilitator who has been through a complete MDRE cycle.

- Schedule modeling sessions in the mornings, three or four times a week. At each session, the subject area to be modeled is known in advance and the appropriate subject matter experts or customers are scheduled into the meeting.

- As the modeling sessions continue, have no more than 5–8 people present. A projector is used so that everyone present can see the model under construction or review. Sessions should last no more than half a day.

- Avoid entering textual descriptions during modeling sessions, as it significantly reduces productivity.

- Assure that the starting or context diagram for a model has only a single entry point in the form of an abstract use case or product feature.

- Define scope and identify "out-of-scope" domains as quickly as possible, and color-code any high-level use cases that are out of scope.

- Review all model diagrams for clarity and completeness.

- Create a Requirements Engineering Artifact Model, identifying all possible traces or links and how they will be maintained (during and after project completion), prior to initial use of the RE tool set.

4.13 Summary

In this chapter, you have seen how the MDRE approach to requirements engineering can be effective on large projects. We believe that as projects increase in size and complexity, the use of hierarchical databases for requirements storage and the review of textual material may be inadequate to ensure a positive outcome.

Visual techniques that combine and improve on traditional modeling and text-based requirements elicitation and analysis techniques have been successfully piloted at Siemens, resulting in work products with consistent high quality and uniformity. While modeling skills are important when using MDRE, it is often possible to use an incremental approach to process and methodology improvement. We suggest experimenting with "lightweight" modeling techniques initially on small projects, and as confidence increases, gradually moving from a natural language approach to a more formal, model-driven process.

4.14   Discussion Questions

1. What are some of the advantages of using models to describe requirements over text-based approaches?

2. What types of tests can be automatically performed on requirements models to help find errors?

3. What are some of the skills required for those who lead requirements elicitation sessions?

References

Alexander, I., "Capturing Use Cases with DOORS," *Fifth IEEE International Symposium on Requirements Engineering (RE '01)*, Toronto, Canada, August 2001, p. 264.

Ambler, S., *The Elements of UML 2.0 Style,* Cambridge University Press, New York, NY, 2005.

Babin, G. and Lustman, F., "Formal Data and Behavior Requirements Engineering: a Scenario-Based Approach," *Proceedings of SEA '99: 3rd Annual IASTED International Conference on Software Engineering and Applications,* N.C. Debnath and R.Y. Lee, eds., Scottsdale, AZ, USA, 1999, pp. 119–125.

Berenbach, B., "The Automated Extraction of Requirements from UML Models," *Eleventh IEEE International Symposium on Requirements Engineering (RE '03),* Monterey Bay, CA, September 2003, pp. 287–288.

Berenbach, B., "The Evaluation of Large, Complex UML Analysis and Design Models," *Twenty-Sixth International Conference on Software Engineering (ICSE 2004),* Edinburgh, Scotland, May 2004.

Berenbach, B. and Borotto, G., "Metrics for Model-Driven Requirements Development," *Proceeding of the 28th International Conference on Software Engineering,* Shanghai, 2006, pp. 445–451.

Berenbach, B. and Gall, M., "Toward a Unified Model for Requirements Engineering," *Proceedings of the IEEE International Conference on Global Software Engineering,* Munich, 2006, pp. 237–238.

Bradley, D.A., Dawson, D., Burd, N.C., and Loader, A.J., *Mechatronics: Electronics in Products and Processes,* Chapman and Hall, London, 1991.

Breu, R., Hinkel, U., Hofmann, C., Klein, C., Paech, B., Rumpe, B., and Thurner, V., "Towards a Formalization of the Unified Modeling Language," *Proceedings of ECOOP '97,* Springer Verlag, LNCS, 1997.

Cheng, B. and Campbell, L., "Integrating Informal and Formal Approaches to Requirements Modeling and Analysis," *Fifth IEEE International Symposium on Requirements Engineering (RE '01),* Toronto, ON, August 2001, pp. 294–295.

Chung, L. and Subramanian, N., "Process-Oriented Metrics for Software Architecture Adaptability," *Fifth IEEE International Symposium on Requirements Engineering (RE '01)*, Toronto, ON, August 2001, pp. 310–311.

Cox, K., "Taking to Scenarios to Improve the Requirements Process: an Experience Report," *IEE Seminar: Scenarios Through the System Life Cycle*, London, UK, 2000, pp. 1–10.

Creighton, O., Ott, M., and Bruegge, B., "Software Cinema-Video-Based Requirements Engineering," *Proceedings of the 14th IEEE International Requirements Engineering Conference (RE '06)*, 2006, pp. 109–118.

Crochemore, M., Verin, R., "Direct Construction of Compact Directed Acyclic Word Graphs," *8th Annual Symposium, CPM 97*, Aarhus, Denmark, 1997, pp. 116–129.

Dulac, N., Viguier, T., Leveson, N., and Storey, M., "On the Use of Visualization in Formal Requirements Specification," *IEEE Joint International Conference on Requirements Engineering (RE '02)*, Essen, Germany, September 2002, pp. 71–80.

Fowler, M., *UML Distilled*, Addison-Wesley, Boston, MA, 2004.

France, R.B. and Bruel, J.M., "A UML Profile for Rigorous Requirements Modeling," *Proceedings of 2000 Conference on Software Engineering and Applications*, M.H. Hamza, ed., Las Vegas, NV, USA, 2000, pp. 86–91.

Gamma, E., Helm, R., Johnson, R., and Vlissides, J., *Design Patterns: Elements of Reusable Object-Oriented Software*, Addison-Wesley, Boston, 1994.

Gane, C., *Structured Systems Analysis: Tools and Techniques*, Prentice-Hall, Englewood Cliffs, NJ, 1979.

Hartmann, J., Vieira, M., and Ruder, A., "UML-Based Test Generation and Execution," *Proceedings of the 21st Workshop on Software Test, Analyses and Verification (GI-FG TAV)*, Berlin, June 2004.

Hsia, P., Samuel, J., Gao, J., Kung, D., Toyoshima, Y., and Chen, C., "Formal Approach to Scenario Analysis," *IEEE Software*, IEEE, Piscataway, NJ, USA, March 1994, pp. 33–41.

IEEE, *IEEE Standard for Conceptual Modeling Language Syntax and Semantics for IDEF1X$_{97}$ (IDEF$_{object}$)*, IEEE Standard 1302.2-1998.

Jackson, M., "Formalism and Informality in RE," *Fifth IEEE International Symposium on Requirements Engineering (RE '01)*, Toronto, Canada, August 2001, p. 269.

Jacobson, I., Booch, G., and Rumbaugh, J., *The Unified Software Development Process*, Addison Wesley Longman, Massachusetts, 1999.

Jarke, M., "CREWS: Towards Systematic Usage of Scenarios, Use Cases and Scenes," *Wirtschaftsinformatik 99*, Springer Aktuell, Saarbrücken, Germany, March 1999.

Jarke, M., "Scenarios for Modeling," *Communications of the ACM, Vol 42, No. 1*, Association for Computing Machinery, January, 1999, pp. 47–48.

Karner, G., "Metrics for Objectory," Diploma thesis, University of Linköping, Sweden, No. LiTHIDA-Ex-9344:21, December 1993.

Kosters, G., Six, H., and Winter, M., "Coupling Use Cases and Class Models as a Means for Validation and Verification of Requirements Specifications," *Requirements Engineering, Vol. 6, No. 1*, Springer-Verlag, London, UK, 2001.

Lau, Y.-T., "*Service-Oriented Architecture and the C4ISR Framework*," *Crosstalk*, September 2004.

Li, X., Liu, Z., and He, J., "Formal and Use-Case Driven Requirement Analysis in UML," *25th Annual International Computer Software and Applications Conference*, Chicago, IL, 2001, pp. 215–224.

Lorenz, M., and Kidd, J., *Object-Oriented Software Metrics: A Practical Guide*, Prentice-Hall, NJ, 1994.

Muthig, J.D., Sody, P., and Tolzmann, E., "Efficient and Systematic Software Evolution Through Domain Analysis," *IEEE Joint International Conference on Requirements Engineering (RE '02)*, Essen, Germany, September 2002, pp. 237–246.

NRC/ERB-1072, January 2000, NRC 43619.

Rational Rose Enterprise Edition is a product of IBM Corporation, www.ibm.com.

Riel, A.J., *Object-Oriented Design Heuristics,* Addison-Wesley, Indianapolis, 1996.

Rugaber, S., Shikano, T., and Stirewalt, R.E., "Adequate Reverse Engineering," *Proceedings of the 16th IEEE International Conference on Automated Software Engineering,* Los Alamitos, CA, 2001, p. 232.

Salazar-Zarate, G., Botella, P., and Dahanayake, A., "An Approach to Deal with Non-Functional Requirements Within UML," *Issues and Trends of Information Technology Management in Contemporary Organizations, 2002 Information Resources Management Association International Conference, vol. 1,* Seattle, WA, 2002, pp. 702–704.

Shulz, J.D., "Requirements-Based UML," *Proceedings of the 39th International Conference and Exhibition on Technology of Object-Oriented Languages and Systems (TOOLS 39),* Q. Li, R. Riehle, G. Pour, and B. Meyer, eds., Santa Barbara, CA, 2001, pp. 307–316.

Singh, Y., Sabharwal, S., and Sood, M., "A Systematic Approach to Measure the Problem Complexity of Software Requirement Specifications of an Information System," *Information and Management Sciences,* Vol. 15, No. 1, 2004, pp. 69–90.

Software Engineering Institute, *The Capability Maturity Model Version 1.1,* CMU/SEI-93-TR-024, www.sei.cmu.edu/cmmi/, 1993.

Stutz, C., Siedersleben, J., Kretschmer, D., and Krug, W., "Analysis Beyond UML," *IEEE Joint International Conference on Requirements Engineering (RE '02),* Essen, Germany, September 2002, pp. 215–218.

Sutcliffe, A., "Requirements Engineering for Complex Collaborative Systems," *Fifth IEEE International Symposium on Requirements Engineering (RE '01),* Toronto, Canada, August 2001, pp. 110–119.

The Object Modeling Group, *OMG Unified Modeling Specification Version 1.4,* Object Management Group, Needham MA, September 2001.

White, P., and Mitchelmore, M.C., *Intelligence, Learning and Understanding in Mathematics: A Tribute to Richard Skemp,* Flaxton, QLD: Post Pressed 2002, pp. 235–255.

Yourdon, E., *Modern Structured Analysis,* Prentice-Hall, Englewood Cliffs, NJ, 1988.

CHAPTER 5

Quality Attribute Requirements

by Raghu Sangwan, Hans Ros, Bob Schwanke

Michael was assigned as a software architect on a project to develop a building security management system. He knew that he would start this assignment by talking to the requirements engineers, review the requirements in the database, and become familiar with the operation of some similar products developed by his company and its competitors. He planned to learn enough about what the new product would do to be able to propose a draft architecture for efficiently meeting the requirements.

He began reviewing the functional requirements that had already been described in the requirements management database and the high-level use cases and scenarios that had been developed. He quickly realized that the architecture would need to be able to meet a large number of nonfunctional or quality attribute requirements. These requirements often were described with a word with "ity" at the end of it, e.g., security, scalability, maintainability. But, the areas Michael became most concerned about were performance and reliability. Since a security event can generate a building alarm, he began to worry about how long it would take after the event occurred for security personnel to be notified. He could imagine many bad outcomes if the security system that he was designing was too slow or unreliable in notifying personnel of the event. As a result, he considered architectural approaches for a system that would respond quickly and reliably to events.

This chapter deals with nonfunctional or quality attribute requirements: their elicitation, analysis, validation, and management. While these requirements are deemed architecturally significant, they must be treated with functional requirements in an integrated manner. A conceptual framework for an integrated approach is described along with its application to an industrial case study.

5.1   Why Architectural Requirements Are Different

Software architecture is defined as "a structure or structures of a system which comprise its software elements, their externally visible properties and relationships among them" [Bass et al. 2003]. Some of the structures consist of static software elements such as classes or modules that are related to each other through inheritance or decomposition. Others include runtime structures, consisting of dynamic software elements such as processes or tasks related to each other by data transmission or invocation. Architecture is concerned with the public interfaces via which these elements interact and the externally visible properties of these elements and their interfaces.

The requirements that drive a product's architecture are often quite different from the requirements that define the functionality of a product.

- They come from many more sources than just the customer, such as stakeholders within the development organization, regulatory agencies, available implementation technologies, and implementations of previous products.

- They have a longer-term impact on the product than most functional requirements, because a good architecture is expected to remain stable through several releases of the product.

- Some of them are highly subjective or difficult to articulate.

- Many have a continuous, quantitative nature, in contrast to discrete, logical functional requirements. Instead of being pass/fail criteria, they are often expressed as measures of the goodness of a system, which must be calibrated to the stakeholders' expectations. Different measures must be traded off against each other to reach an architecture that is "good enough" according to each of the measures.

- They have nonobvious interactions with each other, due to (future) implementation decisions. Many stakeholders don't understand the architectural implications of what they need, so they are likely to overlook some of their quality attribute requirements, i.e., until an architect asks the right question.

- The architecture must anticipate change: in the functional requirements, in business conditions, in available technologies, in the development organization itself, etc. The architecture must also be stabilized while many functional and business requirements are still unstable.

- Architecturally significant requirements (ASRs) can be difficult to test before the system is operational.

- Some ASRs are passive in nature, such as cost and ease of use. Feedback on these may emerge gradually instead of being directly testable.

- They often have cross-cutting impact, making shortcomings difficult to correct after development has progressed, and thus making them high risk.

Terminology

Several different terms are commonly used to refer to requirements that determine the architecture of a system. A *functional requirement* is "a requirement that specifies a function that a system or system component must be able to perform" [IEEE 1990]. In other words, the functional requirements define what the system is supposed to do.

A *quality attribute requirement (QAR)* is specified in terms of observable, usually measurable, characteristics of the system that indicate its fitness for use. Quality attributes may be thought of as modifiers of the functional requirements that indicate how they are achieved. Quality attribute requirements address all "uses" of the system, including those where the system is a passive object rather than an active participant, such as when the system is being sold or when the next version of the system is being developed. Examples of quality attributes include: capacity, security, usability, cost, modifiability, and fault tolerance. The term *nonfunctional requirement*, although still commonly used, has become a synonym for quality attribute requirement.

A *cross-cutting requirement* is a requirement that applies to many different functions of a system, often scattered across diverse functional groups. For example, a system might require all of its "short" interactive commands to display their results within 0.1 seconds, whereas the "long" commands might be permitted to take time proportional to the amount of data they process. Cross-cutting requirements and their implications are described in Chapter 4.

An *architecturally significant requirement (ASR)* is any requirement that is likely to have a substantial influence on a choice among architectural alternatives [Bass et al. 2003]. The most significant of these are sometimes called *architectural drivers*. Any sort of requirement might be architecturally significant, but in our experience, apart from a few "sunny day scenarios" defining the overall functionality of the system, most architectural drivers tend to be quality attribute requirements.

Although architecturally significant requirements are often quite different from functional requirements, they should be analyzed and documented in a coordinated, integrated fashion. Failure to do so can lead to unnecessary duplication of work, or in the worst case, to project failures due to creation of a system that does not meet the needs of its customers [Finkelstein et al. 1996].

Quantifying Quality in Large Software Systems
by Capers Jones

Large software systems, where quality attributes become important, have a typical size on the order of 10,000 function points.

- The failure rate of projects with applications >10,000 function points is about 35 percent. That is, more than one application out of three will never be finished or delivered.

- Of the applications that are delivered, more than 50 percent will exceed their planned schedules by more than 12 calendar months.

- The major cost drivers for large software applications in the 10,000 function point size range are finding and fixing bugs and producing documentation.

- Applications in the 10,000 function point size range generate about 50 different kinds of documents and total about 6,000 pages. More than 200,000 English words, plus about 5,000 diagrams, will be created. More than 30 percent of the cost of software goes to document production.

- There will be about 3 defects per page or 18,000 defects in the documents. Unless document inspections are used, many of these will find their way into the code and eventually go to customers.

- The total volume of defects for applications in the 10,000 function point size range is about 50,000. Defect removal efficiency for this size range averages only about 80 percent. That means that the software will be delivered (if it is delivered at all) with 10,000 latent defects that were not found during development.

- Testing such large applications requires at least 10 different test stages. A total of about 55,000 test cases will be created. Unfortunately, each testing stage is only about 30 percent efficient, or only finds about one bug out of three.

- About 25 percent of the test cases will have defects or bugs themselves. It often happens that the error density of test cases is higher than the error density of the software itself.

- About 7 percent of attempts to fix bugs will be "bad fixes" that accidentally inject a new defect back into the application. If you start with 50,000 defects and find 40,000 of them, then you will create about 2,800 new defects while trying to fix the 40,000 that you discovered. These will probably get delivered with the 10,000 defects that slipped through testing, leading to a delivered total of about 12,800 defects. Of these about 20 percent will be high-severity defects.

- If formal inspections are used for requirements, design documents, architecture documents, and other key information sources, they have a measured defect removal efficiency level of about 85 percent. Inspections should be mandatory for a project of this size.

- If code inspections plus document inspections are used, it is possible to elevate defect removal efficiency up to 96 percent or slightly higher. Doing so will greatly raise the odds of a successful outcome.

More data on software and documentation defects and their implications can be found in [Jones 2007, 2008].

5.2   An Integrated Model

As was discussed in Chapter 2, integrated requirements engineering revolves around an integrated artifact model. Figure 5.1 shows the artifact model that we will use as a guide for this chapter. It shows the artifacts and relationships that integrate functional and architectural requirements engineering disciplines.

In this model, the two subdisciplines (functional and architectural requirements) share artifact types, and specific artifacts, wherever possible. Where this is not possible, trace relationships are established between the artifacts so that consistency and completeness checks can be carried out as needed. In many cases, the integration is achieved by introducing new subclasses of existing artifact classes. For example, *quality attribute requirements* are a kind of *system requirement* and as such are applied to system use cases and system use case scenarios in the same way as functional requirements. On the other hand, a quality

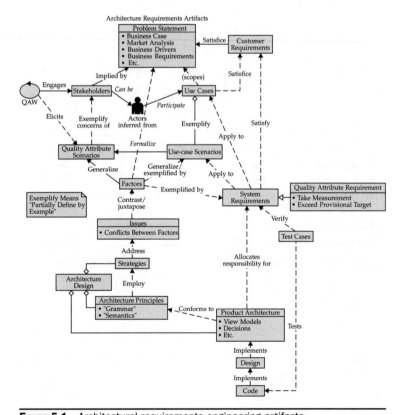

FIGURE 5.1   Architectural requirements engineering artifacts

Document Dependency Diagrams

In the methodology framework diagrammed in Figure 5.1, great attention has been paid to how artifacts (documents) depend on one another. Each arrow represents a *uses* dependency: Artifact X uses Artifact Y (X → Y) *if and only if* the correctness of X depends on the presence of a correct version of Y. For example, it is possible to agree upon a set of architectural principles before the product architecture is complete, but it makes no sense to approve the product architecture before the architectural principles have been signed off. In the case of subclass and composition relations, the subclass depends on the parent class and the component depends on the composite. The arrows do not necessarily represent time sequences for the activities to develop the artifacts. The only way that they represent time sequences is in the sense already defined: a document cannot achieve a sufficient degree of completeness and quality until the relevant parts of the documents it depends on have sufficient completeness and quality. We call this notation a *document dependency diagram* for specifying the overall structure of a software process, whether it is a generic process, like this one, or tailored for a specific project. Describing the overview without control information turns out to make it easy to tailor, even after the project is under way, because the state of the process is captured primarily in the state of the artifacts and does not depend on the control sequence used to reach that state. When you start a new project, you can copy and modify this diagram to suit the needs of your project.

attribute scenario is not a use case scenario in the usual sense, but we often formalize quality attribute scenarios by writing corresponding use case scenarios, which can then be annotated with requirements and tested in the usual way.

Quality Attribute Scenarios

Quality attribute scenarios (QASs) [Bass et al. 2003] are a special kind of structured natural language description of a behavior. They are used for capturing stakeholder concerns, by illustrating each concern with a concrete example. A QAS may have a corresponding use case scenario that formalizes it for the purpose of attaching requirements and testing them.

Quality Attribute Requirements

A *quality attribute requirement (QAR)* is a special kind of requirement that deals with measurable properties (quality attributes), such as capacity, price, and responsiveness, related to stakeholders' expectations.

Factors, Issues, and Strategies

Factors, issues, and *strategies* are artifacts used in a technique called *global analysis* [Hofmeister et al. 1999], [Paulish 2002]. *Factors* (architecture-influencing factors) are statements about the product, the project, or their contexts that potentially influence the architecture. Factors may be inferred from the problem statement or from the engineers' experience or general knowledge. Factors often generalize QASs or use case scenarios. Sometimes, a factor is identified first, and then a use case scenario is written as an example of the factor. Sometimes, product requirements are introduced as examples of factors.

Issues are identified by finding conflicts between factors. The statement of the issue juxtaposes the conflicting factors and explains why they are hard to reconcile.

Strategies are tentative decisions about the architecture or the project plan that address (architectural) issues.

Product Architecture

This artifact maps out all the coarse-grained components and interfaces of the system, preferably using view models [IEEE 2000], [Clements et al. 2003]. It conforms to the architecture principles while allocating responsibility for product requirements to specific components and interfaces. Note that the architecture principles are largely independent of specific product requirements. That is, adding or removing a major piece of functionality could lead to adding or removing the components and interfaces responsible for that functionality without affecting the principles.

5.3   Quality Attribute Requirements

The road to understanding quality attribute requirements starts with a brief detour into the fundamentals of system quality. The quality of a system, in general, is its fitness for its intended uses. ISO Std. 9126-1 defines a quality model with four linked topic areas of quality:

- **Process quality**   Quality of the process that is producing the product
- **Internal quality**   Quality of the intermediate work products (some of which may also be deliverable work products)
- **External quality**   Quality of the finished product, before delivery
- **Quality in use**   Quality of the larger processes in which the delivered product is used

A *quality attribute* is a system or process property indicative of quality in any of these quality topic areas. Note that, for our purposes, the "process" in "process quality" includes not only software development, but all the business functions surrounding the product, including marketing, sales, planning, maintenance, installation, customer support, and preparing to develop the next version.

Naturally, quality in use is the most important area of quality, but it is also the latest one to measure, because it cannot be measured until the product is delivered. Fortunately, quality attributes in the other topic areas give us useful indications of what the quality in use will be; i.e., we say that such quality attributes are "indicative of" quality in use.

As an example, consider a web-based, self-service airline reservation system. We'll focus first on the *completeness* of the system, which is one aspect of its fitness for use. For quality in use, completeness might be measured, in part, by "the percentage of actual reservations that are made successfully without involving airline personnel." This, after all, is a primary goal of such a system: reduce personnel costs for reservations. This percentage will be affected by many things, including bugs, unimplemented use cases, ease of use, response time, server capacity, etc. It will also be affected by the proportions of different kinds of reservations that customers want to make. Figure 5.2 illustrates the many quality attributes, from the four quality areas, that are indicative of the percent of unassisted reservations in actual use.

Before the system is deployed, it has gone through system testing, where testers, acting the part of customers, try to accomplish specified travel reservation tasks. Completeness, here, might be measured by "percentage of use cases passing system test," which would be an external quality measure. It is obviously indicative of the percent of unassisted reservations, but it is different in several ways, including these:

- It attaches equal weight to each use case, instead of accounting for the frequency with which each use case is needed by actual customers.

- Paid testers quickly become experts in using the software they are testing, whereas many real-world customers remain only casual users of the software. So, a tester might complete a task successfully via a user interface that is too frustrating for the typical customer.

- A use case that fails system testing might still work most of the time under real-world conditions.

Before the system even reaches system testing, the development team is tracking their progress toward completing coding. To measure completeness at a finer grain than use cases, they count the requirements associated with the use cases and measure the "percentage of

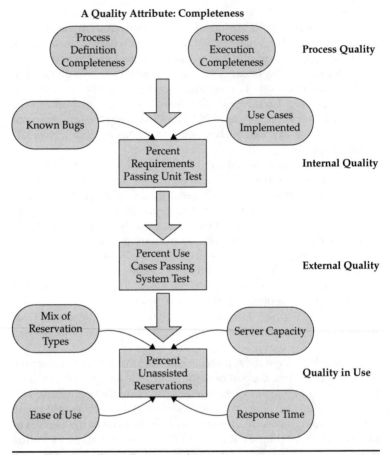

A Quality Attribute: Completeness

Process Definition Completeness

Process Execution Completeness

Process Quality

Known Bugs

Use Cases Implemented

Percent Requirements Passing Unit Test

Internal Quality

Percent Use Cases Passing System Test

External Quality

Mix of Reservation Types

Server Capacity

Percent Unassisted Reservations

Quality in Use

Ease of Use

Response Time

FIGURE 5.2   A quality attribute: completeness

requirements that have passed unit testing." This would be an internal quality measure, both because unit tests can be performed on preliminary configurations of the system and because some of the unit tests represent conditions that cannot be tested via external (system) tests.

Although process quality is in some sense a quite different matter from product quality, we can certainly explore how product completeness is affected by the process. First of all, the process defines the measures of product completeness that are used in the three other topic areas for a given project. Second, the degree to which the organization adheres to the defined process will have a significant effect on the accuracy and timeliness of the completeness measures, and therefore on the ability of the organization to achieve sufficient completeness. For example, the process may define how to count use cases for purposes of measuring the percentage of use cases that have passed their system tests. The project manager needs to update this statistic at regular intervals to keep track of progress. If he doesn't, then the executed process is incomplete, because it does not do everything that the defined process says it should. If the defined process does not specify how to determine whether the set of use cases is sufficiently complete to satisfy the stakeholders, then the defined process itself may be considered to be incomplete as well, which could result in lack of completeness-in-use.

When it comes to defining actual quality attribute requirements, it helps to distinguish two types:

- Requirements that define quality attribute measures and how and when to measure them. For example, "The system shall measure and report 'reservation completion time,' starting from the display of the first flight query screen and ending with the display of the screen giving the reservation confirmation number."

- Requirements that specify what values of the quality attribute measures indicate sufficient quality. For example, "The 'reservation completion time' for an experienced tester on a lightly loaded system making a Type 3 reservation shall be less than two minutes."

From these examples, you can see that functional requirements and quality attribute requirements complement each other, and neither is sufficient without the other. It is not enough to specify all the kinds of reservation functions (the use cases) that the product supports, without specifying how quickly a customer should be able to make a reservation; e.g., it should be much faster than phoning the airline. Conversely, it is not enough to specify that a customer can make a reservation in three minutes, without specifying the kinds of information the customer will be able to examine, the complexity of the itinerary that can be handled, and all the other functional details. Nonetheless, the functional requirements are the basic stuff—the "nouns and verbs"—of the requirements, whereas the quality attribute requirements are typically modifiers of the functional requirements—the "adjectives and adverbs."

Also note that the completeness-in-use of the airline reservation system will be affected by other quality attributes, such as ease of use, because from the user's viewpoint there is little difference between a function being unimplemented and being too hard to use, too slow, etc. In general, quality attributes will overlap within each of the quality topic areas, and each quality attribute in one area will be indicative of multiple quality attributes in other areas.

With these examples in mind, we summarize four related terms:

- **Quality**   Fitness for one or more defined uses
- **Quality attribute**   A property of the system or the process that is indicative of quality
- **Quality attribute measure**   A way of measuring a quality attribute for a specific system or process
- **Quality attribute requirement**   A requirement expressed in terms of one or more quality attribute measures

Table 5.1 gives a broad sampling of other quality attribute topics you might want to consider, with an example measure pertaining to each topic. The topics are drawn from ISO/IEC Std. 9126, but there are many other good sources of topics available on the Internet. The quality attribute measures you use will be very specific to your project, as you will see when we discuss quality attribute workshops.

Quality Attribute Topic	Example Quality Attribute Measure
Suitability	The number of use cases, out of a defined set of use cases that the software supports
Accuracy	The magnitude of error in a specified calculation
Interoperability	The number of interoperation use cases, out of a defined set, that the software supports
Security	The types of security threats against which the software has best-practice protection
Reliability	System performance (e.g., throughput) under specified adverse conditions (e.g., burst of arriving requests)
Maturity	Frequency of disruptions in service due to faults in the software
Fault tolerance	The performance of the system (e.g., throughput) after a specified type of fault (e.g., software, hardware, or environmental)
Recoverability	The time to return to normal system performance and data integrity after a specified type of failure, and the types of data that can be recovered when directly damaged by the failure
Understandability	Average time for a user to decide (correctly) whether the system is well suited for performing a specified task

TABLE 5.1 Quality Attributes

Quality Attribute Topic	Example Quality Attribute Measure
Learnability	The average time for a novice user to perform a specified advanced task for the first time
Operability	The frequency with which users make operational mistakes (attempt to apply the tool to a specified problem incorrectly)
Attractiveness	The frequency with which purchasers choose the product over a functionally similar product
Time behavior	Response time, throughput, and jitter under specified conditions
Resource utilization	Resource consumption (e.g., memory, CPU time, data transmitted) under a specified workload
Analyzability	Average time to diagnose a specified class of bug
Changeability	Average time to design, implement, and self-test a specified type of change to the code
Stability	The frequency with which making a specified type of change introduces unexpected side-effects
Testability	The average time to design, implement, and deploy a specified type of test
Adaptability	The average time to adapt the system to a new type of environment, within a specified range of environment types, exclusively using specified adaptation methods
Installability	Effort to install the software product in a specified type of environment
Co-existence	Frequency of customer-reported, validated system failures due to the presence of other specified, permissible software products in the same computing environment
Replaceability	The list of software products that a given product is suitable to replace
Effectiveness	The proportion of specified use cases that the software correctly implements
Productivity	The proportion of work accomplished to human effort expended, under specified conditions
Safety	The expected monetary cost of harm to people, business, software, property, or the environment when the system is used in a specified context
Satisfaction	The frequency with which trial users of the software go on to purchase the software within 30 days

TABLE 5.1 Quality Attributes *(continued)*

Besides making reservations, there are many other "uses" of an airline reservation system. It is used to make money for the software house that built it. It is used to make a better airline reservation system later. In fact, each major class of stakeholders will have a different idea of what "fitness for use" means for them. For example,

- The business team cares about process speed and efficiency: time to market and value for money spent on development. They also care about the product's capacity and efficiency.

- The development manager cares about code understandability and modifiability.

- The IT department at the customer site cares about the product's resistance to viruses and other penetration attempts.

Choosing a good set of quality attribute requirements requires a judicious blend of stakeholder focus and expert knowledge. You have to satisfy the stakeholders in the short term, to keep the project going. But, you also have to anticipate problems that the stakeholders haven't thought about yet. For that, you draw on your own experience and the experience of other architecture experts. Be careful not to bloat your requirements database with every conceivable quality attribute, but you might want to keep a private list of attributes that you think will become important later.

Setting Performance Targets Too Soon

Timing can be important when setting quality attribute targets. In a recent project, the leadership team had an estimate for the throughput needed from a certain subsystem but decided to withhold the information from the subsystem team because

- They lacked confidence in the throughput estimate.

- The estimate would demand a high-performance design, which would be costly and take a long time to develop.

As it turned out, the throughput estimate was correct, but the subsystem designer had chosen a simpler design that could not provide the required throughput. Major rework was performed, delaying the project.

In retrospect the leadership team could have

- Documented the risk associated with uncertainty in the estimate, and managed it along with other risks.

- Mitigated the risk, by giving the subsystem designer two throughput estimates, and asking for a quick-and-dirty analysis of the implications of choosing one over the other.

Stages of Quality Attribute Grief

The stages that a project team goes through when dealing with quality attributes can be compared with the stages of grief that an individual may experience.

- **Denial** Early in the project, quality attributes are poorly understood and therefore given less attention than they deserve. They are treated superficially, as in "the system shall have good performance."

- **Shock** When the first realistic end-to-end scenarios are executed, and it becomes possible to observe the quality attributes, everyone suddenly realizes how poorly the system measures up, and panic sets in.

- **Anger** Everyone tries to blame someone else.

- **Depression** Fixing the quality problems seems overwhelming. Developers waste energy grumbling or worrying. Productivity decreases.

- **Bargaining** The architect begs and cajoles stakeholders to approve tradeoffs among quality attributes.

- **Acceptance** Stakeholders adjust their expectations to close remaining gaps between actual and desired quality.

We've come to recognize that treating quality attribute requirements effectively is partly a matter of timing.

- Many team members will not be ready to talk much about quality attributes until the broad functional requirements have been defined.

- Before the quality attribute requirements can be defined, one must define the units of measure of the quality attributes, and focus on a manageable number of such attributes.

- Many quality attributes need to be traded off against other quality attributes. The relative importance of them will be different for different stakeholders. For external stakeholders, the stakeholders' understanding of these tradeoffs will evolve based on external events of which you might not be aware.

- Setting an ambitious target value for, say, a performance requirement can push the designers toward a complex, high-performance solution. Project leadership needs to think carefully about such impacts before committing to specific targets. In worrisome cases, it may be worthwhile to discuss the implications with the affected subteams and see if it is worth commissioning a comparative study to see whether a simple solution may be good enough to justify the savings compared to a higher-performance, costlier design.

- For resource-related attributes, we have to deal with configurations of resources and associated quality attribute requirements (see Chapter 6).

5.4   Selecting Significant Stakeholders

Earlier chapters have mentioned stakeholders as the sources of requirements, but for architecturally significant requirements, you need to think carefully about identifying *all* of the stakeholders. We recommend writing a stakeholder analysis document and updating it from time to time. This document will likely have some frank and unflattering opinions in it, as stakeholders have different views of important requirements, so it must not be widely circulated.

A stakeholder is any person whose opinions, needs, or preferences are likely to be relevant to the success of the project. An obvious example is the customer: if we want someone to buy the product, that person's opinions matter. However, even with this simple example, it is important to note subtle differences between the buyer and the primary users. For example, for medical imaging, the purchasing decisions for million-dollar CT scanners and MRI devices are often driven by the opinions of a small number of influential research faculty staff at major teaching hospitals. However, the primary users of such machines are medical technicians, who care more about ease of use than the latest technical advances.

Examples of stakeholders include

- **Installer**   In some fields, such as telecommunications or manufacturing, installing the software and configuring it to operate correctly with diverse preexisting equipment constitute a labor-intensive, mentally challenging task. Especially in businesses that use indirect sales channels, ease of installation can have a huge impact on profitability, so including installers as stakeholders is important.

- **Tech support**   In many businesses, the staff who answer phone calls from irate customers need good remote diagnostic tools, as well as easy-to-explain user interfaces.

- **Competitor**   Some stakeholders want to see the project fail! But things get even more complicated when the same company is a partner in one part of a business and a competitor in another.

The term "stakeholder" may have any of three meanings, depending on context

- **Stakeholder class** A group, category, or type of individual with a certain set of concerns.

- **Individual stakeholder** A particular, named person who is a member of one or more stakeholder classes. You might need to engage several individuals from the same class.

- **Stakeholder representative** An individual selected to represent a stakeholder class for the purposes of a project. In some cases, a stakeholder representative is not a member of the class he or she represents but is chosen as a proxy for them because, for one reason or another, no member of the class can be made available to represent them.

Identifying Potential Stakeholders

It is very important for you to brainstorm a list of potentially important stakeholders before settling on which ones you will actually engage, because if you miss a significant stakeholder, you are likely to miss a significant requirement.

Your project will undoubtedly present you with several obvious individual stakeholders. Some additional sources that can help identify significant stakeholders are

- **The problem definition** This should tell you why the project is important, which will give you clues as to whom it is important to.

- **Other projects and departments in your organization** Other departments may, for example, provide field support to the product you are developing, giving them a stake in it.

- **Checklists** There are several good published lists of potential stakeholder classes, including those from the Software Engineering Institute [Clements et al. 2003] and the Atlantic Systems Guild.

- **Use-case context diagram** In Chapter 4, you learned how to identify use case categories top-down and breadth-first. The top-level use case diagram identifies all the types of actors that interact with the system you are building. Each type of actor suggests a stakeholder class. Tip: If the use case context diagram hasn't been created yet, offer to help draft it.

- **Quality attributes** As you consider potentially important quality attributes, ask the question "important to whom?" This will sometimes uncover new stakeholder classes worth considering.

Begin to document each stakeholder class as you identify it. For each potentially important stakeholder class, you may want to describe

- Major concerns of that class of stakeholders
- Their stake in the project (how the project benefits or hurts them, including how big the impact is)
- Expertise and other inputs they bring to the project
- How much of their time you expect to need
- When you expect them to spend significant time talking to you about the project, considering both when you need them and when they will begin to see the project as urgent enough to spend time on
- Candidates to represent the class of stakeholders

Prioritize the stakeholder classes as you go along, both in terms of importance and urgency. You don't need to complete the analysis if you are sure a stakeholder class is unimportant, but it helps to at least mention the class and why it is not important, so that others know you have thought about it.

Next, choose the stakeholder representatives. For each stakeholder class, consider how the candidate fits or differs from the rest of the class members. Pay particular attention to

- The political importance of the individual within the organization
- Availability
- Importance of the project to the individual personally
- Potential for conflicting agendas

Conflicting agendas are an inevitable part of the analysis. For example, if your project is building a software platform or library that will be used in several different products, each product will have a different development schedule and will use your software in a different way. When you find that candidates to represent the same class have conflicting agendas, you may want to do one of the following:

- Give preference to the candidate for whom the project is most important and/or urgent.
- Split the stakeholder class into two or more classes.

5.5   Methods for Architectural Requirements Engineering

In this section, we describe a number of methods that architects use for defining and analyzing quality attribute requirements as part of starting system design.

Quality Attribute Workshop

A quality attribute workshop (QAW) [Bachmann et al. 2002], [Barbacci et al. 2000] brings together a diverse set of stakeholders in a one- or two-day meeting to elicit their quality attribute concerns and help them understand one another's concerns. As a concern is being described, the facilitator helps the stakeholder write a quality attribute scenario (QAS) that describes what he wants (and thinks might be hard to achieve). Each stakeholder captures at least two of his or her biggest concerns in the form of QASs and presents them to the group. The group then selects a handful of QASs to explore in more detail. The facilitator helps them see some of the architectural significance of the QASs, and begins the process of trading them off against each other.

A QAS is a structured textual description of how a piece of a system responds to a stimulus, including measuring the quality of the response. It was invented by software architecture researchers at the Software Engineering Institute (SEI) as a medium of communication between stakeholders and the architecture team [Bass et al. 2003].

A QAS is typically structured to have the following parts:

- A stimulus

- A stimulus source

- An artifact being stimulated

- An environment in which the stimulus occurs

- A response to the stimulus

- A response measure (to quantitatively define a satisfactory response)

For example, a configurability scenario might be written as

"A customer requests support for a new type of sensor after the software has been installed and activated. The customer support engineer reconfigures the system to support the new sensor without writing any new source code, without extraordinary downtime, and commencing operation with the new sensor within one calendar week of receiving the necessary documentation on the sensor."

For this example, we can define

- **Stimulus**   Requests support for a new type of sensor

- **Stimulus source**   The customer

- **Artifact**   The system and the customer support organization

- **Environment**   After the software has been installed and activated

- **Response**   The customer support engineer reconfigures the system to support the new sensor

- **Response measure** No new source code, no extraordinary downtime, and commencing operation within one calendar week

Note the quality attribute, measure, and requirement implied by this scenario:

- The quality attribute is "configurability to accommodate new sensors."
- The measure is "the amount of new source code written, the amount of downtime, and the amount of calendar time to bring a new sensor online."
- The requirement is "zero new source code, no extra downtime, and less than one calendar week."

Also, notice how the QAS nails down some details that an unstructured scenario might have left open:

- Since no new source code is permitted, there must be a limit on the range of new sensor types that can be handled. With enough programming, any type of sensor could have been handled.
- Shutting the system down to reconfigure it is probably not an option, because that would require extraordinary downtime.
- Reconfiguration will be done by an expert, not a novice.
- The expert is part of the installation organization, not the customer organization.

But the most important aspect of the scenario is that it gives a concrete example of configurability, which is easy for both the stakeholder and the architecture team to understand.

When eliciting QASs, it is helpful to consider the following types of scenarios, as a way of bringing out issues that might not have been considered:

- **Normal operations** These are the most obvious scenarios.
- **System-as-object scenarios** In these, the system is a passive object that is being manipulated by, say, a programmer or an installer.
- **Growth scenarios** These scenarios deal with likely or plausible changes to the requirements in the future, such as a 50 percent increase in capacity requirements. They help develop a system that is (somewhat) future-proof.
- **Exploratory scenarios** These are improbable scenarios, such as the loss of power from an "uninterruptible" power supply.

They are used to stimulate thinking about implicit assumptions underpinning the architecture, which may turn out not to be true.

We recommend using QASs, not just in workshops, but whenever you are capturing stakeholder concerns. You will want to manage them similarly to how you manage other high-level requirements. However, it is important to remember that

- The QAS is only an example of the concern. It is up to you to investigate the topic and propose good quality attribute measures and requirements.

- The stakeholders' priorities will change over time. The prioritization work done in a workshop helps you know where to focus your attention first, but the official prioritization of concerns will need to be done later and more systematically.

- QASs do not replace use case scenarios. A QAS generally treats the system as a black box, with a stimulus and a response, whereas a use case scenario is attached to a particular use case and can be as rigorous and detailed as necessary. We recommend that you establish trace links between QASs and the use cases or use case scenarios they correspond to, indicating that the QAS is part of the rationale for the quality attribute requirements attached to the use case.

Goal Modeling

One of the challenging differences between functional requirements and quality attribute requirements is that functional requirements usually have a yes/no flavor to them, whereas quality attribute requirements have a more-is-better character. For example, if an airline reservation system is required to display a certain list of available flights within 15 seconds, the information displayed in the list is either correct or incorrect, but nothing very bad happens if the list is displayed in 16 seconds instead of 15, and displaying it in 10 seconds is even better than 15, although the additional benefit may not be very important.

Another challenging difference is that the logical linkage between design decisions and functional requirements is normally clear-cut, whereas the linkage between design decisions and quality attributes often remains subjective during development. The easiest example is user interface design, where many design decisions affect ease of use, but it is mainly guesswork to say which ones will have a big impact, and whether the aggregate ease of use will be sufficient for the end user's needs.

One way to deal with "more is better" logic is by using the goal modeling approach we have discussed in Chapter 3. A goal model is a graph of nodes and edges, where the nodes are goals and other decisions, and the edges are "satisficing" relationships. The term "satisfice" means "satisfy sufficiently." So, if a design decision seems to achieve a goal well enough for the purposes of a particular project, we say that the decision satisfices the goal.

More typically, a single decision contributes toward satisfying several goals but also interferes with achieving other goals. Some goal modeling notations therefore support both positive and negative satisficing relationships, and some even provide for "double-plus" and "double-minus" links. In these models, an edge A → + B means "A contributes to satisficing B." A → − B means "A interferes with satisficing B." To decide whether a given node N is satisficed, one must consider all the edges leading to it, both positive and negative, and analyze the combined effect of those decisions on the goal. While this representation can be useful in visualizations, diagrams of large graphs can be in practice quite unreadable. Their value comes more from their use in a trace link database, when analyzing the impact of changing a decision (see later Figure 5.4).

Global Analysis

Global analysis is a methodology for organizing a broad variety of soft, uncertain information gathered in the early stages of architectural requirements analysis [Hofmeister et al. 1999], [Paulish 2002]. It is "global" both in the sense that it looks at the system from all directions (all external interfaces, all stakeholder concerns, plus any sort of other constraint, whether from the organization, the marketplace, available implementation technologies, the job market, or whatever), and the topics addressed frequently have a broad impact on the system as a whole, cutting across many subsystems and multiple architectural views.

Global analysis classifies this information into three types of entries: factors, issues, and strategies. Architecture-influencing *factors* are (alleged) facts that are likely to have significant influence upon the architecture. *Issues* are potential conflicts or tradeoffs among factors. *Strategies* are proposed decisions that address the issues. All three types of entries are collected concurrently, as new information becomes available, opportunities to ask questions arise, and ideas come to mind. Classifying them this way helps the analysts keep from confusing external constraints with proposed solutions, helps them focus on the hard problems first, and helps them build their rationale for the emerging architecture.

Factors: Beyond Requirements

Any requirement or stakeholder concern might be a factor, but there are many factors that are neither requirements nor stakeholder concerns in the usual sense. We normally expect requirements to state properties of the product, whereas a factor may describe something other than the product itself, for example, "Our programmers don't know application service provider (ASP) technology." Rather than arising from a stakeholder concern, a factor might arise from general knowledge, from architectural experience, from legacy products, from the history of the development organization, or from any other source. Finally, global analysis deals simultaneously with requirements, architecture, and project management, so some of the factors may only bear on the product indirectly.

Here are some example factors, illustrating their diversity:

- "The product developers are spread across three locations."

- "The license fees for a key third-party software component will likely be around $1500 per server."

- "There is significant market demand for both large-screen and cell-phone versions of this type of product."

Factors can come from anywhere. For convenience they are grouped into three categories: product factors (typically derived from features); technology factors, which involve the technologies available to implement the product; and organizational factors, which involve properties of the company or other organization that is developing the product. These categories are further grouped into subcategories, such as product performance, services provided, programming tools, technical standards, staff skills, and schedule constraints. These categories and subcategories should not be considered exhaustive; any significant factor should be captured and addressed, whether or not it fits neatly into one of the categories.

We try to capture the following information to describe factors:

- **Category and Subcategory** These are specific to the project and are just used to help organize the factors as you collect them.

- **Name** This is a short phrase that makes it easy to refer to the factor within the team and in other documents.

- **Brief statement of the factor** This statement typically consists of a single sentence, as in the preceding examples.

- **Negotiability (optional)** This is the "wiggle room" in the factor today. For example, in the case of the three development sites, one of the sites might be optional, depending on the overall staffing needs and the skill mix required.

- **Change over time (optional)** This describes how the factor might change in the future. For example, the demand for the product on a cell phone may not be significant for another two years. Negotiability and changeability should not be confused with *stability*, a property indicating how strong the consensus is for the current wording of a requirement.

- **Impact**   This explains how the factor is likely to influence the architecture.

- **Authority**   This is the justification for including the factor in the analysis. For example, it could be the name of a stakeholder or a team member, references to requirements, stakeholder requests, or other project documents, or a phrase like "general knowledge" or "past experience." External authorities are generally better than just listing a team member, but since you are the architects, others do expect you to be the authority some of the time. Also, there will be cases where you identify a factor that you expect will become important to certain stakeholders later. You can list yourself as the authority temporarily, and comment on who else may become interested.

- **Expert**   This is the subject matter expert for the factor.

In addition, each factor has other attributes equivalent to those usually attached to requirements, such as unique ID, owner, status, or stability.

An example textual description of a factor is given in Figure 5.3.

Although storing factors, issues, and strategies in an ordinary text document can be adequate for small efforts, we would recommend managing them with a general-purpose requirements management tool, such as *Teamcenter*, *Doors*, or *Requisite Pro*, if your organization is already using one. The key advantage of using a tool is being able to look at the same text either as a narrative document or as a requirements catalog.

---

1. Organizational Constraints
1.3 Management
1.3.5 Buy reporting subsystem
(Factor-37)
The reporting subsystem should be based on a commercial product, e.g. Crystal Reports
Negotiability Previous reporting system was implemented in-house, so buying COTS is not a rigid requirement. But competitors are already doing this.
Changeability Reporting features may become more specialized, making the "buy" option less advantageous.
Impact Buying the market leading product has low development cost, risk, and time to market, but introduces licensing costs and reduces product differentiation.
Authority Features 135, 136, and 139, and SR 174 are from Jim Smith, who has interviewed customers concerning reporting features.

Figure 5.3   Textual presentation of a factor

"Softness" is a hallmark of architecture-influencing factors. Softness is inevitable because much of the analysis must be performed before the hard facts are known. We find that factors often need to capture four kinds of softness: range, change over time, uncertainty, and negotiability. These can all be present in a single factor. For example,

"Customers' networks currently have 100 to 100,000 nodes. The upper end of this range will increase every two years by a factor of 1.5 to 3. Our architecture may not have to cover the low end of the range, if expected sales don't justify the cost."

This factor illustrates range (100 to 100,000 nodes), evolution over time (will increase every two years), probability (factor of 1.5 to 3), and negotiability (expected sales vs. cost). Although this example expresses probability with numbers, a factor is permitted to use qualitative words like "probably," "likely," "might," and "could" to express uncertainty. Negotiability links this factor to other factors, giving some idea of how variations in one affect the other. Although it may be tempting to split such a factor into four different factors, each addressing one kind of softness, don't make the split unless you are confident that the different factors are relatively independent of each other. Allowing softness in an architecture factor thus allows the architect to document a factor and make plans concerning it before the uncertainty is resolved.

Unlike requirements catalogs, the collection of architecture factors does not have to be complete. Global analysis prioritizes them, finds conflicts and tradeoffs between them, and finally reduces them to a set of key issues that shape the architecture. The less important factors will likely be ignored, for most purposes, so missing a few of them is okay.

Issues

The purpose of documenting issues is to identify the aspects of the project that are going to be hard to accomplish. A global analysis issue is a potential conflict or tradeoff between two or more factors—usually many more! For example, the issue "Aggressive Schedule" might be described as, "The project probably can't be completed in the 14 months currently budgeted if we have to train our programmers in Java, add new tools to our development environment, and implement all 75 major features, using a novel user interface concept." Implicit in that statement are the factors

- Develop in 14 calendar months
- Programmers don't know Java
- Seventy-five major features
- Novel user interface concept

To document an issue, record

- **Name**   A short phrase
- **Brief description**   One or two sentences
- **Factors involved**   Names of, and links to, the factors that conflict with each other to create this issue.
- **Why it's hard**   The challenges facing the project team; e.g., meeting functionality, schedule, budget, schedule, quality, performance constraints.
- **Expert**   The subject matter expert
- **Owner, status, priority, etc.**   The usual requirements management attributes
- **Discussion**   Additional information that came up when the issue was uncovered. This may include potential strategies for resolving the issue, before the strategies have been separately documented.

Sometimes, an issue is identified that does not seem to reflect a conflict between factors. That's okay. Document it first, and figure out the factor conflicts later.

- If you're lucky, thinking about what makes the issue hard will suggest a new factor.
- Sometimes the factor conflict won't become apparent until you consider the architectural alternatives surrounding the issue.
- If nothing else, there will usually be a conflict with cost and/or schedule.
- Or, it may turn out that something that appeared to be difficult didn't really make a difference to the architecture after all.

Strategies

A *strategy* is a proposed decision that addresses one or more significant issues. Many strategies are simply architectural design decisions, such as the decision to implement asynchronous communication using loosely coupled event channels instead of tighter-coupled publishers and subscribers. However, in global analysis, an issue can involve both technical and managerial factors, and so the strategy may be technical, managerial, or a combination. For example, if the issue is "ASP programming is best done in Java for this product, but our programmers only know C++," the architect and the project manager could choose to "retrain our programmers in JSP," "buy an ASP development environment for C++," or "use some C++ programmers to write C++ applets, and retrain others to write JSP."

To document a strategy, record

- **Name**   A short phrase
- **Brief description**   One or two sentences
- **Issues and factors affected**   Names of, and links to, the issues and factors that are addressed by this strategy
- **Explanation**   A lengthier description of the strategy
- **Why it works**   Why the strategy satisfices the factor-goals and issue-goals
- **Expert**   The subject matter expert
- **Unique ID, owner, status, priority, etc.**   The usual requirements management attributes
- **Discussion**   Additional information about the strategy, including references to additional reading

Factors vs. Requirements

Although a factor is similar to a requirement, there are important differences, as summarized in Table 5.2.

We expect both factors and requirements to be correct. However, a requirement is supposed to be a true statement about a set of products, whereas a factor is a true statement related to the architecture of a product family. "Related to" is important because an architecture is constrained by many stakeholders, not just the market requirements. "Product family" implies that the architecture should reflect "family planning," leaving room for family members to grow and for new ones to be added.

Although they must be unambiguous, factors are allowed to be explicitly variable. The idea is that a factor expresses a multidimensional region of values within which a combination of product requirements will fall.

Requirement	Factor
True of the product(s)	True and *related* to the architecture of a product *family*
Unambiguous	Explicitly variable
Verifiable	Arguable
Modifiable	Readable
Consistent	Conflicting
Complete	Important
Traceable	Yes, eventually

TABLE 5.2   Requirements and Factors

Instead of being verifiable, factors are only expected to be arguable, meaning that someone can make a convincing case that the factor is true. This relaxation of rigor is important for capturing assumptions before the "true facts" are known.

Modifiability is less important than readability, because the number of important factors should remain small (under 100), making them relatively easy to maintain in any case. In the customer network example given earlier under "Factors: Beyond Requirements," conventional wisdom on modifiability would recommend breaking the factor into three or four separate factors, but in truth it is a single factor that varies in four dimensions. We also prefer not to restrict the sentence structure of factors (as some requirements standards do), in favor of greater expressiveness. For example, is it clearer to write, "The architecture shall facilitate developing the framework and products using programmers whose previous experience does not include ASP technology" or "Our programmers don't know ASP"? The first alternative is verbose, vague, and might actually be incorrect, if there is an option to hire a few ASP developers. The second alternative succinctly captures one fact that constrains the architecture.

We expect to record contradictory factors, both because they can represent different points of view and because one purpose of global analysis is to discover conflicting factors and find ways to reconcile them. For example, one stakeholder may ask for a fast, powerful system, while another asks for a low-cost, small-footprint system. Only later analysis will determine whether one of the stakeholder requests is rejected, a good compromise is found, or two system family members are produced, where one is fast and powerful and the other is cheap and small.

The collection of factors will be incomplete because only the most important ones can be addressed. Experience has shown that, in practice, architects address only the top 5–10 concerns when defining the architecture principles. So, the process of collecting factors needs to be systematic but limited in duration, ending when the team is reasonably confident that they have reached a point of diminishing returns (or time has run out). Completeness has a secondary meaning here as well: some factor descriptions will be left incomplete if they are deemed not important enough to finish, but will not be deleted so that they can be revisited later.

Finally, traceability of factors is important, both backward and forward. Each factor that is deemed important must eventually be traceable back to a source, which is typically an expert or a stakeholder. Without such a trace, the factor has no authority over the project, either because it isn't true or because no stakeholder thinks it is relevant.

Goal Modeling of Factors, Issues, and Strategies

Goal modeling is a useful way to describe the relationships among factors, issues, and strategies. Each factor represents the goal of developing a product compatible with that factor. Each issue represents a derived goal, namely to develop a product that satisfices a particular combination of factor-goals, even though they appear to conflict with each other. Each strategy, if adopted, represents a design decision that contributes to satisfying some issue-goals and some factor-goals and detracts from satisfying others. Finally, the engineering requirements sponsored by the architecture team have satisficing relationships to the chosen strategies. Figure 5.4 uses goal modeling to depict relationships among factors, issues, and strategies.

Managing Factors, Issues, and Strategies

As with functional requirements, it is important to have a definite procedure for managing factors, issues, and strategies. We have already mentioned that it is useful to put them in a requirements catalog, if a suitable tool is already in use in the organization. However, unlike conventional requirements management, the whole purpose of Global Analysis is to identify a *small number* of *high-priority* issues and corresponding strategies that shape the architecture. If you don't manage toward this goal, global analysis can grow into a very large,

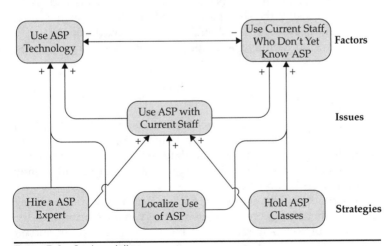

FIGURE 5.4   Goal modeling

unwieldy effort that is vulnerable to analysis paralysis. Therefore, we recommend these approaches:

- Use brainstorming to identify factors, issues, and strategies, but don't insist on fully documenting every idea that comes up. Use priority and status attributes to mark certain items as *deferred* (we've decided not to work on it right now), and/or *low priority*.

- Use face-to-face prioritization meetings within the analysis team to narrow down the list of high-priority issues to less than 20. Eventually, the architects will most likely focus on fewer than 10 issues, but they need a longer list to choose from. Simple voting can help focus the meeting's attention, but then you should discuss the borderline cases to seek consensus on whether to include them or exclude them from the high-priority list.

- Use time-boxed scheduling (e.g., *sprints* in agile terminology) to limit the amount of time you spend on global analysis; then pull together what you know and assess whether additional time is needed, and how it should be spent.

- Drive the analysis toward the document in which it will be published for outside review. The purpose of this document will typically be to win buy-in for the early architecture concepts you've selected, by showing how they address stakeholder concerns and other dangers you've uncovered. The document only needs to include the factors and issues that justify the strategies selected and the key architectural concepts adopted. It should be a persuasive document with a flowing narrative, and not just a catalog of factors, issues, strategies, and architecture concepts.

5.6   Testing ASRs

Although we have argued that architecturally significant requirement (ASRs) carry high risk because they *cannot* be *fully* tested until very late in development, we now argue almost the opposite: critical ASRs *should* be *partially* tested early in development, and retested frequently as development proceeds.

The problem with not testing ASRs is that whatever is not being tested tends to be ignored. Therefore, once you have prioritized the ASRs on a project, you must devise a way to test the most important ones, in order to keep the team's attention focused on them. However, the most important ASRs are typically based on quality-in-use attributes, which by definition cannot be measured until the system is put into use. Fortunately, as you saw in our earlier example, one can usually find internal quality attributes that are indicative of quality-in-use attributes.

Partially measuring key ASRs can therefore be accomplished by selecting indicative quality attributes, internal and/or external, that can be measured early, and measuring them. When results of these measurements change significantly, it is time to review them and decide whether the key ASRs that they indicate are in trouble.

For example, in a recent project, we saw that having adequate performance of the messaging infrastructure was going to be an important quality attribute and a difficult challenge. Focusing the project's attention on it was particularly difficult because the project was globally distributed and cross-divisional. Therefore, we set out to create an early testing strategy for the relevant quality attribute scenarios.

First, we discovered that the QASs were written in terms of complex functionality that could not be tested until late in the project. But since we were really interested in the infrastructure performance, we selected much simpler functionality to test, whose performance would be indicative of the complex functionality's eventual performance. We also limited our attention to just four use case scenarios. We then defined three independent variables to describe the space of performance tests, with a choice among a handful of ordinal values on each dimension (see Table 5.3).

We then defined quality attribute measures for four performance attributes:

- Real-time database memory consumption
- Message throughput
- Message latency
- Command response time

We specified numerical parameter values for each of the independent variables and wrote automated testing scripts to execute each of the functional scenarios under each sensible combination of traffic load and network sensor size. Finally, we specified plausible success thresholds for each of the performance parameters under each combination of independent variables.

As soon as the functional scenarios were implemented, we were able to begin executing these performance tests. We found two

Independent Variable	Values
Traffic load	Normal, Peak, Burst, Max
Sensor network size	Embedded, Small, Medium, Large
Functional scenario	Scenario A, Scenario B, Scenario C, Scenario D

TABLE 5.3 Independent Variables

clusters of pain points: in one cluster of failed tests, memory consumption was excessive; in the other, latency and response time were too slow. At first, the test results pointed to low-hanging fruit: obvious design flaws that had obvious fixes. Once these were taken care of, the tests continued to show deficiencies, but the causes were much less obvious.

Therefore, we conceived and convened *Quality Attribute Testing Workshops* where we brought together cross-functional teams of architects, implementers, and testers, to dig deeper into the performance problems, to *prototype* solutions to the problems, and to specify internal resource measurements that would better quantify what a successful solution looked like. Armed with the test findings, diagnoses, and prototyped solutions, we then conducted *Quality Attribute Design Workshops*, where we designed the solutions in detail, including looking for secondary problems exposed by the solutions to the primary problems.

To summarize, our ASR testing strategy will

- Use quality-in-use attributes to identify corresponding internal quality attributes.

- Test the internal QAS by measuring simple scenarios that are built early.

- Keep the number of ASR test scenarios small, but with multiple combinations of resource parameters (or other independent variables).

- Automate the testing early, so that it is repeatable and cheap.

- Use the tests to drive QA Testing Workshops and QA Design Workshops to improve the quality.

For a more sophisticated approach to testing critical system qualities, see [Cleland-Huang et al. 2008].

5.7   Case Study: Building Automation System

For the purpose of illustration, consider a company that manufactures devices for the building automation domain and software applications that manage a network of these devices. With the hardware being commoditized, its profit margins have been shrinking. The internal development costs for the software applications that manage different devices have also been rising.

To sustain their business long term, the company decides to create a new integrated building automation system. The intended system would broadly perform the following functions:

- Manage field devices currently used for controlling building functions.

- Define rules based on values of field device properties that trigger reactions.

- Issue commands to set values of field device properties.

- For life-critical situations, trigger alarms notifying appropriate users.

Taking this approach would allow the company to reduce internal development costs, since several existing applications will be replaced with the new system. The company could also achieve market expansion by entering new and emerging geographic markets and opening new sales channels in the form of value-added resellers (VARs).

It is clear that some of these business goals will have a significant impact on the development of the building automation system; e.g., hardware devices from many different manufacturers would need to be supported; consideration would have to be made to take the language, culture, and regulations of different markets into account; tradeoffs would need to be made and risks assessed to determine the extent to which the product should support these goals; and depending on the company's comfort level with the tradeoffs and risks, these goals might need to be refined, e.g., scaling back on the intended markets. Therefore, it is highly relevant to use these as a starting point for deriving not only the features that the building automation system must support but also the forces (architectural drivers) that will shape its architecture. Table 5.4 shows these business goals and their refinement.

Features That Define the Product

Business goals play a significant role in defining the critical features that a product must support. For instance, integration implies that the features of existing applications to be integrated must be

Business Goal	Goal Refinement
Reduce internal development costs	Integrate existing applications into a single unified software package: the building automation system
Expand by entering new and emerging geographic markets	Support international languages
	Comply with regulations impacting life-critical systems, such as fire alarms, to operate within specific latency constraints
Open new sales channels in the form of value-added resellers (VARs)	Support hardware devices from different manufacturers
	Support conversions of nonstandard units used by the different hardware devices

TABLE 5.4   Business Goals for the Example Building Automation System

supported in the new system. This may require innovative ways of displaying information in the user interface and providing fine-grained access control over who is allowed to interact with what part of the system. Supporting international languages implies personalization capabilities. Regulatory policies for safety-critical parts of the system would require alarm-handling capabilities for situations that could cause loss of life. Supporting hardware devices from different manufacturers would require dynamic configuration capabilities. Table 5.5 shows a mapping of business goals to the features of the building automation system.

These features can be refined into specific use cases based on how the external actors shown in the context diagram in Figure 5.5 intend to use the system. For instance, the field engineer intends to manage field systems and dynamically reconfigure them. The facilities manager intends to manage alarms generated by field systems that monitor a building. Alarms related to events that could cause loss of life also result in notifications to the public safety system. The system administrator intends to manage the users of the building automation system.

Goal Refinement	Features
Integrate existing applications into a single unified software package: the building automation system	User Management
	Access Control
	Field Device Management
	Event Management
	Alarm Management
Support international languages	Internationalization and Localization
Comply with regulations covering life-critical systems, such as fire alarms, to operate within specific latency constraints	Alarm Management
Support hardware devices from different manufacturers	Dynamic Reconfiguration
Support conversions of nonstandard units used by the different hardware devices	Dynamic Reconfiguration

TABLE 5.5   Features Derived from Business Goals

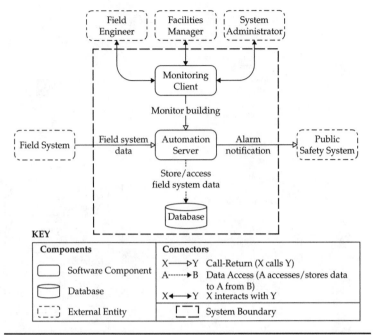

FIGURE 5.5   Building automation system context

Some of the use cases related to the goals of the actors of the building automation system are shown in Figure 5.6. These use cases are grouped by product features they realize and provide a broad functional context of the system under development.

Forces That Shape the Architecture

The business goals also correspond to quality attributes the system must exhibit. In order to support a multitude of hardware devices and consider different languages and cultures, the system must be modifiable. In order to support different regulations in different geographic markets, the system must respond to life-threatening events in a timely manner. It is, therefore, critical that the business goals and their implied quality concerns be fully understood.

One way to do this is to employ the SEI's Quality Attribute Workshop (QAW) [Bachmann et al. 2002], [Barbacci et al. 2000]. As we have discussed, this is a technique for eliciting quality attribute requirements that are mapped to business goals. Through workshops, the business goals provided by management and technical stakeholders are used to elicit concrete scenarios for the quality

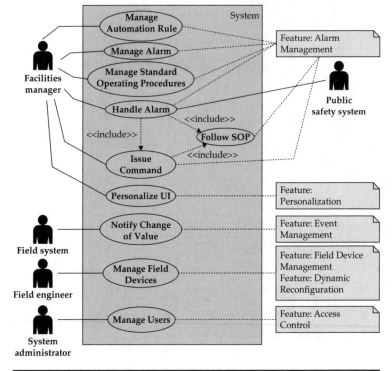

Figure 5.6   Use cases

attributes corresponding to these goals. These scenarios must be specific enough that a system can be evaluated to determine if it satisfies a given scenario. Table 5.6 shows a mapping of the business goals to quality attribute scenarios for the building automation system.

Constraints on the Architecture

While the features define a product and the quality attributes play a significant role in shaping its architecture, there are additional factors that may constrain how the architecture will be designed. For instance, it may be the case the system under consideration has to be developed on the Microsoft .NET platform and needs to use the Oracle DBMS. This *a priori* choice of technology will limit the ability of an architect to make design decisions such as how the system is partitioned into tiers; the communication mechanisms across these tiers; and the strategies for security, failover, and transaction management.

As discussed earlier, global analysis is a technique for analyzing a wide variety of factors that may become constraints for creating the architecture. Table 5.7 enumerates a few such factors for the building automation system.

Refined Business Goal	Quality Attribute	Quality Attribute Scenario
Support hardware devices from many different manufacturers	Modifiability	Two developers are able to integrate a new device into the system in 320 person hours.
Support conversions of nonstandard units used by the different devices	Modifiability	A system administrator configures the system to handle the units from a newly plugged-in field device in less than three hours.
Support international languages	Modifiability	A developer is able to package a version of the system with new language support in 80 person hours.
Comply with regulations requiring life-critical systems, such as fire alarms, to operate within specific latency constraints	Performance	A life-critical alarm should be reported to the concerned users within three seconds of the occurrence of the event that generated the alarm.

TABLE 5.6   Quality Attributes and Scenarios Derived from Business Goals

Architectural Drivers

From the features, quality attributes and factors enumerated in earlier sections, we distill a list of significant architectural drivers. A prioritized list of such drivers for the building automation system is shown in Table 5.8.

Architectural drivers 1–5 relate to the quality attribute scenarios enumerated in Table 5.6. In addition, architectural drivers 1 and 3 also correspond to dynamic reconfiguration, 2 corresponds to personalization, 4 corresponds to event management, and 5, to alarm management features respectively enumerated in Table 5.3. Most architectural drivers relate to the factors identified in Table 5.7. For instance, the organizational factor concerning new market segments is reflected in architectural drivers 1–5. These drivers take into account the flexibility needed to accommodate new field devices and their calibration, language, and cultural aspects, as well as regulatory concerns regarding the responsiveness of the system to safety-critical events. The technological factor related to scalability and responsiveness and the product factor related to performance and scalability are addressed through architectural drivers 4, 5, and 6.

Category	Factor	Description	Strategy
Organization	New Market Segments	Limited experience with some market segments the organization would like to enter.	Incrementally grow the solution into market segments with limited experience.
Technology	Scalability and Responsiveness	System must be scalable to handle large number of field devices and improve responsiveness.	Consider the possibility of scaling upward by adding additional processors in one server computer or additional server computers.
Product	Performance and Scalability	System must handle a wide range of configurations, say, from 100 field devices to 500,000 field devices.	A scalable distributed solution is necessary to meet performance requirements.

TABLE 5.7   Factors in Designing the Building Automation System

Architecture Design

Given a prioritized list of architectural drivers, we can begin to create an architecture that reflects them. To accomplish this, we can employ Attribute-Driven Design (ADD) [Bass et al. 2003].

#	Architectural Driver	Priority
1	Support for new field system	(H, H)
2	International language support	(H, M)
3	Nonstandard unit support	(H, M)
4	Latency of event propagation	(H, H)
5	Latency of alarm propagation	(H, H)
6	Load conditions	(H, H)

TABLE 5.8   Architectural Drivers for the Building Automation System

ADD begins by prioritizing the architectural drivers. This is done by soliciting input from both the business and technical stakeholders. The business stakeholders prioritize scenarios based on their business value (High – H, Medium – M, Low – L), whereas the technical stakeholders do so based on how difficult it would be to achieve a given scenario during the system design, resulting in nine different combinations in the following order of precedence: HH, HM, HL, MH, MM, ML, LH, LM, and LL. Table 5.8 shows the prioritized drivers for the building automation system.

From here we decompose the system by applying a series of architectural tactics corresponding to each architectural driver. Figure 5.7 shows the result of applying these tactics to the building automation system. The sequence of decomposition reflects the priority order of the quality attribute drivers in Table 5.8.

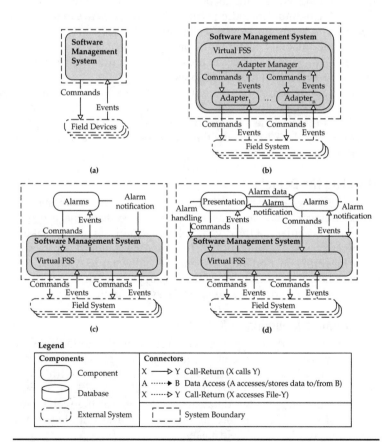

FIGURE 5.7 (a) Monolithic system, (b) support for adding new hardware, (c) support for life-critical systems to operate within specific latency constraints, and (d) support for internationalization

Starting with a monolithic system in Figure 5.7(a), ADD applies the modifiability tactics to limit the impact of change and minimize the number of dependencies on the part of the system responsible for integrating new hardware devices. This is shown in Figure 5.7(b), where an adapter is introduced for each field system (anticipation of changes tactic) with each adapter exposing a standard interface (maintain existing interface tactic) and a virtual field system is introduced to further limit the ripple effect when removing or adding field systems (hiding information tactic).

The performance tactic (concurrency), shown in Figure 5.7(c), is applied next to add support for critical systems so that they operate within specific latency constraints and can handle specified load conditions. The parts responsible for evaluating rules and generating alarms for life-threatening situations are separated out into an alarms module. This module can now be moved to a dedicated execution node, reducing latency, and its performance can be further enhanced by introducing multithreading within the module. We can also add execution nodes for horizontal scalability.

The modifiability tactic (anticipation of changes) is applied in Figure 5.7(d), and a separate presentation module is created to support several international languages.

It should be noted that the only driver from Table 5.8 that does not appear to be addressed is the one dealing with conversion of nonstandard units used by various devices. We use the adapters shown in Figure 5.7(b) to do the conversions into standard units (intermediary modifiability tactic).

Modeling the Domain

Figure 5.8 shows a domain model for the building automation system. In describing various artifacts related to the system, the use of a standard vocabulary of the domain plays a significant role in making the descriptions less ambiguous. The closer the standard vocabulary is to the problem domain, the smaller is the representation gap between how the stakeholders of the system perceive their world and how the software engineers describe the system under design.

Performance Modeling

In the event that data from the field systems begins to indicate the possibility of an alarm, the facilities manager (and possibly, the public safety officials) needs to know about this possibility within one minute of its occurrence. Under normal operating conditions, a single field system generates ten data samples/second in the worst case. Sample size is approximately ten bytes. A typical building in the worst case may have 100 field systems.

This section creates a performance model for the proposed architecture for the building automation system based on the end-to-end

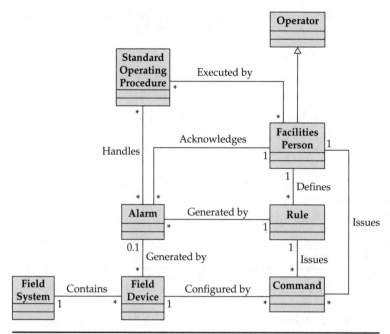

FIGURE 5.8 Domain model

scenario just described. Once the model is created, the computational needs of the software and hardware resources are determined. Finally, this model is evaluated against the specified performance objectives. The purpose of this exercise is to ensure the proposed architecture meets the stipulated performance objectives and explore alternatives if any serious design flaws are discovered. In some cases, a simulation of the system performance is created in addition to or instead of a performance model; e.g., for a nuclear reactor, simulation may be the only way to verify that the design meets the requirements prior to construction.

Figure 5.9 shows the key end-to-end scenario or workflow for the building automation system. Many field systems concurrently transmit data to the virtual field system. The virtual field system processes the raw data and persists it to a database after gaining secure access through the access control component. This data is then made available for analysis by the alarm subsystem, and when alarms are detected, they are reported to the monitoring clients for the facilities manager and the public safety system for the public safety officials. This execution snapshot can be used as a basis for creating a performance model when sufficient information is available on data volumes, data arrival rates, and processing requirements of the individual software elements shown in this figure.

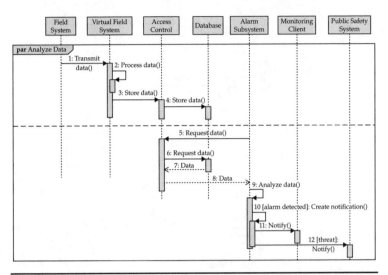

Figure 5.9 Execution snapshot of the building automation system showing message flow across communicating hardware and software elements

Figure 5.10 shows the execution graph for the building automation system corresponding to the scenario in Figure 5.9. Each data sample from the different field systems is first collected by the virtual field subsystem. On the virtual field subsystem, data from all the field systems within a building is stored into a database and made available for analysis by the alarm subsystem. If an alarm is detected, the alarm subsystem generates a notification for necessary action.

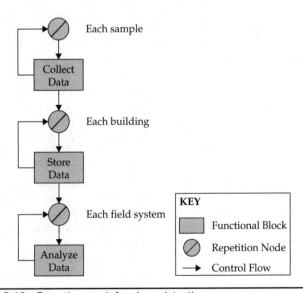

Figure 5.10 Execution graph for alarm detection

Processing Step	Work Unit	Database Access	Network Message
Collect data	1	0	1000
Store data	3	1	1
Analyze data	5	100	100

TABLE 5.9   Software Resource Requirements

Table 5.9 specifies the software resource requirements for each of the processing steps shown in the execution graph. Work units represent CPU consumption, the range being 1 to 5. Here, 1 represents a simple task, whereas 5 represents a complex task. Database accesses represent data persistence or query. We assume data is stored or retrieved in blocks approximately equivalent to 1000 samples of four bytes received from all the field systems every second in a building. For example, the store data task needs one database access to save data from all the field systems within a given building. Network messages represent outbound messages from a processing task. We assume store data and analyze data tasks send packets carrying 10KB of data. Therefore, to transmit data from each building requires approximately one network message.

Table 5.10 shows the processing overhead or computer resource requirements for each of the software resource requirements.

In the top section of the table, the names of devices in a typical server (for instance, an application server) appear in the first row, the quantity of each is in the second row, and the units of service provided by these devices are in the third row. The values in the center section of the table define the connection between the software resource

Device	CPU	Disk	Network
Quantity	1	1	1
Service Unit	Thousand Instructions	Physical I/O	Messages
Work Unit	20	0	0
Database Access	500	2	0
Network Message	10	2	1
Service Time	0.00001	0.02	0.01

TABLE 5.10   Processing Overhead (Courtesy of Connie U. Smith and Lloyd G. Williams, 2002)

Processing Step	CPU Instructions (K)	Physical I/O	Network Messages
Collect Data	10,020	2000	1000
Store Data	570	4	1
Analyze Data	51,100	400	100
Total	61,690	2404	1101

TABLE 5.11 Total Computer Resource Requirements for Alarm Detection

requests and computer device usage. For example, a database access requires 500K CPU instructions, two physical I/Os, and 0 network messages. The last section specifies the service time for the devices. For example, a CPU uses 10 microseconds to execute one thousand instructions.

This processing overhead table can be used for calculating total computer resource requirements for the execution graph for alarm detection in Figure 5.10. We show this in Table 5.11.

The best-case elapsed time for the alarm detection execution graph, therefore, is $(61690 \times 0.00001) + (2404 \times 0.02) + (1101 \times 0.01) = 59.7$ seconds

Thus 59.7 seconds is the best-case elapsed time and does not take into account any network latency, unavailability, or queuing delays. Any increase in the number of field devices and the arrival rate of data samples could also affect the system performance. Given the best-case time is so close to the expected performance, certain other design decisions may need to be made to achieve further improvements. These include but are not limited to

- Concurrent processing at each processing step to avoid bottlenecks
- Filtering and preprocessing of data that avoids transmitting all raw data to the alarm subsystem

5.8 Practice and Experience

Our experience in applying these methods has shown benefits in a number of areas.

Impact of Business Goals

Every system has a rationale for its creation. This rationale takes the form of business goals set forth by the organization creating the system and has a strong influence on the architecture of the system under consideration [Sangwan et. al. 2007].

All of these business decisions require input from technical staff to determine the impact of such requirements and to inform the technical staff of the importance of these requirements. Too often in practice, however, there are some differences between what an organization wants and what its technical team delivers. For example, a business unit wants to create a high-performing infotainment system for a luxury line of cars in a compressed time-to-market. The technical team is forced to distribute the development of parts of this system across geographically distributed teams to achieve the compressed schedule via parallel development efforts. When the components developed by the teams are integrated together, they exceed the memory and performance budgets. While individual components are carefully crafted, not enough attention has been given to the overall system goal of achieving high performance within the given resource constraints. The result is that the business unit is not able to produce the desired product. In this example, the difference between what was desired and what was delivered cost the company hundreds of millions of dollars spent developing the system and billions of dollars in potential lost revenue.

The Notion of Quality

Quality attribute requirements are important both in terms of customer satisfaction and in driving the design of a software system. Yet asserting the importance of quality attribute requirements is only an opening for many other questions [Ozkaya et al. 2008].

There is no shortage of taxonomies and definitions of quality attributes. The best known is probably ISO 9126, which defines 22 different quality attributes and subattributes (which we refer to as quality attribute concerns) [Glinz 2008]. There are questions concerning the extent to which practitioners use the terminology defined in ISO 9126, and which quality attributes defined in ISO 9126 cover the qualities about which practitioners are most concerned. We have observed during architectural evaluations that practitioners sometimes do not use consistent terminology and have concerns that are not covered in relevant taxonomies. Our approach to resolving terminological ambiguities is to use quality attribute scenarios as a means of capturing the precise concerns of the stakeholders. This allows us to supplement the terms used by various stakeholders with a specification that is independent of quality attribute definitions and taxonomies.

For example, ISO 9126 does not have an explicit performance category; the concerns are listed under efficiency and only two concerns are listed, which are time behavior and resource utilization. Another commonly used taxonomy is the FURPS+ scheme, which refers to functionality, usability, reliability, performance, and supportability. FURPS+ lists recovery time, response time, shutdown time, startup time, and throughput as concerns under the performance category. All of these concerns appear in our data, along with some others such as accuracy and stability during overload conditions. However, several concerns in the FURPS+ taxonomy, such as configurability, testability, and maintainability under the supportability category, or availability under the reliability category, appear at the quality attribute level in our data.

A conclusion from these mismatches is that there is clearly a gap between the vocabulary used by stakeholders and practitioners in specifying quality attributes and those that are used in commonly referred-to reference material and taxonomies. Our observation using the integrated approach is when it comes to specifying quality attributes, eliciting the concern supported by the description of the quality attribute scenario is more expressive than going down a list of classifications, which may not give a complete coverage of quality issues.

Integration of Functional Requirements, Quality Attributes, and Architecture

Of the mainstream design methodologies, object-oriented analysis and design (OOAD) has taken a center stage since the early 1980s, and almost all programming languages developed since the 1990s have object-oriented features [Budgen 2003]. OOAD makes use cases and domain modeling its starting point and primarily uses functional decomposition to drive the architecture of a system. There is, however, a need for integrating these activities with the architecture-centric approaches to gain an understanding of the quality attribute requirements used in the elaboration of the architecture for a software-intensive system [Sangwan et al. 2008]. Our experience with the integrated approach is that such a synergy between the OOAD and architecture-centric approaches also provides a linkage from high-level design models to detailed design models that is important for preserving the integrity of the architectural design as the system evolves.

5.9   Tips for Quality Attribute Requirements

Tips for effectively handling quality attribute requirements are given below.

- Empower the chief architect to be the technical leader and decision maker for the project team.

- Establish traceability from soft goals through ASRs and use cases to test cases, so that testing the architecture can become a relatively routine part of the software development process.

- Write a stakeholder analysis document and periodically update it to identify the key stakeholders. Give preference to the stakeholders for whom the project is most important and/or urgent.

- Be careful not to bloat your requirements database with every conceivable quality attribute, but you might want to keep a private list of attributes that you think will become important later.

- Use quality attribute scenarios not just in workshops, but whenever you are capturing stakeholder concerns.

- When conducting QAWs, ask stakeholders to capture their QASs on their laptops and e-mail them to the workshop facilitator.

- During a QAW, stakeholders should be encouraged to seek clarifications on QASs, but any other issues for discussion should be captured and e-mailed to the facilitator. Avoid side discussions on QASs during a QAW.

- Manage factors, issues, and strategies using a general-purpose requirements management tool, if your organization is already using one.

- Address the top 5–10 concerns when defining the architecture principles.

5.10   Summary

Following an integrated approach to requirements engineering and architecture design provides the following major benefits:

1. Joint awareness and a shared understanding, among all stakeholders, of the system context and its problem domain, together with an overarching vision of the system to be designed, helping to properly frame decisions

2. Clear traceability of requirements specification and architecture design to business goals ensuring a higher probability of delivering the "right" system

3. A shared project context that avoids costly duplication of work across the requirements engineering and architecture design disciplines

4. A clear focus on business goals making it easier to communicate, to all concerned stakeholders, the vision of the system being developed, its requirements specification, and its architecture design

5. 11   Discussion Questions

1. Which requirements engineering artifacts are likely to be used by both requirements engineers and software system architects?

2. What kinds of practices can be used to elicit architecturally significant requirements from stakeholders?

3. How does one analyze design tradeoffs and the associated risks with implementing a system that best meets requirements?

References

Bachmann, F., Bass, L., and Klein, M., *Illuminating the Fundamental Contributors to Software Architecture Quality (CMU/SEI-2002-TR-025)*, Software Engineering Institute, Carnegie Mellon University, Pittsburgh, August 2002.

Barbacci, M., Ellison, R., Weinstock, C., and Wood, W., *Quality Attribute Workshop Participants Handbook (CMU/SEI-2000-SR-001)*, Software Engineering Institute, Carnegie Mellon University, Pittsburgh, July 2000.

Bass, L., Clements, P., and Kazman, R., *Software Architecture in Practice*, 2nd ed., Addison-Wesley, Boston 2003.

Berenbach, B., "The Automated Extraction of Requirements from UML Models," *Eleventh IEEE International Symposium on Requirements Engineering (RE '03)*, Monterey Bay, CA, September 2003, pp. 287–288.

Budgen, D., *Software Design*, Addison-Wesley, Boston, 2003.

Cleland-Huang, J., Marrero, W., and Berenbach, B., "Goal Centric Traceability: Using Virtual-Plumblines to Maintain Critical Systemic Qualities," *IEEE Transactions on Software Engineering*, June 2008.

Clements, P., Kazman, R., and Klein, M., *Evaluating Software Architectures: Methods and Case Studies*, Addison-Wesley, Boston, 2001.

Clements, P., Bachmann, F., Bass, L., Garlan, D., Ivers, J., Little, R., Nord, R., and Stafford, J., *Documenting Software Architectures*, Addison-Wesley, Boston, 2003.

Cortellessa, V., Di Marco, A., Inverardi, P., Mancinelli, F., and Pelliccione, P., "A Framework for the Integration of Functional and Non-functional Analysis of Software Architectures," *Proceedings of the International Workshop on Test and Analysis of Component Based Systems (TACoS 2004)*, 2005, pp. 31–44.

Dardenne, A., Lamsweerde, A., and Fickas, S., "Goal-Directed Requirements Acquisition," *Science of Computer Programming*, Vol. 20, Nos. 1–2, 1993, pp. 3–50.

Finkelstein, A. and Dowell, J., "A Comedy of Errors: the London Ambulance Service Case Study," *Proceedings of the 8th International Workshop on Software Specification and Design*, 1996, pp. 2–4.

Glinz, M., "A Risk-Based, Value-Oriented Approach to Quality Requirements," *IEEE Software*, March–April 2008.

Hofmeister, C., Nord, R., and Soni, D., *Applied Software Architecture*, Addison-Wesley, Boston, 1999.

Hofmeister, C., Krutchen, P., Nord, R., Obbink, H., Ran, A., and America, P., "Generalizing a Model of Software Architecture Design from Five Industrial Approaches," *Proceedings of the 5th Working IEEE/IFIP Conference on Software Architecture (WICSA '05)*, 2005, pp. 77–88.

IEEE Std. 610.12-1990.

IEEE Std. 1471-2000.

ISO/IEC 9126 (2001). *Software Engineering—Product Quality—Part 1: Quality Model.* International Standards Organization.

ISO/IEC 25030 (2007). *Software Engineering—Software Product Quality Requirements and Evaluation (SQuaRE)—Quality Requirements*. International Standards Organization.

Jackson, M., "The Meaning of Requirements," *Annals of Software Engineering*, Vol. 3, 1997, pp. 5–21.

Jones, C., *Applied Software Measurement*, 3rd ed., McGraw-Hill, New York, 2008.

Jones, C., *Estimating Software Costs*, 2nd ed., McGraw-Hill, New York, 2007.

Lamsweerde, A., "Requirements Engineering in the Year 00: A Research Perspective," *Proceedings of the International Conference on Software Engineering*, Limerick, Ireland, 2000, pp. 5–19.

Nuseibeh, B., "Weaving Together Requirements and Architectures," *IEEE Computer*, Vol. 34, No. 3, 2001, pp. 115–119.

Nuseibeh, B. and Easterbrook, S., "Requirements Engineering: A Roadmap," *Proceedings of the International Conference on Software Engineering*, Limerick, Ireland, June 2000, pp. 35–46.

Ozkaya, I., Bass, L., Sangwan, R., and Nord, R. "Making Practical Use of Quality Attribute Information," *IEEE Software*, March–April, 2008, pp. 25–33.

Paech, B., Dutoit, A., Kerkow, D., and von Knethen, A., "Functional Requirements, Non-Functional Requirements, and Architecture Should Not Be Separated," *Proceedings of the International Workshop on Requirements Engineering: Foundations for Software Quality*, Essen, Germany, September 9–10, 2002, pp. 102–107.

Paulish, D., *Architecture-Centric Software Project Management*, Addison-Wesley, Boston, 2002.

Peraire, P., Riemenschneider, R., and Stavridou, V., "Integrating the Unified Modeling Language with an Architecture Description Language," *OOPSLA '99 Workshop on Rigorous Modeling and Analysis with the UML: Challenges and Limitations*, 1999.

Robbins, J., Medvidovic, N., Redmiles, D., and Rosenblum, D., "Integrating Architecture Description Languages with a Standard Design Method," *Proceedings of the 20th International Conference on Software Engineering*, Kyoto, Japan, 1998, pp. 209–218.

Sangwan, R., Bass, M., Mullick, N., Paulish, D., and Kazmeier, J., *Global Software Development Handbook*, Auerbach Publications, New York, 2007.

Sangwan, R. and Neill, C., "How Business Goals Drive Architectural Design," *IEEE Computer*, August 2007, pp. 101–103.

Sangwan, R., Neill, C., El Houda, Z., and Bass, M. "Integrating Software Architecture-Centric Methods into Object-Oriented Analysis and Design," *Journal of Systems and Software*, May 2008, pp. 727–746.

Smith, C. and Williams, L., *Performance Solutions: A Practical Guide to Creating Responsive, Scalable Software*, Addison-Wesley, Boston, 2002.

Zave, P. and Jackson, M., "Four Dark Corners of Requirements Engineering," *ACM Transactions on Software Engineering and Methodology*, Vol. 6, No. 1, 1997, pp. 1–30.

CHAPTER 6

Requirements Engineering for Platforms

by Xiping Song, Hans Ros

Steve was assigned as a requirements engineer on a project that was developing a new platform for real-time control systems. Although he had worked on platform projects before, he had not worked with so many different stakeholders. The stakeholders came from the different business divisions who were planning to develop their future applications on the platform. In some cases these divisions were former companies that were acquired by his company, and they had previously competed with each other. Steve began to sense that the stakeholders were competing to promote their features to be developed earliest in the platform project, and they were attempting to influence the platform development schedule. He realized that this project would not necessarily be technically challenging, but it would be very difficult to manage the requirements coming from so many competing stakeholders.

This chapter deals with how to carry out requirements engineering when developing software platforms. It describes some of the challenges that arise when developing the platforms. In order to address these issues, a practical approach is presented for how to unify, normalize, and reconcile the nonfunctional requirements in the platform development.

6.1   Background

Software product lines have been an active area of software systems engineering for the past few years [Clements et al. 2002]. Building a product line on top of a common *platform* with shared services is commonly practiced in many industries. For example, the use of platforms has been widely practiced in the automobile industry, where a standard drive train and body are used for multiple models and variations of automobiles. One may read automobile model reviews with statements like, "a new ES 350 will grace the Lexus lineup for the 2007 model year, sharing its platform with the Toyota Camry." "Of course, Lexus doesn't want you to think of the ES 350 as an upscale Camry, but as a full-scale luxury car."

Siemens has initiated a number of development projects using software product line concepts that are referred to as "platform initiatives." In this case, a platform refers to a common set of lower-level software services such as operating system and middleware. Applications are written on top of the platform to create products within one or more product lines for potentially differing business units. For example, the Building Automation System (BAS) project described in [Sangwan et al. 2007] required that multiple application disciplines be integrated to run on a single workstation platform. The applications were developed by different business organizations, at different development sites, with different skills, and for different domains.

6.2 Challenges

Requirements engineers working on platform projects accept stakeholder requests where the stakeholders are from different organizations interested in developing products in different application domains. In such a platform project, it is very likely that stakeholder requests will be quite different and sometimes conflict with each other. As each business unit is eager to get their new products quickly to market, setting priorities for the platform features will be difficult. Furthermore, there will likely be many feature requests as the stakeholders from different business units are motivated to put as much functionality as possible (from their view) into the platform.

Although the platform developers will likely push back on functional requirements coming from the stakeholders, they will need to have confidence that the intended platform will be able to support a wide variety of applications. As future applications will likely be vaguely defined, the services that the platform will provide will also be vague. Functional requirements will drive the definition of the components that make up the software system architecture. Nonfunctional requirements drive the quality definition of the platform upon which the components will execute. Thus, requirements engineers will need to address both functional and nonfunctional requirements, and the requirements analysis feeds directly into the software system architecture design.

Requirements engineers and software architects working on platform projects will necessarily focus on the nonfunctional requirements that the platform will be designed to meet. As you have seen in Chapter 5, developing and implementing nonfunctional requirements (NFRs) is probably one of the most challenging tasks in developing large software systems. The nonfunctional behaviors of software systems are difficult to elicit, describe, and quantify. Many research and industrial standardization efforts have been made to enable the NFR development to become more systematic and unify NFR specifications [ISO 2001, ISO 2007]. However, due to the high complexity and large scale of industrial software development, software practitioners are still having difficulty in developing and implementing NFRs. Some example challenges follow:

- The NFRs (quality attribute requirements) defined in the standards may be incomplete, since each software product has its own unique needs. Thus, software engineers must customize the standard NFR definitions to their needs and make them more effective to categorize their specific NFRs. For example, the *hostability* quality attribute may be simple when the software is operated at only one central location, but it may grow complex when the software is operated across a number of service locations in order to provide fast services to many widely distributed customers. This is specific to the nature (e.g., for an ASP [application service provider]) of the software being delivered. For example, *scalability* is the ability for a system to size its capacity either up or down to fit a variety of computing devices. However, some software applications may operate on only one or two types of computing devices. Selecting and customizing NFRs often needs to be done iteratively during the NFR development process, based upon continuous inputs from the stakeholders.

- Software platforms coming from a large software system company tend to support a large variety of customers with different application situations. The customer situations are different financially and operationally. The customer businesses are likely based upon different hardware infrastructures and service support models. To reduce development and maintenance costs, however, it is most desirable for the software system company to have some software platforms to support all of those application situations and maintenance needs. How to reconcile and organize NFRs for the platforms that support such a wide variety of application situations and maintenance needs is often very challenging.

6.3   Practices

Based upon our experience in developing NFRs for large software systems, we have developed a software process that helps us to more systematically develop NFRs for platforms. This process is called the Platform NFR Development (PND) process. It complements existing NFR development methods by emphasizing iterative development, interacting with other development activities (e.g., prototyping, testing, and release management), and reconciling the stakeholders' inputs. It provides detailed descriptions for how the stakeholders' NFR inputs can be collected, and how such inputs can be organized to facilitate the reconciliation activity as necessary for platform projects. The process targets the NFR development of software systems that are to be installed on a distributed computing environment that uses a variety of computing devices for different purposes (e.g., database, user interface, data collection). Simple systems, such as single-user desktop software, are not the target of this NFR development process. The PND process has been used for defining hundreds of NFRs for a large software system; thus, the techniques described here are capable of managing NFRs for medium- to large-sized industrial software systems.

Figure 6.1 illustrates the PND process, and each activity of this process is described in the sections that follow.

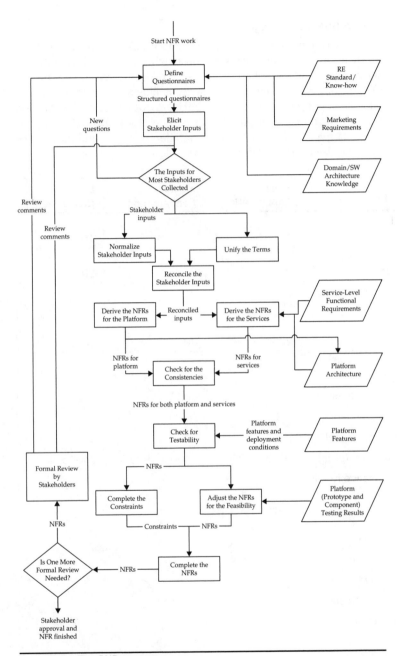

FIGURE 6.1   The PND process

Define Questionnaires

This activity defines the questionnaire that will be sent to the stakeholders for their inputs. Requirements engineers will also use it during the on-site requirements elicitation meetings to collect the stakeholder inputs. One major artifact used in this activity is illustrated in Table 6.1. The table as shown here is not complete, but it provides sufficient information for showing how we can structurally organize the stakeholders' inputs. The data filled in Table 6.1 is for illustration purposes and may not be fully consistent and realistic. An example row may represent only a

	Small Configuration	Medium Configuration	Large Configuration
# of server computers	1	4	10
# of local client computers	3	8	20
# of remote client computers	10	30	100
# of managed objects	2000	40,000	100,000
Hard-disk needs			
Networking conditions (Mbps)	100	100	1000
UI Display Needs			
Operator screens	3	12	40
Picture size (pixel)	1600 × 1200	6400 × 4800	6400 × 4800
Performance Needs			
Normal load			
Peak load			
Burst load			
Burst period			
Burst load			
Archiving Needs			
# of archive servers	0	1	2
# of redundant servers	0	4	10
. . .			

TABLE 6.1 Example NFR Questionnaire

category that defines a set of rows (bolded text indicates a category). Our experience indicates that such a table in practice could have well over 200 rows related to NFRs (e.g., reliability, availability). Thus, the ISO standards [ISO 2001, 2007] for quality attributes are a good source to start to define the questionnaires, but many more details need to be added for collecting the stakeholders' inputs.

Elicit Stakeholders' Inputs

This activity collects inputs from the stakeholders. Requirements engineers will organize workshops with the stakeholders from each of the organizations that will use the future software platform for their products. The goal is to complete the answers to the questionnaires and avoid any misunderstandings by having discussions during the on-site workshops. Table 6.1 does not include any explanations for each row, so it is most important for the requirements engineers to collect the stakeholders' inputs when they are together on site.

Unify Terminology

This activity aims to unify the terms used in the stakeholders' inputs. After this, only the unified terms will be used in the NFRs to replace a set of similar terms. Since a software platform may aim to support the users of different application situations and organizations, stakeholders may use varying terms in describing their business applications. For example, terms such as alarms, telegrams, events, requests, messages, change of value (COV) events, etc., may have similar meanings, depending on the application. Thus, we may just use a unified term "message" to represent all these terms for all applications of the product platform.

For this activity, the Language Extended Lexicon (LEL)–based requirement analysis approach [Cysneiros et al. 2004], [Boehm et al. 1996] should be very useful for identifying the terms. Requirement engineers can effectively unify/conceptualize terms by analyzing their relationships (e.g., a-type-of, a-part-of, etc.). Depending on how complex the analysis is, users can choose to use simple modeling notations (e.g., Structured Table) and visual modeling notations (e.g., Entity-Relation).

Normalize Stakeholders' Inputs

This activity aims to make the stakeholders' inputs comparable with each other on the same scale and operating conditions. For example, for performance requirements, one stakeholder's input might be 50 alarms per 10 seconds while another stakeholder's input might be 20 alarms per 1 second. Such differences are often caused by the different nature (e.g., how frequently an alarm would usually come and how quickly the system must respond to it) of their application domains or the existing (legacy) products from which the performance requirements are derived. Sometimes, such performance needs are based upon competitors' product specifications to ensure an edge over the competitors (e.g., so that the inputs are comparable to the competitors' quality attribute requirements values). In order to make those stakeholders' inputs directly comparable for an NFR for the platform, requirements engineers must convert them into the same scale (e.g., number of alarms per second). Sometimes, this normalization changes the stakeholder's original intent. For example, "Processing 50 alarms per 10 seconds" as a performance need for certain applications reflects more precisely the stakeholder's real need than an alarm processing rate (alarms/second). Normalizing the need to "Processing 5 alarms per second" would make a more specific and demanding requirement than the original stakeholder's need. However, in order to reconcile the stakeholders' inputs, such normalization is necessary.

Reconcile Stakeholders' Inputs

This activity identifies and groups the similar stakeholders' inputs, and then requirements engineers can define a single NFR to address this group of similar stakeholders' inputs. By doing this, requirements engineers can also identify a range of variations on the similar requirements. Depending on how much they vary, some constraints might be added to ensure the NFRs are feasible to implement. For example, the performance requirements within a narrow latency range might be grouped together. If one stakeholder requests less than 2 seconds for transmitting an alarm while another stakeholder requests less than 4 seconds (assuming they are easily achievable with low-end hardware), then the requirements engineers can define that a low-end, small deployment of the system shall support an alarm latency that is less than 2 seconds. However, if another stakeholder requests a 0.5-second alarm latency that is far more demanding, a constraint might be added to ensure that such a short latency can be implemented and acceptable for the targeted application situation. For example, the constraint might be that some high-speed networking device should be used when achieving this short alarm latency. By doing this, we can address the stakeholders' needs with similar NFRs by specifying different constraints.

Define the NFRs for the Platform

This activity defines the NFRs for the platform from the stakeholders' inputs that address the end-user needs. The reconciled stakeholders' inputs will be used for specifying the NFRs. The NFRs will use the specific values from the reconciliation. The worksheets used in the reconciliation should be put into the NFR specification, possibly as an appendix, referred from the main context of the NFR specification.

Derive the NFRs for the Components

This activity allocates the NFRs to the related functional requirements, which are often defined in terms of services in a service-oriented platform. The stakeholders' inputs usually describe the functions they need in their products. The software platform would have to provide either a program-callable service or an end user–level (application-level) service to support the implementation of such functions. This activity derives what NFRs certain services must satisfy. For example, a NFR might be that the service for subscribing a value change event must have a latency that is less than 0.1 seconds. Such NFRs may depend on the high-level architectural design to some degree. However, since the development of NFRs will be performed in parallel or intertwined with the architecture design, the NFRs can be adjusted according to the architectural design changes.

This activity should document the NFRs' traces to the original stakeholders' inputs so that the NFR reviewers (often a stakeholder) can understand from which inputs the NFRs are derived.

The NFRs resulting from the two preceding activities are grouped into NFR categories. For each category, the following structure is used to define its NFRs.

NFR Category (e.g., Performance)

We give an example of how a platform-level NFR model can identify lower-level NFRs.

- *The platform-level NFR model*
- **Platform-level NFRs**
  - [Perf-PLATFORM-1]
  - [Perf-PLATFORM-2]
  - . . .
  - [Perf-PLATFORM-N]
- **Component-level NFRs for component 1**
  - *The component-level NFR model*
  - [Perf-COMP1-1]
  - [Perf-COMP1-2]
  - . . .
- **Component-level NFRs for component 2**
  - *The component-level NFR model*
  - [Perf-COMP2-1]
  - . . .

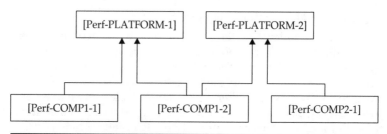

Figure 6.2   Example platform-level NFR model

The platform-level NFR model captures how the platform-level NFRs are refined into the components and their relations. The major relation is "support" that shows which component-level NFRs support which platform-level NFRs. For an example, see Figure 6.2.

The *component-level NFR model* shows the relations among the NFRs at the component level. The major relations are "reference," "replace," and "deprecated" (a self-relation). It also shows what platform-level NFRs they support as well. The reference relation indicates that one NFR is built upon another NFR. For example, one performance requirement might be that a rate should be two times faster than the rate defined by another NFR. The replace relation shows one NFR has been replaced by another NFR. One NFR could also be replaced by more than one NFR, as shown in Figure 6.3.

Check for Consistency

This activity checks the consistency between the NFRs at the platform level with those at the component level. The NFRs at the platform

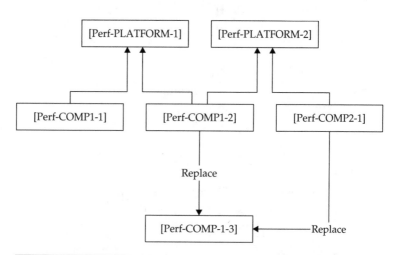

Figure 6.3   One NFR [Perf-COMP-1-3] replaced by two NFRs, [Perf-COMP1-2] and [Perf-COMP2-1]

level are concerned about the quality of the services that can be directly used by the end users to provide the product functionalities (e.g., those for handling alarms in a monitoring product) or the quality of the platform as a whole (e.g., ease of installing the platform). The NFRs at the component level are for those services that can only be used as a part of the implementation for the product functionalities. For example, an alarm forwarding latency requirement must be consistent with the performance of the low-level messaging system, since the latency of alarm forwarding (as a platform-level function) depends on the performance of the messaging system (e.g., message transmit latency).

Check for Testability

This activity checks if the NFRs that have been developed are generally testable or not. The requirements engineers would play the role of a tester and examine if the NFRs provide sufficient information that the test procedures (including the testing environment) can be specified to test the NFRs. This activity is integrated with feature release management to focus on the features that are to be released soon (e.g., the next major platform delivery time). That is, for the features to be released, the related NFRs must be clearly testable. This strategy avoids requiring all NFRs to be testable, since some of them may still be unstable and may not be implemented at all. Such an incremental approach can be integrated well with agile development methods [Schwaber 2004].

Complete the Constraints

This activity identifies the missing constraints (e.g., operating conditions, deployment conditions, prerequisite software systems) under which the NFRs should be defined. The activity "check for testability" will provide inputs for completing the constraints, since it helps identify the unspecified conditions under which the tests should be performed. For example, for testing the platform startup latency, a necessary condition is whether the operating system has been started or not. Without this condition specified, the platform startup latency cannot be tested to verify whether the latency requirement has been fulfilled or not.

Tune the NFRs for Feasibility

This activity aims to ensure that the NFRs are implementable; i.e., the NFRs can likely be satisfied with the technologies that the platform will be based upon. For example, this activity examines whether the performance requirements are achievable by analyzing the available results from testing the platform prototypes or finished components. If the analysis shows that the NFRs may not be achievable, the constraints might have to be added or modified to make the

NFRs more specific so that they will be satisfied only under certain conditions. For example, the deployment constraints might be modified to use a more powerful computing infrastructure to support high performance requirements. This can certainly lead to architectural changes or the use of other implementation technologies.

Complete NFRs

This activity completes the NFR definitions and makes them ready for external review by the stakeholders. This activity should include conducting an internal review of the NFRs by the requirement engineers, software architects, software testing lead, and project lead. In particular, this activity should check if each NFR has a trace to some original stakeholder's inputs and if the traces are documented in the NFRs.

Formal Review by Stakeholders

This activity aims to collect feedback comments and get approvals from the stakeholders. The review results may either lead to modifications of the NFRs or generate new questionnaires for the stakeholders. For example, if a stakeholder's comment is that some NFR might be missing, a questionnaire about this potentially missing NFR could be defined and sent to all the stakeholders in the next iteration of the NFR definition process. From our experience, we expect that at least three iterations that involve external reviewers are needed for completing an NFR document.

6.4   Experience

We have applied the PND process for developing a software platform that supports the running and implementation of diverse industrial software systems (e.g., factory control, automation, transportation). For this example, each of the stakeholders represented either a Siemens company or a division of such a company. In the following sections, we describe our experiences in carrying out the activities of the PND process.

Define Questionnaires and Elicit the Stakeholders' Inputs

Defining the questionnaires for the NFR elicitation is very much an iterative activity, since multiple elicitations are often needed. At the beginning of NFR development, the questionnaires can be drafted based upon the standard quality attribute requirements as defined by ISO-9126 or other standards in relation to the key business drivers of the software platform to be developed. An example business driver could be increasing software reusability to reduce the software development cost. Based upon ISO-9126, the questionnaires could include questions regarding software functionality (e.g., accuracy, interoperability, compliance, and security), reliability, usability, efficiency, maintainability, and portability. The questionnaires organized around those attributes should help elicit the first set of the stakeholders' inputs. Analyzing the answers to those questionnaires often helps identify the needs that are beyond the scope covered by the questionnaires. In addition, some answers may be incomplete when providing insufficient details such as those that describe the related operating environments. This often needs to be corrected by carrying out the next round of stakeholder elicitation. During this elicitation, the NFR Questionnaire Table as illustrated in Table 6.1 will most likely be used. This table is precise and structured with built-in mathematical formulas to automatically calculate (derive) the stakeholders' inputs.

Some quality attributes that were not covered by the standards will be added into the questionnaires as well. For example, the ISO standard does not have the safety and localizability (i.e., defines how easily the software can be localized) attributes. For a real-time, embedded system that controls physical equipment, safety is often very important and thus needs to be added. For a large software system company, its products often need to be localized to the regional markets all over the world. Thus, localizability-related questions could be added to the questionnaires.

Note that although our experience reported herein emphasizes using the NFR Questionnaire Table, it cannot take the place of the face-to-face elicitation meetings we have described in Chapter 3. Complete understanding of functional and nonfunctional requirements requires much discussion and communication between stakeholders and requirements engineers.

Unify Terminology

This activity is particularly important for developing NFRs for a software platform that is potentially applied in multiple application domains. For example, a software platform may support the applications in multiple application domains or different applications (e.g., image analysis for different purposes) in the same application domain (e.g., the medical imaging domain). Not unifying and differentiating those key terms in the stakeholders' inputs will make many NFR-related discussions very difficult.

Our experience indicates that carrying out this activity is actually not very difficult if it is well supported by the stakeholders. In our practice, we used only two to five structured tables that modeled the relationships among the similar terms. The table can be used to indicate the relations among the terms and list the differences and commonalities. Some of those tables were documented into the NFR requirements as the term definitions. However, during the NFR documentation development, we must be very disciplined at using the unified terms to ensure the use is appropriate. This requires that the NFR writer clearly understands the differences among the terms and decides if it is appropriate to use the unified terms rather than the terms that came directly from the stakeholders. Though the different terms used by the stakeholders were very similar, they could indeed be different, depending on where those terms are used in the NFRs. For example, for an NFR that defines the rate of transmitting data, a value change as data that is being transmitted is the same as an alarm. However, for an NFR that defines the limit on the specific data size, the two terms are different and the unified term (e.g., message) would not be used. When NFRs are bound to specific platform services, more service-oriented terms (e.g., alarm), and not the unified term (e.g., message), would be used, since this would make the NFR more readable and specific.

Normalizing and Reconciling Stakeholders' Inputs

It is essential to normalize the stakeholders' inputs before we can reconcile their requests. Our practice indicates that normalizing (hence, changing) the original stakeholder's input is usually acceptable to the stakeholder as long as a clear trace to the original stakeholder's request is maintained. Such traces helped answer the stakeholders' questions concerning the origins of the normalized stakeholders' inputs. Without such traces, there could be a great deal of confusion when the stakeholders review the NFRs.

In our practice, Excel spreadsheets are used to perform the normalization and reconciliation, since the spreadsheets help build the links and enable automated computations from the original stakeholders' inputs to the normalized results. Furthermore, the spreadsheets help to identify and manage the value ranges represented in the stakeholders' inputs. For example, a performance requirement "alarms processed per 10 seconds" from one stakeholder was normalized to alarms processed per second (APS). Then, the APS needs that were collected from all the stakeholders were listed in the spreadsheet. More specifically, each stakeholder provided the APS range for different deployment configurations (i.e., those defined earlier also through the normalizing and reconciling process). The spreadsheet automatically calculated the combined range (see Table 6.3: 40–120 alarms per second). In most cases, such simple, automated calculations can work well, for example, when the ranges are not too wide to provide specific enough information for design decision making. However, it is necessary to review the automated calculations results. Sometimes, in our practice, we did override the results to make sure that the range was not too wide. If the values of the combined range were acceptable (e.g., approved by the architects), we manually put them into the reconciled range, which was further turned into a NFR. Sometimes, in our practice, we checked with the stakeholders as to why they provided either an unusually small or unusually large number, to ensure the performance need was for similar load and deployment configuration situations. It was possible that one stakeholder had some special application situations that led to a very wide range of data in the stakeholder input.

The examples provided in Tables 6.2, 6.3, and 6.4 are a very small part of what we develop in practice. Each of the stakeholders' inputs on the NFRs or the reconciliation sheet had hundreds of spreadsheet cells that captured the stakeholders' inputs for a variety of situations; e.g., loading conditions, system deployment conditions. The inputs from one stakeholder often were a set of collective/combined inputs within one Siemens business division that planned to use the platform to develop their products. Such semiautomated analysis was very useful and greatly improved our productivity for both creating and maintaining the NFRs.

Stakeholder A	. . .	Large Configuration		. . .
Alarm processed per second (APS)		50	100	
. . .				

TABLE 6.2 Stakeholder A's Inputs

Stakeholder B	. . .	Large Configuration		. . .
Alarm processed per second (APS)		40	120	
. . .				

TABLE 6.3 Stakeholder B's Inputs

All Stakeholders	. . .	Large Configuration		. . .
APS for stakeholder A		50	100	
APS for stakeholder B		40	120	
. . .		. . .	. . .	
Combined range		40	120	
Reconciled range		40	120	
NFR			<120	

TABLE 6.4 Example Reconciliation Worksheet

Derive the NFRs for the Software Platform

The derivation is to identify and conceptualize the NFRs for the platform services based on the stakeholders' inputs. For example, one stakeholder's input could be, "If an unauthorized user attempts to access the X product, the platform should detect the attempt and cut off the accessing PC from the network." Another input might be, "If an unauthorized user attempts to access the Y product, the software should detect the attempt and raise an alarm." The platform requirement could be, "The software shall provide a service(s) for detecting the unauthorized access, and upon the detection, execute a predefined handling action." Our experience indicates that this activity actually performs two tasks: one is to identify a required service (e.g., a platform security service) to support this platform-level security requirement; another one is to reconcile/combine the stakeholders' inputs. Such activities have an impact on the software architecture and services the software platform should provide (e.g., functional requirements).

Check for Testability and Complete the Constraints

These two activities are highly related in developing software systems. As the products we develop often support a variety of application situations (e.g., loading conditions and deployment configurations), without sufficient description of those situations, the NFRs would not be testable. The testers would not know how to set up the testing environment to perform the NFR testing. The tester review of the NFRs often provides many inputs for completing the NFR constraints.

Using structured templates is a way to ensure the constraints are more complete. For example, we could enter certain attributes (e.g., loading conditions, deployment configurations, redundancy status) for each requirement. Our experience, however, was that this is too much work for defining the NFRs for all of the attribute combinations. Stakeholders would not likely provide all the inputs for all of the combinations. This is because some of those combinations are rare in the intended applications (e.g., small deployment configurations with redundancy). Thus, it was not necessary to provide NFRs for all combinations.

6.5   Tips for RE for Platforms

The following tips may be useful when developing and analyzing platform requirements.

- Use a standard set of quality attribute requirements to structure the first version of the NFR questionnaire.
- Unify the terminology used by different stakeholders for defining platform requirements.

- Add constraints to ensure that the NFRs are feasible to implement.

- Describe NFRs with sufficient information so that the test procedures (including the testing environment) can be specified to test the NFRs.

- Define NFRs for only the attribute combinations that are likely to be deployed for the product line.

- Use structured templates to ensure that constraints are complete.

- After the NFRs are reasonably stable, create draft marketing literature for the platform (as though it is a standalone salable product) and use as an aid when conducting requirements reviews with stakeholders.

6.6   Summary

This chapter introduces an approach for

- Developing NFRs for large software systems that might be deployed in a variety of computing infrastructures and operate under a variety of application situations. We call the lower-level common software (e.g., operating system, middleware) a platform. We have described a detailed process (called PND) and related artifacts that can be used to help reconcile the stakeholders' inputs.

- The PND process complements the existing NFR approaches by integrating the NFR development with other software engineering processes. It describes how testing and release management could be integrated with the PND process.

6.7   Discussion Questions

1. What are some of the differences between a software product line and platforms?

2. How can one determine which functions should be implemented in application software and which in the platform?

3. When should the ISO standards be used within the PND process to define a list of NFRs?

References

Bachmann, F., Bass, L., Klein, M., and Shelton, C., "Designing Software Architectures to Achieve Quality Attribute Requirements," *IEEE Software Proceedings*, Vol. 152, No. 4, August 5, 2005, pp. 153–165.

Bachmann, F., Bass, L., and Klein, M., *Illuminating the Fundamental Contributors to Software Architecture Quality (CMU/SEI-2002-TR-025)*, Software Engineering Institute Carnegie Mellon University, Pittsburgh, August 2002.

Barbacci, M., Klein M., Longstaff, T., and Weinstock, C., "Quality Attributes," Technical Report, CMU/SEI-95-TR-021, ESC-TR-95-021, December 1995.

Bass, L., Clements, P., and Kazman, R., *Software Architecture in Practice*, 2nd ed., Addison-Wesley, Boston, 2003.

Boehm, B. and In, H., "Identifying Quality-Requirement Conflicts," *Proceedings of the Second International Conference on Requirements Engineering*, 1996.

Clements, P., and Northrop, L., *Software Product Lines*, Addison-Wesley, Boston, 2002.

Cysneiros Luiz Marcio and Leite, Julio Cesar Sampaio do Prado, "Nonfunctional Requirements: From Elicitation to Conceptual Models," *IEEE Transactions on Software Engineering*, Vol. 30, No. 5. May 2004.

Doerr, J., Kerkow, D., Koenig, T., Olsson, T., and Suzuki, T., "Non-Functional Requirements in Industry: Three Case Studies Adopting an Experience-Based NFR Method," *Proceedings of the 13th International Conference on Requirements Engineering*, 2005, pp. 373–382.

ISO/IEC 9126 (2001), *Software Engineering—Product Quality—Part 1: Quality Model*, International Standards Organization.

ISO/IEC 25030 (2007), *Software Engineering—Software Product Quality Requirements and Evaluation (SQuaRE)—Quality Requirements*, International Standards Organization.

Kuusela, J. and Savolainen, J., "Requirements Engineering for Product Families," *Proceedings of the 2000 International Conference on Software Engineering*, June 2000, pp. 61–69.

Mylopoulos, J., Chung, L., and Nixon, B., "Representing and Using Non-Functional Requirements: A Process-Oriented Approach," *IEEE Transactions on Software Engineering*, June 1992.

Sangwan, R., Bass, M., Mullick, N., Paulish, D., and Kazmeier, J., *Global Software Development Handbook*, Auerbach Publications, New York, 2007.

Schwaber, K., *Agile Project Management with Scrum*, Microsoft Press, Redmond, WA, 2004.

CHAPTER 7
Requirements Management

by Brian Berenbach, Beatrice Hwong

C hris was assigned as a requirements engineer on a project that was much larger than the last project he had worked on. On the smaller project, the product manager had maintained a spreadsheet listing all the features and their status. For this new project, there were thousands of features that were kept in a requirements database. Chris began to be concerned how he would understand a system with so much functional complexity, and how he would track the status of all the features that were assigned to him.

This chapter introduces and explains some of the requirements management practices that are used on large projects. Requirements engineering is a continuous activity across the entire product development life cycle, and it must be managed accordingly. This includes practices for traceability, measurement, change management, quality, and scalability.

7.1   Background

As development projects grow in complexity and new products are released to the market with many features, the importance of good practices in requirements management grows. Requirements must be identified, documented, and analyzed, and the various downstream development artifacts must be traced back to the requirements and original business goals.

The purpose of *requirements management* is to manage all of a project's or product's requirements post-elicitation, and to identify inconsistencies between those requirements and a project's plans or work products [Chrissis et al. 2003].

We discussed in Chapter 2 the use of requirements engineering artifact models as an aid in defining tool integration and usage. The RE processes most impacted by such planning are those associated with requirements management. Requirements management (RM) encompasses several major activities and some lesser ones. Furthermore, there is significant overlap between some project management activities, such as tracking and oversight, and requirements management activities that provide some level of transparency into the various requirements engineering tasks. Requirements management makes requirements engineering possible for large projects and helps reduce project chaos. The remainder of this chapter is organized as follows: first, some of the important requirements management activities are described; then some of the issues associated with those activities are discussed. Tips for requirements management are also provided.

7.2   Change Management

Change inevitably happens, so we must plan for changes to requirements over the course of a development project as well as after the product is released to the field. Thus, we must establish processes and tools to manage changing requirements.

Requirements management includes the version control of all artifacts that are the sources of requirements or the products of the requirements management process. Examples of artifacts that would be controlled include

- Source documents, pictures, and blueprints

- Memos and meeting minutes

- Requirements and stakeholder requests

- Documents produced from requirements, including requirements, design, and test specifications.

There are a large number of version control or configuration management tools available that can be used to control requirements artifacts [White 2000].

Initially, requirements will be fluid and uncertain. While requirements elicitation is ongoing it is very difficult to create a somewhat stable set of requirements. Consequently, a baseline is usually created when nearing the end of the requirements elicitation phase after stakeholder requests have been reviewed and an initial set of requirements has been created and approved. A *requirements baseline* is the set of requirements, source documents, and all documents derived from the set of requirements at a specific point in time. If, however, a supplier is receiving the requirements from a customer as part of a negotiated contract, then the set of requirements contained in the contract is normally considered the initial baseline.

Until a baseline is created, changes to stakeholder requests and the evaluation of potential requirements make it difficult to track changes. However, once a baseline has been established, the tracking of changes to requirements becomes mandatory.

The term *feature creep* applies when many small changes are permitted without control or formal review. Such changes can severely impact the profitability and delivery date of a project or product. In order to prevent this from happening, proposed changes must be reviewed by a control group often called a *change control board (CCB)*. The role of the CCB is to provide a central control mechanism to ensure that every change request is properly considered, authorized, and coordinated. The CCB considers *modification requests (MRs)*, and after considering the impact of the proposed change, some of the MRs will result in changes to requirements or other artifacts. The CCB is analogous to an *engineering review board (ERB)* that is used to review proposed changes to the form, fit, or function of the electrical components in electronics design and manufacturing. In this case, *engineering change requests (ECRs)* are made, analyzed, and some of the requests are implemented as *engineering change orders (ECOs)*. A summary of the decision-making components for requirements engineering change management is given in Table 7.1.

The degree of formality in change management—e.g., the makeup of any CCB—is a function of the nature of the project, contract, or the like. For example, in research projects frequent changes are sometimes expected, and consequently, reviews may be frequent and informal. On the other hand, some projects require the delivery of electromechanical systems with well-defined software and hardware features (e.g., a railroad signaling system where unauthorized feature changes can have a catastrophic effect on the project's bottom line or delivery date), so these systems must have formal CCB processes.

Several different types of analyses are done by the members of a change control board (or project management staff) to support change management. Note that any kind of CCB analysis relies on in-place traceability mechanisms. They will be discussed in the next section. A summary of the major types of analyses done by CCB members is given in Table 7.2.

Change Control Decision-Making Components	Description
Summary	Deciding whether to accept a proposed change to the requirements of a system
Inputs	Proposed requirements change, including justification and rationale
Steps	Considering the impact of the proposed change, costs, benefits, ROI
Deliverables	"Yes," "No," "Defer," or "Yes," but with modifications
Responsible	Change control board (CCB)
Contributors	Proposer and CCB members
Methods	Tradeoff analysis
Tools	Costing tools, tracing tools, tradeoff tools

TABLE 7.1   Requirements Engineering Change Management

Type of Analysis	Description	Processes Supported
Impact analysis	Follow incoming links, to answer the question: "What if this were to change?"	Change management
Derivation analysis	Follow outgoing links, to answer the question: "Why is this here?"	Cost-benefit analysis
Coverage analysis	Count statements that have links, to answer the question: "Have I covered everything?" Most often used as a measure of progress.	General engineering, management reporting

TABLE 7.2   Main Types of RE Analysis Initiated by a CCB

Impact Analysis

The objective of *impact analysis* is to determine the financial, resource, or temporal cost of a change request or new feature. To do this, the responsible CCB member (usually the architect) or his/her delegate must trace from the impacted features to the actual system design in order to determine how significant any modifications or enhancements would be, and then from that derive the cost and risk of such modifications.

Analyzing the impact of a change request requires tracing down the left side of the example engineering project traceability model (see later Figure 7.1). Traces go from requirements → design. If the requirement being analyzed is nonfunctional (e.g., performance, capacity), then additional effort may be required to simulate the impact of the proposed change to determine if it is feasible.

Customer Management and Change Control

A software developer was sent to do installation work on a control system for an offshore oil platform. While the developer was seated at a terminal performing a software installation, the customer representative sat down alongside him and asked if a specific change was feasible. The developer replied that it was. The customer then asked how much it would cost, and the developer, not giving it much thought, said "a few days." Several weeks later the project manager received a letter of understanding from the client stating that there had been agreement between our representative (the developer) and the customer to make the change at no charge. Upon doing an impact analysis, it was determined that the cost of the change would completely wipe out the project contingency. The developer barely remembered the conversation. Heated discussions with the customer then ensued.

Derivation Analysis

Derivation analysis is concerned with discovering the origin or rationale of a function, module, etc. The relevant designs are traced back first to the requirements, and then from the requirements to the stakeholders' requests (or market demands or business goals) that led to the decision to add the requirement to the product. Alternatively, a product component or component requirement is traced back to the original rationale for creating it. Derivation is necessary to understand why a feature or function is in a product, without which intelligent decisions regarding a change to the requirement cannot be made.

Coverage Analysis

Coverage analysis measures the ratio of defined to actual product features. It is used to determine whether the requirements or features of interest have been implemented in the product. This is accomplished by tracing from the original system (or contract) requirements directly to test cases. Note that the tests are the best way to measure completion or compliance as designs may not have been implemented. If a product is released to the market without the features deemed as being important, it may fail. If the product is being delivered as part of a contract, then coverage analysis is used to measure contract compliance; e.g., what was agreed on versus what is currently being delivered. The architect can also use coverage analysis to assist with an impact analysis; that is, the cost of making a change may be lower if implementation of a product feature has not yet started.

7.3   Routine Requirements Management Activities

Routine requirements management activities are those that take place on most, if not all projects. They may not involve a lot of manual effort, but depending on the nature of the project, they may be crucial to a positive outcome.

Identifying Volatile Requirements

Volatility is usually measured by gathering statistics from a *requirements data management system (RDMS)*. One of the advantages of an RDMS is that whenever a requirement is changed, version management is transparent to the user. Most, if not all, RDMS products can provide volatility reports. If they do not, then it is usually a simple matter to create such a report. Two metrics are of special interest: the volatility of the overall requirement set and the volatility of individual requirements. A baseline typically cannot be established until aggregate volatility (number of requirements changing per unit of time) drops to a sufficiently low value that the requirements are deemed stable. The point at which that occurs will be different for different types of projects. Keep in mind that a volatility metric is only valid where all the requirements analyzed are at the same level (e.g., high-level customer requirements).

Establishing Policies for Requirements Processes and Supporting Them with Workflow Tools, Guidelines, Templates, and Examples

A common mistake on large projects is to start executing the project without having well-defined processes, guidelines, templates, examples, or integrated toolsets. As was mentioned in earlier chapters, not planning (omission) can cause problems as a project matures. For example, not having high-quality examples of requirements and specifications may result in lower quality requirements and a large initial number of defects. Furthermore, not planning for tool integration can result in a rapid increase in workload as the number of requirements explodes during analysis. Tool integration will not be discussed in more detail here, as a wealth of information is available in texts and on the web, and the actual implementation of tool chains can be organization or project specific. We suggest, for example, that the reader explore the many white papers published by the RDMS vendors.

Prioritizing Requirements

Prioritization and ranking of requirements has been discussed briefly in prior chapters. It is a nontrivial activity that requires decisions such as what algorithms will be used, how prioritization will be calculated and stored, the impact of dependencies on priority, and propagation issues (up and down). Furthermore, any work in this area will most likely be domain and organization specific. If the reader is interested in this topic, there are many fine texts available, for example [Wiegers 2003].

Establishing and Updating the Requirements Baseline

As was discussed in the preceding section, once the requirements stabilize, a baseline is established so that changes can be tracked. Most RDMS tools have facilities for establishing baselines; however, that may not be the end of the story. External documents, blueprints, government standards, and so on may also need to be baselined. For example, a change in a government standard may result in a reevaluation of hazards, followed by modified or additional mitigation requirements (see Chapter 11).

Documenting Decisions

The documentation of decisions is required for both project and requirements management. As there is overlap, it may be necessary to have a coordinated strategy. For an example of what can happen when decisions are not documented, see the sidebar.

Planning Releases and Allocating Requirements to Releases

Planning releases can be a product or project management activity, depending on the type of project. During the planning, requirements are allocated to releases so that product versions will be released in a cost-effective manner, depending on the business goals (e.g., positive

Why Decisions Should Be Documented

On a large nuclear power plant project in the early 1990s, a multiprocessing supercomputer had been purchased. Because of feature creep, the computing capacity had been exceeded and an additional processor had to be added at a cost of several hundred thousand dollars. The client agreed to pay for the change, the agreement was documented in the project meeting minutes, a change request was issued to purchase and install the additional processor, and the project proceeded. A year later, the client refused to pay for the processor, claiming that the supplier had agreed to pay for it. The project manager had not retained copies of the meeting minutes and as a result could not find a written record of the agreement. Just before the issue went to litigation, a copy of the agreement was found in a set of files that were about to be thrown out, and the client agreed to pay the full cost of the upgrade.

cash flow, preempt competition, etc.). If requirement dependencies and traces are not maintained, planning can be difficult. Derivation analysis may be needed to determine the potential return-on-investment for a feature, and that, in turn, requires a stable in-place tracing strategy (see the next section).

7.4   Traceability

"Requirements traceability is the ability to describe and follow the life of a requirement, in both a forward and backward direction; i.e., from its origins, through its development and specification, to its subsequent deployment and use, and through periods of ongoing refinement and iteration in any of these phases" [Gotel et al. 1994]. We discuss traceability in some detail here, as it can be a difficult, daunting task, and it may be vital to the success of a project.

Traceability is the key to coverage, derivation, and impact analyses. A requirement is traceable if and only if the origin of each of its component requirements is clear; and if there is a mechanism that makes it feasible to refer to that requirement in future development efforts [IEEE 1998].

A suggested approach to defining a traceability strategy is to look at the roles on the project and their needs, implementing tracing mechanisms only where necessary. Several different categories of stakeholders are listed in Table 7.3, along with their tracing needs. Because the actual needs differ depending on the kind of organization, tracing needs are defined by organization and by role.

Different projects will have different trace mechanisms for different reasons. A purchaser of a product or services (referred to as the *buyer*) will need traces that are different from those of the vendor providing the services (referred to as the *contractor*). These two sets of traces will, in turn, be different from the kinds of traces used by a development

Role	Manufacturer	Buyer	Contractor
Marketing/Sales	Is development implementing all the features? What features are in the current product? In each release?	Has the contractor fulfilled the contract? Are all my product features appropriately implemented and operational?	Are we in compliance with the contract? Has every line item in the contract been successfully implemented per test cases?
Requirements Analyst	Has each feature been sufficiently explored? What requirements are associated with which feature? Do the requirements have sufficient detail?	Do all the features and related requirements in the RFP trace to the contract? Does the contractor understand each feature? Is the contractor's test plan correct?	Are all the requirements in the contract feasible and testable? Are there any cost drivers? Do the requirements trace to test cases? Is there full coverage testing for the delivered solution?
Architect	Why is this feature needed (e.g., what is the context)? What is the cost to change a product feature? Does the architecture of the product adequately support all the features that are in scope? What is the impact of a feature or constraint change?	Not applicable. A buyer will often not have an architect.	Do all the contract requirements trace to the appropriate design elements? Does the design fully meet the terms of the contract? What is the impact of a change request?
Developer	What is the context of this requirement? Why is it necessary? Do I have enough information to develop or manufacture it?	Will this product be maintainable after deployment? If changes are needed will the trace mechanisms support an impact analysis?	What is the context of this requirement? Why is it necessary? Do I have enough information to develop or manufacture it?
Tester	Are all the product features covered by test cases? Are all the test cases traceable back to product features?	Can we trace our contract requirements to test cases? Can we ensure that we are getting the product we contracted to receive? Can we detect noncompliance?	Can we ensure that we are in compliance with the contract? Will the delivered product pass an acceptance test?

TABLE 7.3 Traceability Needs Based on Role and Organization

organization to create a product to fulfill a need defined by marketing and sales. A typical, sometimes costly mistake on projects is to wait until the analyses are needed before implementing a trace strategy.

Goal-Based Traceability

Goal-based traceability starts with business goals or objectives, and traces are then used to determine that the business objectives have been met. On many of the projects that we have worked on, goal-based traces are sometimes absent. However, without the traces in place back to the original goals, it can be very difficult, especially for nonfunctional requirements, to make the necessary tradeoffs when prioritizing features. Goal modeling, as described in Chapter 3, has the advantage of implicit tracing; that is, when relationships are created between goals and subgoals, the traces are implicitly defined. Problems may arise because different organizations define business goals, product features, and detailed requirements. For example, a building alarm system has the low-level requirement that alarms shall have three different blink rates. The developer implementing the requirement does not understand why the requirement is there (e.g., blink or no blink should be good enough, especially with multiple colors), but going back to the business goals, we see that the different blink rates are needed so that the product will sell in markets where security staff may be color blind.

Types of Traces

We can group traces into categories as defined in [Jarke 1998]. These categories include

- **Forward from requirements**   Allocation to system components to establish accountability and support change impact

- **Backward to requirements** Verification of system compliance to requirements, and avoidance of gold plating

- **Forward to requirements**   Changes in stakeholder needs or assumptions that may require radical reassessment of requirements relevance

- **Backward from requirements** Contribution structures crucial for validating requirements

Trace types are related to analysis; that is, derivation analysis requires backward tracing, while coverage analysis and impact analysis require forward tracing.

Example Engineering Project-Based Traceability Model

Starting points for defining a requirements trace strategy are the creation of a traceability model ("V" model) and the creation of a project metamodel (see Chapter 2). The "V" model (see Figure 7.1) can be used as a guide to assist in defining a tracing strategy. An alternative approach

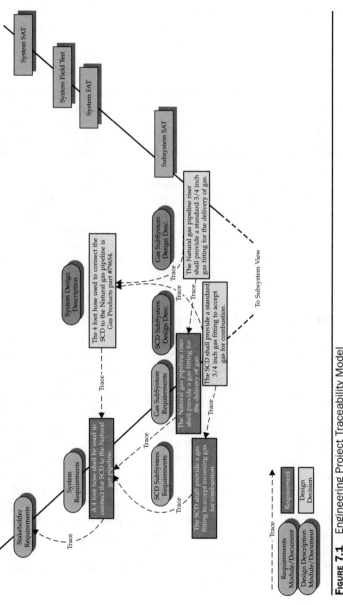

FIGURE 7.1   Engineering Project Traceability Model

> **Incomplete Traceability May Result in Inefficiency**
> On a medical project, a doctor was asked to write a use case document explaining how orders were used to schedule operations at hospitals. After spending several weeks creating the document, he discovered that the requested use case already existed but had no traces to or from it, and therefore it was "invisible" to analysts.

is to define a metamodel, and then derive a trace strategy from the metamodel. The "V" model approach to defining traceability is often used where there are significant regulatory concerns, and is almost always used when product development is outsourced. The metamodel approach is typically used where there are many disparate sources of requirements or the RE process is relatively complex.

The left side of the "V" model is concerned with requirements, design, and implementation and the right side deals with testing. At the top of the "V" model, the requirements and acceptance test plan are associated with traces. Moving down the "V" model, the traces connect lower-level requirements (more highly detailed) with corresponding tests, and at the very bottom, units or components are associated with their unit test plans.

7.5   Measurement and Metrics

The application of *measurement* practices to obtain *metrics* is a technique for effectively managing the software development and maintenance process [Jones 1991], [Moeller et al. 1993]. The origins of software and system measurements are grounded in code complexity measures [McCabe 1976], software project cost estimation [Boehm 1981], software quality assurance [Moeller 1988], and software development process improvement [Basili 1980]. In 1987, Grady and Caswell wrote a book on the application of a management by metrics approach that was practiced at Hewlett-Packard [Grady et al. 1987]. Process, product, and quality metrics are used for monitoring and improving a software development process and for managing software development projects [Jones 1991].

Requirements engineering has practices and measures that are used to measure the progress of RE activities and the quality of RE artifacts. These RE metrics may be used to provide guidance on improving the RE process. They may be applied across the full life cycle or applied to specific phases of development or to specific RE artifacts.

For example, measurements can be used to perform analyses that are compared to benchmark values. RE metrics may be used to determine these points:

- Was the RE staff adequately trained?
- Was the team paying enough attention to the RE process (e.g., was the defect rate acceptable)?
- Was the quality of the overall work products adequate?
- Were the requirements traceable?
- Were the work products suitable for a) in-house manufacturing/development or b) outsourcing?

To effectively use metrics, they should be planned at the beginning of the project. It may also be beneficial to retain metrics postproject and use them for overall organizational process improvement.

Metrics can loosely be divided into two categories: project and quality. Project measurements, of use to management, assist in understanding progress and productivity. Quality metrics provide information on the quality of the various work products. Example quality and project metrics are described in more detail in the following sections.

Project Metrics

Project measurements are used for day-to-day evaluation of project status, and to determine the completeness of an artifact or task to trigger the review process. Process, measurements, and tools are mutually interdependent. That is, without the process there could be no measurements; without the measurements, project progress and work product quality could not be accessed; and without tool support, taking measurements would be extremely time consuming, possibly to the point of being impractical. Table 7.4 lists a few suggested project metrics.

Quality Metrics

Quality metrics are those metrics that measure the quality of requirements artifacts (including the final product) but do not necessarily convey information about project progress or productivity (see Table 7.5). As quality is measured against a standard, quality standards need to be defined in order to utilize quality metrics; e.g., does the requirements specification meet or exceed the standard for good requirements specifications?

Metric	Description	Computation
Completeness	An indicator of project progress	Each requirement or feature has a completeness attribute. For a high-level requirement, the completeness is measured by aggregating all the derived or child requirements. Requirements progress can then be determined by evaluating all high-level requirements at the same level and using a normalized value.
Coverage	Indicates percent overall project completion	For each requirement, determine whether the traced leaf test cases have been successfully completed. This analysis requires a tree traversal down the requirements pyramid to traced test cases.
Volatility	Normalized requirement change rate	Uses requirement change history to determine change rate for requirements. Can be used as an indicator of implementation risk as well as project progress. Requirements change rates should asymptotically approach zero as the project reaches the completion date.

TABLE 7.4   Example Project Metrics

Metric	Description	Computation
Derivation	All requirements are traceable back to stakeholder requests	Every root requirement (parent) needs to trace from an external document or stakeholder request.
Requirement Quality	Percent of requirements passing a first review	The percentage of requirements that passed a review the first time. This is an indication of the skill of the requirements analysts.

TABLE 7.5   Example Quality Metrics

7.6   Scalability

Processes put in place at the beginning of a project may not take into consideration the number of requirements that may need to be managed as requirements definition nears completion. For example, a project with 50 features to start may not appear to be a large project. But, if we consider the not unreasonable explosion of each feature to 100 or more "high-level" requirements, we now will have over 5000 high-level requirements. Adding an additional explosion layer of detail needed to implement the product and create test cases (assume an explosion of 10:1), we'll wind up with a total of 50,000 requirements and at least the same number of traces. Such a number of requirements to manage and trace is not unreasonable for today's large projects. It is therefore imperative that trace mechanisms be, to the extent possible, intrinsic to routine processes without a burdensome manual effort. Some techniques for mitigating issues of scale are described in the section "Best Practices" later in this chapter.

7.7   Creation of a Requirements Management Process

It is easy to underestimate the effort necessary to properly manage requirements on a project. Unfortunately, process problems tend not to show up until it is late in the project, and it can be very difficult and labor intensive to make changes to in-place processes. Consequently, it is important to plan early for handling large quantities of data, requests for change, and high productivity through automation. For example, requirements, especially nonfunctional requirements, may impact other requirements, and so search and modification mechanisms are best automated. In this section, we will walk through the process of creating a requirements management environment. In following sections, we will provide additional details about specific aspects of requirements management.

1. The definition of processes or process improvement begins with the definition of work products that are needed for the organization. They can be defined in a taxonomy or an artifact model (see Chapter 2), but the important thing is not to leave out anything that may be needed.

2. The next step is to scope the artifacts based on business need; e.g., what is in and what is out.

3. Automation and tracing strategies are defined by evaluating the relationships between the artifacts and determining if traces are necessary and, if they are, whether they will be created and maintained manually or automatically.

4. For each artifact that needs to be created (e.g., specifications such as a customer requirements document), templates need to be created and reviewed.

5. If activities to create the artifacts are not in place, they need to be defined, along with roles, standards, and quality assurance procedures. Creating idealized sample documents or reports is a great way to ensure good quality.

6. Be sure to define interface processes for interacting with product management, manufacturing, and testing.

7. Don't forget maintenance and version control! After a project is completed, it may be necessary to manage change for future product releases or repairs.

A requirements engineering management process is often described in a document called a requirements engineering management plan (REMP). A table of contents for an example REMP is given in Figure 7.2.

FIGURE 7.2   Example Requirements Engineering Management Plan (REMP) Table of Contents

7.8   Measuring Savings with RE Processes

When improving requirements processes in an organization, it may not be possible to quantify savings by looking just at the RE work products and productivity improvements. The real savings can only be determined by looking at a project holistically. However, that may require changing mindsets. For example, one organization that we looked at during a process improvement effort used the category "software defect" for nearly all reported software bugs. After a root cause analysis, it was found that the majority of the software bugs were actually problems with requirements. After some training of the RE staff to do a better job of writing requirements, the number of defects fell markedly. Some sample defect indicators are shown in Table 7.6.

Cause of Defect	Suggested Remedy
Requirement was ambiguous	Train analysts to write unambiguous requirements.
Requirement was incomplete	Review the amount of time spent on analysis. Determine if the requirement reviews are done with the right participants.
Conflicting requirements	Modify the RE process to adequately address requirements conflict resolution.
Requirement was incorrect	The process may need to be modified to include additional interaction and reviews with stakeholders.
Product feature did not meet client expectations	Communication with client may need to be more frequent or comprehensive.
Performance or quality was below expectations	Nonfunctional requirements may need to be addressed early enough in the elicitation process and/or maybe architects and designers ought to be involved early enough to do an effective analysis of the nonfunctional requirements.
Failure to meet regulatory requirements	Tracing techniques may need to be improved such that designers can understand any regulatory constraints from which the requirements derive.

TABLE 7.6   Using Defects for Process Improvement

7.9   Organizational Issues Impacting Requirements Management

A requirements engineering management plan (REMP) should not be created without taking a holistic look at other processes associated with systems development; e.g., manufacturing, hardware development, software development, testing, and maintenance. A typical mistake when setting up a REMP is to ignore upstream and downstream processes. They are very necessary to understand the context of any RM processes put in place, for example,

- How are business goals and policies created?
- Where are they kept?
- How can we maintain traces between goals, policies, and requirements such that the impact of a change in business direction (e.g., change in goal) can be measured?

Since business rules derive from policies, the impact of policy changes must be measurable; e.g., what rules will have to change if this policy changes?

Note that for smaller projects, processes should not be top-heavy but rather as lean as possible. Most important, when leaving activities and work products out of a process, is to leave them out by commission and not by omission (e.g., forgetting about them).

Another organizational issue is that of distributed engineering work (see Chapter 10). Distributing the effort carries with it additional challenges, as shown in Table 7.7.

In general, any distributed effort should have strong leadership at the project management and technical lead levels, face-to-face relationship building and training prior to project initiation, a clear chain of command, clear definition of roles and responsibilities, a well-defined, well-understood requirements engineering process, and a liaison at each site with responsibility for all communications activities.

Creating a Requirements Database

For small projects, requirements can be managed using spreadsheets. However, as a project reaches a critical size, say 100 requirements or more, it becomes necessary to use a database to hold information. Activities such as configuration management, managing traceability, generating specifications, and extracting metrics are accomplished with much less effort using one of the commercially available requirements engineering data management facilities.

Commercial data management tools can do a very nice job of tracking requirements changes as they do fine-grain version control. For example, just changing the priority of a requirement will result in a new requirement version being created as well as an audit trail, so

Observed Problems	Suggested Remediation
No cross-location reviews	Frequent collaborative reviews using web or network hosting tools.
Varying documentation styles	Availability of standards and sample documents *prior* to the initiation of work; face-to-face kickoff meetings.
Weak configuration management	Strong technical leadership; close, frequent coordination between team members at different sites; use of a central requirements repository.
Communication difficulties between analysis and design organizations	Strong technical leadership; process definition prior to project initiation; well-defined tool strategy.
Pushing detailed analysis to remote development organizations	If the detailed analysis is pushed to a remote site, push a senior analyst to the site also; it is important that remote team members not feel remote. Also, if analysis is done remotely, the remote staff will need the requisite skills or training.
Late feedback	Technical management needs to be highly visible and preemptively address potential problems with the distributed locations before minor problems snowball into crises.
Requirements suitable for in-house development are incomplete and confusing to remote sites	The best way to mitigate incomplete requirements is to perform thorough reviews. If that is not feasible, then it may be necessary to collocate analysts with the development staff and subject matter experts.

TABLE 7.7   Organizational Challenges in Requirements Management

that the history of the requirement can be viewed. Assuming that a requirement is stored as a single record with a unique ID, the record will have attribute fields that can be customized for an organization or project. Usually the data management tool will come "off-the-shelf" with a standard set of attributes. Those attributes almost always need tailoring and extending to be useful. A suggested (but not necessarily comprehensive) set of fields for inclusion in a data management schema are listed in Table 7.8. Note that not all fields would be associated with all types of requirements. For example, Kano values would be best associated with product features and may have no meaning in the context of other requirement types.

While potentially difficult to set up initially, an RDMS with an adequate amount of information can result in a wealth of information

Field	Description
Owner	Stakeholder who "owns" the requirement.
Requirement type or subtype	Create a requirements pyramid and then use the levels defined in the pyramid as requirement types.
Requirement category	Fine grain, typically taken from the requirement taxonomy. The values available in this field might change based on the requirement type (see the preceding item), e.g., performance, security. Combining the two types can make a noun phrase, e.g., "Performance goal."
Trace from	Sources of the requirement (possibly several different types).
Trace to	What artifacts the requirement impacts (possibly several different types).
Priority	Once a measurement is decided on, e.g., "high, medium, low," 1 to 5, etc., the scope of the priority also needs to be defined, e.g., product, product line, release. This can be a multidimensional field and will be described in more detail in the coming section "Managing Requirements for Product Lines."
Ranking	Ranking and priority are different in that while many requirements can have the same priority, e.g., "High", only one requirement in a set can have a rank, e.g., 5 out of 50. Requirements at the same level are unequivocally ranked from high to low, based on a scheme defined in the requirements management plan.
Category	Functional category, e.g., maintenance, product, training, etc.
Status	Draft, accepted, obsolete, sunset . . . .
Verification status	Whether the requirement has been met (measured through product testing or customer acceptance).
Risk of implementation	This is the implementation risk. It is usually associated with potential difficulties in meeting the requirement, such as difficulties in quantifying or meeting a performance requirement.
Volatility	The likelihood that the requirement will change prior to product freeze.
Kano values	Fields used to measure the emotional value of a requirement to customers.
Estimated cost of implementation	Projected cost to implement a feature.
Actual cost of implementation	Compared against the estimated cost and then used to improve the quality of estimates.

TABLE 7.8 Suggested Requirements Fields for an RDMS *(continued)*

Field	Description
Quality characteristics	Marked as the result of requirement reviews. Includes, for example, ambiguity, traceability, completeness, correctness, modifiability, consistency. These fields are used as the foundation for quality metrics reporting and process improvement. The characteristics are typically those described in Chapter 1.
Product release	Product and release or version to which the requirement has been assigned.
Component	Hardware or software component or components implementing this requirement.
Reported defect	Defect caused by a problem with this requirement (defect type, e.g., caused by ambiguity, incomplete, infeasible to implement, etc.).
Product line description	Describes whether a requirement is associated with core assets, platform, or specific products in a product line.

TABLE 7.8 Suggested Requirements Fields for an RDMS

downstream through queries and metrics analysis that can be used to increase transparency, identify organizational weaknesses, and perform process improvement. The easier it is for the responsible staff to provide the information, the more likely it is to be used.

One technique we use is to periodically query the database, retrieving statistics on how well the fields are being filled in. After a review, for example, the review results are all placed with the reviewed requirement; e.g., the ambiguity field gets a "fail" or "conditional acceptance" value. By observing quality field values over time, an organization can monitor improvements in requirements elicitation and analysis.

Another technique that can be used to reduce the manual effort in defining requirement attributes is to automatically propagate attribute values from parent to derived or from derived to parent. For example, if all the derived requirements for a parent quality goal have been "satisficed", then the parent goal can automatically be marked as being satisficed. Going in the opposite direction, if a high-level requirement is marked as priority "high," then all its derived requirements automatically inherit the same priority. Remember, it is less risky to have information you don't need in an data management tool than to need information you don't have!

Managing Requirements for Product Lines

Product lines, their processes, and their artifacts have been well documented [Clements et al. 2001], [Pohl et al. 2005] (see Chapter 6). However, the management of requirements for product lines is a difficult task for which few standard practices exist. This section briefly describes extensions to an RDMS for handling product lines.

First, the requirement or its parent has to be marked as to where it belongs; e.g., a platform, a core asset of the product line, or one or more of the products in the product line. This can be accomplished with one requirement attribute. Downward propagation would be appropriate for this field; e.g., if the requirement belongs to one product in a product line, then all the subrequirements or derived lower-level requirements would also apply to that one product.

The most challenging aspect of managing product line requirements is the multidimensional nature of some of the requirement attributes. For example, instead of a requirement having a priority, it can now have a priority that is a function of which product and product release it is in. Since requirements may have dependencies (e.g., feature "B" cannot be implemented until feature "A" is completed), defining the requirement set for a release of a product may require some level of optimization. Mark Denne and Jane Cleland-Huang in their text, *Software by Numbers*, define a release strategy based on cash flow and the measurement of the return-on-investment (ROI) that a product feature can offer [Denne et al. 2003]. Such an algorithm would then be complicated by the fact that the same feature might have different values in two different products in a product line. For example, while offering a leather interior in a low-end car might increase its market share, offering the same leather interior in a high-end car might not increase market share at all. A summary of some of the major differences between managing requirements for a product and product line are shown in Table 7.9.

Topic	Product	Product Line
Change control board	Only one necessary	There may be more than one; e.g., one for the platform or core assets and an additional one for each product.
Requirement priority or ranking	Only one per requirement	May be two-dimensional; e.g., a requirement may have a different priority for different products.
Requirement attributes	Standard attributes	Additional attributes may be needed to specify whether a requirement is assigned to a core asset or to several of the products in the product line.
Release assignment	Only one	May be multidimensional; e.g., for product 1 the requirement is assigned to release V2.1 but for product 2 the requirement is assigned to release V3.0.

TABLE 7.9 Comparison of Requirements Management for Products vs. Product Lines
(continued)

Topic	Product	Product Line
Stakeholder categories	Simple	May be complicated by the driving force behind the product line; e.g., regional stakeholders.
Tracing	Single thread from feature to testing	May be complicated by regionalization or other factors. For example, tracing paths may diverge for products created for different regions, where final testing is done by a regional organization.

TABLE 7.9   Comparison of Requirements Management for Products vs. Product Lines

7.10   Tips for Requirements Management

Table 7.10 summarizes some important tips for an effective requirements management process.

Best Practices

A real problem with many requirements engineering processes is that they do not scale well. A process that works with 100 requirements may explode with 10,000. The following practices can help with medium- to large-scale projects.

- Requirements hierarchies should be well defined (e.g., parent/child relationships depending on the level of abstraction of the feature or requirement). Failure to create a hierarchy (such as a tree structure) in turn leads to a two-dimensional trace table of size $N \times N$, where N is the number of requirements associated with traces, and after several thousand requirements, the traces are no longer maintainable or usable. Mitigation techniques include the creation of requirement hierarchies in the database schema that permit database trace queries to return a more meaningful subset of traces.

- Create a glossary of terms and use the terms consistently throughout the project. Failure to define a standard glossary of terms may result in different terms being used to mean the same thing, causing ambiguity and making it difficult to mine for trace relationships at a later date.

- Create a project metamodel or artifact model at project initiation. Creation of such a model will reveal all the possible types of traces that may be possible and enable the creation of an automated (if necessary, manual) trace strategy.

Issue	Suggestion
Only possible to review 4–10 requirements per hour	Conduct reviews at the highest level possible. As the requirements become more detailed, the reviews should have fewer participants and be less formal.
Toolsets not integrated	Create a full metamodel for the environment. Use the metamodel to plan and implement a tool integration strategy.
Navigation of text documents	Use web pages with hyperlinks. Associate documents with keywords. Use nontraditional techniques like Wikipedia's or web-based visual models, with text behind the symbols.
Difficulty managing traces	Use metamodels to define and automate a tracing strategy. If possible, use advanced dynamic tracing tools to minimize manual effort and eliminate problems associated with traces breaking.
Very large, complex product	Use formal modeling techniques instead of pure text. Minimize the number of documents by keeping the text in the model symbols and generate documents on the fly.
Large numbers of requirements	Use requirement attributes in the database for levels and types of requirements to ensure that a query does not bring back too much.
Quality assurance of requirements	Put the quality attributes for requirements in the database. Use automated scripts to propagate quality attributes up to parents or down to children.
Difficulty managing nonfunctional requirements	Use formal goal models to visualize NFRs and their relationships, with algorithms to compute the "satisfice" level and to do tradeoff studies, e.g., quality vs. low cost.
Difficulty understanding extensibility requirements	Use feature/variability models to formally define exactly what features are given to which clients. Generate skeleton test plans semiautomatically from the programmatically linked product map/feature model.
Lots of rework due to major discrepancies	Be sure to do a root cause analysis on discrepancy sets to determine if there are any weaknesses in the requirements processes.
Difficulty getting reviews done because of the volume of material	Use visual/graphical techniques and do online reviews with a web conferencing tool. Feature, goal, and process models are much easier to review than large amounts of text.
Lots of use case documentation, trace problems	Use automated techniques to generate requirements from use cases.

TABLE 7.10 Tips for Effective Requirements Management

- Plan for navigational facilities. As projects get large, the volume of documentation associated with the project can make document management unwieldy. For example, what happens if a requirement is added that cross-cuts other requirements? Navigation techniques should be defined that will ensure that important information is not lost, and that there is no duplication of effort.

- Carefully define the requirements database schema. Requirements databases are a good source of project metrics, but query retrieval is only as good as the metrics built in and adherence to the process to record them. For example:

  - **Percent of requirements failing review because of ambiguity** An excessive number of requirements that do not pass review because of ambiguity indicates that analysts have not had enough training in requirements writing or perhaps need additional mentoring. Ambiguous requirements are a major source of software defects.

  - **Percent of requirements failing review because of incompleteness** This can be an early indicator of several problems: not enough time is being spent on the analysis phase of the project, analysts may be time boxed or rushed to deliver, or subject matter experts are not available sufficiently to clarify the material.

  - **Percent of requirements covered by test cases** This is a measure of project progress. If automated tracing mechanisms are in place, a project dashboard can be created to display indicators of project progress.

- Include business goals and policies in change management; define business artifacts such that requirements traces can flow back to originating policies or goals.

7.11 Summary

In this chapter, we have introduced some of the practices used for requirements management. These practices become increasingly important as projects grow larger. Requirements and RE artifacts must be controlled and traced. When changes are proposed, processes must be used to analyze the impacts of the changes.

7.12 Discussion Questions

To review the practices described in this chapter, please consider the following discussion questions.

1. How do you measure the quality of a requirements document?

2. How do you measure the completeness of a requirements document?

3. How do you decide if a modification request is implemented or not?

4. What are the central questions that tracing tries to answer?

References

Basili, V., *Tutorial on Models and Metrics for Software Management and Engineering*, IEEE Computer Society Press, Los Alamitos, CA, 1980.

Boehm, B., *Software Engineering Economics*, Prentice-Hall, Englewood Cliffs, NJ, 1981.

Chrissis, M.B., Konrad, M., and Shrum, S., *CMMI: Guidelines for Process Integration and Product Improvement*, Addison-Wesley, Boston, 2003.

Clements, P., and Northrop, L., *Software Product Lines: Practices and Patterns*, Addison-Wesley, Boston, 2001.

CMM Practices Manual, CMU/SEI-93-TR-25, L2, Carnegie Mellon University, Software Engineering Institute, Pittsburgh, PA, 1993.

Denne, M., and Cleland-Huang, J., *Software by Numbers: Low-Risk, High-Return Development*, Prentice-Hall, Englewood Cliffs, NJ, 2003.

Gotel, O., and Finkelstein, A., "An Analysis of the Requirements Traceability Problem," *Proceedings of the First International Conference on Requirements Engineering*, Colorado Springs, CO, pp. 94–101, April 1994.

Grady, R.B., and Caswell, D.L., *Software Metrics: Establishing a Company-Wide Program*, Prentice-Hall, Englewood Cliffs, NJ, 1987.

IEEE Standard 830, *IEEE Recommended Practice for Software Requirements Specifications*, 1998.

Jarke, M., "Requirements Tracing," *Communications of the ACM*, 41(12), pp. 32–36, 1998.

Jones, T.C., *Applied Software Measurement*, McGraw-Hill, New York, 1991.

McCabe, T.J., "A Complexity Measure," *IEEE Transactions on Software Engineering*, Vol. 2, No. 4, December 1976.

Moeller, K., "Increasing of Software Quality by Objectives and Residual Fault Prognosis," *First European Seminar on Software Quality*, April 1988.

Moeller, K., and Paulish, D., *Software Metrics: A Practitioner's Guide to Improved Product Development*, London, IEEE Press, 1993.

Nurmuliani, N., Zowghi, D., and Fowell, S., "Analysis of Requirements Volatility During Software Development Life Cycle," *Proceedings of the 2004 Australian Software Engineering Conference (ASWEC '04)*.

Pohl, K., Boeckle, G., and van der Linden, F., *Software Product Line Engineering: Foundations, Principles, and Techniques*, Springer, Berlin, 2005.

White, B., *Software Configuration Management Strategies and Rational ClearCase: A Practical Introduction*, Addison-Wesley, Boston, 2000.

Wiegers, K., *Software Requirements, Second Edition*, Microsoft Press, Redmond, WA, 2003.

CHAPTER **8**

Requirements-Driven System Testing

by Marlon Vieira, Bill Hasling

J	ohn was a recent Purdue graduate who for his first job was assigned to test a real-time vehicle control system. He had studied the "V" model in school and had written some small test programs with a team of students. But, he was never exposed to a system as large and time-critical as the one he was about to test. He knew that he should "test to validate the system requirements," but he had a difficult time understanding the requirements as he browsed through the requirements database. Furthermore, his boss explained to him that the project was behind schedule, and he may be asked to work some evenings and weekends as they were trying to get through their test suite in a shorter time than originally planned by working multiple shifts. John began to become concerned for his social life, since he realized he will be spending many hours in the test lab.

This chapter deals with system testing that is based on requirements. It introduces concepts and discusses techniques that can be successfully used to create test cases using some of the RE artifacts. It discusses model-based testing (MBT), focusing on the types of RE models and specifications that are useful to the test engineer.

8.1   Background

Software Testing is the process of executing software with the intent of finding errors [Myers 1979], and it basically supports validation & verification (V&V) activities. The CMMI (Capability Maturity Model Integration) guidelines describe validation as the activity that demonstrates if a product will meet its intended use, and verification as the activity for ensuring that the product meets specified requirements. Verification is mainly done by the development and testing teams, and it typically includes other non-testing-based techniques such as peer reviews, inspections, and debugging. On the other hand, validation activities are based on specified requirements, and the requirements engineers are very much involved. Thus, there is a strong link between testing and requirements engineering. Test engineers must understand the requirements so that they can validate that the system's behavior is such that it meets the requirements. Validation activities can be based on both functional and nonfunctional requirements.

The role of testing to requirements validation can be seen in various life cycle models such as the "V" model [VModel-XT 2008]. Testing is done to validate life cycle artifacts that are generated by requirements engineering and design. For example, testers will use a requirements specification as the starting point for defining their acceptance test suite. Ideally, there should be a system test suite that runs on the actual target system such that each requirement can be satisfied. When the system behavior does not satisfy the requirements, defect reports are written by the testers such that the developers can correct the deficiencies before the product is released to customers.

System testing is a well-defined industrial process; in many cases, however, it remains a manual process. Typically, test engineers derive their test data, that is, their required system input and expected output information, from a variety of sources, including textual-use case specifications and business-process rules. They then create a set of test procedures comprising individual test steps, which can be executed manually by test executors against the system under test (SUT). Whenever an automated-test execution environment is available, tests are translated into executable test scripts. This process usually occurs in a late phase of the development process during which system testers strive to discover as many defects as possible (i.e., no conformance with the specified requirements) before the product is released to the market.

As system testing is relatively expensive and occurs during the back end of the development process, test teams are usually large and overworked. For many systems where end-user discovery of defects can have significant financial or safety consequences and regression testing is necessary, the execution of tests is often highly augmented by automated tools; i.e., tools that are used to stimulate the SUT, discover, and document defects. The automatic generation of test cases can be accomplished using model-based testing (MBT) approaches, to be described later in this chapter.

Defects in Requirements

Although this chapter is focused on system testing, the "V" model envisions many stages of testing, review, and inspection used to detect defects. In many cases, defects in requirements will be discovered during these downstream V&V activities. Capers Jones reports that: 1) requirements in U.S. projects seem to have about 1 to 1.2 defects (bugs) per function point [Jones 2008] and 2) most forms of testing are only about 35 percent efficient in finding defects, so some requirements defects will still be present even at customer delivery. Also, even good requirements will be incomplete, so there will be gaps that can't be tested, because the requirements are missing. About 7 percent of attempts to fix requirements defects, once they are identified, will accidentally include new defects as part of the fix itself.

8.2 Requirements Engineering Inputs for Testing

In Chapter 1, we discussed that a "good" requirement must be verifiable, such that the finished product can be tested to ensure that it meets the requirement. This means that requirements must be quantifiable and easily tested. In addition, for automated test generation, requirements must be described in a form that can be understood by computers or specialized testing equipment or the requirements engineering artifacts must be easily translated to such a form. This implies that requirements described as models will make the tester's job easier.

When testers have access to requirements specifications that are verifiable, complete, unambiguous, and so on (see Section 1.7), they will be able to understand what the intended system should do and how it should perform. With a clear understanding of the functionality and performance of the intended system, they should be able to write "good" test cases.

In addition to requirements or system specifications, other artifacts that are useful to test engineers include user manuals and prototypes (see Chapter 9). Since much of the system testing typically is done through a user interface, RE and design artifacts that describe the operation of the user interface (e.g., the user interface design specification) will be useful to the tester [Vieira et al. 2006], [Song et al. 2006]. For automatically generating test cases and executing those tests, artifacts that contain models will be helpful [Hasling et al. 2008]. A scenario where it is possible to generate test cases automatically from a requirements specification is: (i) requirements engineers create models describing the requirements for the system under test, and then (ii) the testing engineers use those models as inputs to a model-based testing tool, which can automatically produce a set of tests. Typically those tests are "abstract" (i.e., not ready for execution yet), but they provide early test documentation and a test plan that can guide future test creation.

8.3 Model-Based Testing

Model-based testing attempts to derive test cases from a given model of the system under test (SUT) using a variety of test selection criteria. A model is an abstract view of the system and specifies typically (parts of) the behavior of the system in terms of its control flow and/or data flow. Three different types of models typically can be created

- *Requirements models* that specify the intended behavior of the system
- *Usage models* that reflect the behavior of a potential user
- Models constructed from the *source code* directly (where the system under test is a software product)

The test derivation approaches applied on the different model types are sometimes classified into specification-based testing (or black-box testing) if they are based on requirements models, and program-based testing (or white-box testing) if source code is used as the underlying model.

In recent years, MBT gained importance in connection with the model-driven architecture (MDA) initiative of the Object Management Group (OMG) and concepts of test-driven development for software products. Other advances in software and systems engineering, like the use of executable specification languages, the pattern-based detection of faults in source code, or the inference of program behavior from runtime observations, contribute to a renaissance of MBT approaches, although the roots of MBT go back to the early beginnings of computer science [Moore 1956].

To apply MBT successfully in today's industrial software development projects, it is important to automate the execution of the tests that are generated. Today, a wide range of test automation solutions of varying abstraction levels exist, depending on the actual application domain and project history.

From the perspective of their current practical usage, MBT approaches based on requirements models and appropriate coverage criteria are dominant. They can be easily implemented using graphical specification techniques like UML [Gross 1998], [Hartmann et al. 2005], [Utting et al. 2006] and the UML 2.0 Testing Profile [Schieferdecker et al. 2003]. In particular, these approaches benefit from methodologies for test-driven development that are currently in vogue. They also circumvent the test adequacy problem associated with the tests derived from design models that occurs if production code from the same model is automatically generated.

We have discussed how UML diagrams can be used for describing requirements models in Chapters 4 and 5. For model-based testing, test engineers may utilize the following diagrams: use case diagrams, package diagrams, activity diagrams, sequence diagrams, state machine diagrams, and class diagrams. In our experience, use case models and activity diagrams are particularly effective because they bridge requirements to system tests, and they can be created early in the development life cycle. The use case models can be created based upon the system requirements and also from the use case descriptions that are created as part of the system requirements.

The use cases for testing can be developed early in the project life cycle as soon as requirements are available. In the early phases of the project, these use cases are somewhat abstract. In later phases, the use cases are populated with enough information to create executable system tests. An approach to use models for test generation is described as follows:

1. Use case diagrams are used to identify the usage scenarios of the system. Abstract use cases represent related collections of

use cases, and concrete use cases are the basis for test generation.

2. Package diagrams are applied to provide a hierarchy to divide a large model for easier navigation, and they also can be used to split a large model into multiple files to support multiple users.

3. Activity diagrams are used to show details of each use case in relation to steps on using the system. Activities are used not only to show test steps, but also to show expected results or validation steps. Swim lanes are used to distinguish between test steps and validation steps. Activities can be annotated with properties to provide information to be used in test generation.

4. Class diagrams are used to define equivalence classes to represent data variations used in testing. Variables are described as notes within an activity diagram to reference an equivalence class of data variations defined in a class diagram.

In this approach, the use case model refers to a model that describes the use cases from a tester's point of view. Each use case describes how to test the various scenarios. This is different from the use cases that describe the implementation of the system. The tester's use cases do not describe how to implement each use case, but describe how to test each use case by describing the inputs and expected results.

Test cases can be automatically generated (with tool support) using this MBT approach. Each test is represented by a series of test steps. Each test step is represented by an activity. Decision points in the activity diagram represent alternative usage scenarios. Guard conditions on transitions provide a way to restrict infeasible test scenarios. Figures 8.1, 8.2, and 8.3 show examples of use case and activity diagrams that can be used to support model-based testing.

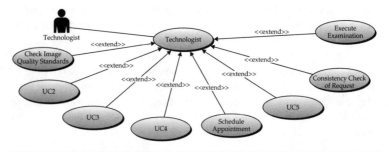

FIGURE 8.1 Use case diagram

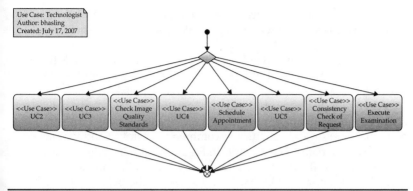

FIGURE 8.2   Activity diagram of an abstract use case

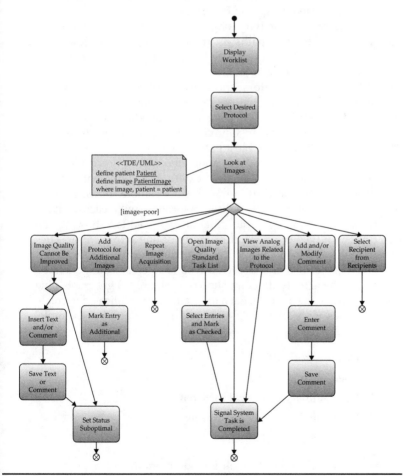

FIGURE 8.3   Activity diagram of a concrete use case

Figure 8.1 shows an abstract use case that is extended by various concrete use cases that describe the possible operations of the modeled abstract use case. An abstract use case typically has a generated activity diagram, as shown in Figure 8.2, which explicitly models the fact that there are several independent alternative ways to test the abstract use case.

Figure 8.3 is an example of a concrete use case that shows alternative test paths of different scenarios to test a particular use case. Note there are several activities in common to each test and various alternative test paths. The example in Figure 8.3 also introduces a test variable as a UML note to declare data variations. In this case, two variables are declared. One variable represents the object "patient" and the other variable represents the object "image" to be used. Each possibility of a patient or image in the equivalence classes results in a different test case. A constraint in the note reflects the relationship between the selected image and the selected patient.

A transition in the activity diagram contains a constraint on the data for one of the test paths. In the example, this specifies that the test path should use a test data image with poor image quality. The constraint language is an Object Constraint Language (OCL) subset with logical operators 'and', 'or', 'implies', and 'xor'; unary operator 'not'; and relational operators '=' and '<>'; using literal terms and variable terms. During test generation, variables are bound to one choice of an equivalence class subject to all the constraints in the generated test path.

Each activity in the model is annotated with a description and expected result and also related external requirements. These annotations can be specified in the diagram as notes or assigned as properties using a property editor associated with each activity. Figure 8.4 shows an example of a property editor showing the description and expected result property of one activity. Properties of variable choices and properties of activities can be substituted into the descriptions and expected results to create the generated test steps. The activity diagram shown in Figure 8.3 generates nine test paths to test the use case. Each test path can be replicated to create different tests with different patient and image data. For example, here is one test path:

1. Display work list.

2. Select desired protocol.

3. Look at images ${image} for ${patient}.

4. Image quality cannot be improved.

5. Set status as suboptimal.

More complex examples will include more decisions points, or decision points that join back and split again to other decisions.

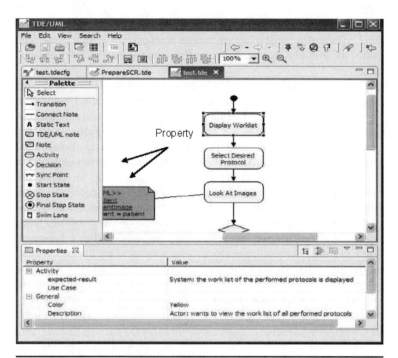

FIGURE 8.4   Editing properties of a selected activity

Activities can also reference other use cases, which can be used to break up larger diagrams or to achieve reuse of modeling activities.

Using use case models for model-based testing means that we are interpreting the use case models for the purpose of test generation. This means that errors in the model can prevent the ability to generate tests. Thus, before test generation, we check the model for errors that would prevent the generation of a correct test. We check for errors such as: use cases without activity diagrams, activities without transitions, illegal constraints, illegal constructs in note declarations, and missing start/stop states.

8.4   Testing Performance and Scalability Requirements

We describe here an approach to efficiently build optimized simulation models using UML diagrams [Avritzer et al. 2008] that can be used to assist with testing performance and scalability requirements. We annotate the deployment diagram models and sequence diagram models with arrival rates and departure rates, and automatically generate performance modeling scenarios from these diagrams. The UML models are used to specify the message flow among objects as well as the arrival and departure rates. In addition, we use a library of node types optimized for simulation solutions. A platform node on the UML deployment diagram model is associated with a node type that has already been implemented by an expert performance engineer.

Using the UML models that were generated by the requirements engineers to specify complex activity diagrams has the potential of generating performance models that are not optimized for solutions, because the perspectives of the requirements engineer and the performance engineer are significantly different. While the requirements engineer focuses on eliciting as much detail as required to correctly specify a certain system feature, the focus of the performance engineer is on modeling the bottleneck resources to an efficient solution of the performance model. We recommend that requirements engineers focus their efforts on developing good sequence diagrams by understanding the application's behavior, while performance engineers focus on understanding the best way to model the nodes on which the application executes. Thus, performance engineers develop libraries of node types. Software architects could use the library of node types when developing the deployment diagrams to make a mapping between the software components used in the sequence diagram model and the node types.

Activity diagrams are used to completely specify system behavior at the UML model level. The UML activity diagram modeling approach was designed to be used by requirements engineers and is well suited to requirements engineering work. However, for large industrial systems, activity diagram–based model specifications may not be well suited to be applied to the model transformations that should result in an efficient simulation model. For example, while we have encountered limitations to model the behavior of dynamic load balancing algorithms using UML activity diagram models, we could easily model these algorithms using the following approach:

1. Construct a library of node types.

2. Define the goals of the analysis, and develop a set of use cases to describe the message flow.

3. Develop the deployment diagrams and select the appropriate node types.

4. Generate the performance model.

5. Evaluate the results obtained from the performance model to analyze if the requirements of the system are met.

8.5   Rules of Thumb/Best Practices

In our experience, we found several advantages of using use case models as the basis for model-based system testing.

Reviewing Models

We have found that it is easier for domain experts and other stakeholders to review models such as use case diagrams than to review test specifications. A use case model is written from the perspective of the end user, and this is the perspective understood best by the product stakeholders. Reviewing the use case models not only finds gaps in the testing but also discovers gaps in the requirements, so the models have multiple benefits.

The activity diagrams that describe the scenarios specify the desired tests in the same way as a test suite, but the diagrams are easier to review than, say, 500 pages of test specifications written in plain text. There are fewer activity diagrams than test cases, since an activity diagram can represent several test cases because of the decision points and data variations described in the activity diagrams.

We also have observed that the development of use case models forces requirements to be testable and documents ambiguities in requirements. When requirements are not testable or ambiguous, either the requirement is rewritten or the use case description documents a testable interpretation of the requirement.

Improved Test Coverage

Generating tests from activity diagrams allows us to specify a basis for test coverage. We can choose to create tests for every path in the activity diagram or every transition in the diagram, and we can be assured that we have created test cases for each of these cases. Missing test cases are only a result of incomplete models, and the models provide transparency to what is tested and what is not tested.

Tracing to Requirements

System tests are required to be traced back to requirements in order to demonstrate verification of requirements. When use case models are used as the basis for model-based testing, the mapping back to requirements is more natural than with other types of models such as state machines, which typically are associated with implementation components.

Since use cases can be easily associated with requirements, the generated tests can also be more easily associated with requirements. When tests are generated, it is also possible to automatically generate traces back to the associated requirements.

Start Early in the Development Life Cycle

For most of the projects we work on, the use case models for automated testing are developed during the system test phase of the project. However, we recommend beginning the development of the use case models as early as possible in the project so that the testing team can effect the definition of requirements early in the process to ensure that testable requirements are specified.

As the use case modeling occurs earlier in the development process, we expect to see many improvements in system testing. The following improvements are expected:

- Improvement in the overall quality of general customer use cases in granularity and variations

- Reduction in the overall validation effort for system tests

- Improved communication to all stakeholders about requirements issues that result from the development of the testing use cases

- Finding defects as early as possible because you can discuss inconsistencies and impacts to the workflow model when it is defined and released

Improved Efficiency

In traditional testing the challenge is how to efficiently create the tests. In model-based testing, by contrast, the problem is often how to not generate too many tests. The test generation tools that we use have features to prune the number of test paths through the model to reasonable numbers while still covering all activities or all transitions through the model. It is easier to create a large number of tests using this technique than using traditional testing methods [Ostrand et al. 1988], [Balcer et al. 1990]. This creates the need for some sort of prioritization scheme to decide which of the generated tests have higher priority and should be executed first. Although we are currently able to manage the number of tests we work with, it would be desirable to be able to assign priorities to the tests. Multiple factors affect priorities; for example, giving priority to recently changed code, giving priority to scenarios that are more likely to be executed by users, giving priority for scenarios with more serious consequences if they fail. Just as we can model the test scenarios, it is possible to add features to perform risk-based testing as well.

We have used activity diagrams for describing use case diagrams, and we have explored using sequence diagrams to describe test scenarios. This works adequately, but we would also like to be able to use UML 2.0 semantics with combined fragments to represent conditional execution of sequences. In some cases, sequence diagrams may be a more efficient representation of scenarios.

8.6 Summary

In this chapter, we have discussed the relationship between requirements engineering and system testing. Requirements engineers generate use cases which are the basis for the models used by the test engineers to generate test cases. Good requirements are necessary for applying model-based testing approaches. Having test engineers develop the models and tests early in the development project helps to review and clarify the requirements.

8.7 Discussion Questions

1. What are some of the requirements engineering artifacts that test engineers use to develop system tests?

2. What types of models are used by test engineers to develop tests?

3. How can performance engineers work with the models generated by requirements engineers to test for performance and scalability?

References

Avritzer, A., Cai, Y., and Paulish, D., "Coordination Implications of Software Architecture in a Global Software Development Project," *Proceedings of WICSA 2008*, IEEE Press, 2008.

Balcer, M., Hasling, W., and Ostrand, T., "Automatic Generation of Test Scripts from Formal Test Specifications," *Proceedings of ACM SIGSOFT '89: Third Symposium on Software Testing, Verification, and Analysis (TAVS-3)*, ACM Press, New York, 1990, pp. 257–271.

Beer, A., Mohacs, I. S., Stary, C., and IDATG, "An Open Tool for Automated Testing of Interactive Software," *Proceedings of the COMPSAC '98: 22nd International Computer Software and Applications Conference*, August 1998, pp. 470–475.

Gross, H., *Component-Based Software Testing with UML*, Springer, Berlin, 1998.

Hartmann, J., Vieira, M., Foster, H., and Ruder, A., "A UML-Based Approach to System Testing," *Innovations in Systems and Software Engineering (A NASA Journal)*, Vol. 1, No. 1, ISSN: 1614-5046, Springer-Verlag London, April 2005, pp. 12–24.

Hasling, B., Goetz, H., and Beetz, K., "Model Based Testing of System Requirements Using UML Use Case Models," *Proceedings of the International Conference on Software Testing (ICST) 2008*, April 2008.

Jones, C., *Applied Software Measurement*, McGraw-Hill, 2008.

Mingsong, C., Xiaokang, Q., and Xuandong, L., "Automatic Test Case Generation for UML Activity Diagrams," *Proceedings of the AST '06*, ACM Press, 2006.

Moeller, K. and Paulish, D., *Software Metrics: A Practitioner's Guide to Improved Product Development*, IEEE Press, London, 1993.

Moore, E.F., "Gedanken-Experiments on Sequential Machines," *Automata Studies,* Princeton University Press, Princeton, New Jersey, 1956, pp. 129–153.

Myers, G., *The Art of Software Testing,* Wiley, New York, 1979.

Ostrand, T. and Balcer, M.J., "The Category-Partition Method for Specifying and Generating Functional Tests," *Comm. ACM,* vol. 31, no. 6, 1988, pp. 676–686.

Schieferdecker, I., Dai, Z.R., Grabowski, J., and Rennoch, A., "The UML 2.0 Testing Profile and Its Relation to TTCN-3, Testing of Communicating Systems," *Proceedings of the 15th IFIP International Conference on Testing of Communicating Systems (TestCom 2003),* LNCS 2644, Springer, May 2003, pp. 79–94.

Song, X., Hwong, B., Matos, G., Rudorfer, A., Nelson, C., Han, M., and Girenkov, A., "Understanding Requirements for Computer-Aided Healthcare Workflows: Experience and Challenges," *Proceedings of the 28th International Conference on Software Engineering, ICSE '06,* ACM Press, 2006.

Utting, M. and Legeard, B., *Practical Model-Based Testing: A Tools Approach,* Morgan-Kaufmann, San Francisco, CA, 2006.

V-Modell XT. http://www.v-modell-xt.de/, 2008.

Vieira, M., Leduc, J., Hasling, B., Subramanyan, R., and Kazmeier, J., "Automation of GUI Testing Using a Model-Driven Approach," *Proceeding of the 2006 International Workshop on Automation of Software Test, AST '06,* ACM Press, 2006.

CHAPTER 9

Rapid Development Techniques for Requirements Evolution

by Beatrice Hwong, Gilberto Matos,
Arnold Rudorfer, Brad Wehrwein

B ill was working with a group of stakeholders with whom he was having a difficult time getting decisions and clarifications about their new product requirements. He began to realize that the reason they were so reluctant to precisely define the requirements was that they did not know what they wanted. The product was new to the business, and the stakeholders did not have a clear vision of what the product should do.

Bill suggested that an approach to define the requirements for this new product could be to quickly develop a prototype of the user interface of the new product that could be evaluated by the stakeholders. He found that although they did not know what they wanted, they could more easily determine what they did not want. Implementing a user interface that the stakeholders could navigate seemed to be a good way to define the product requirements and collect feedback from the stakeholders. Since Bill was able to quickly change the prototype user interface and show the stakeholders a number of different options, they began to make good progress on requirements definition. Over time, the prototype became the primary artifact for describing the desired features of the new product.

This chapter identifies some requirements elicitation and evolution challenges and shows how rapid development practices can be used to help stakeholders evolve the requirements. Sometimes, the many stakeholders of a complex system lack a common and unambiguous representation of the system requirements. While architects and developers often favor using requirements models and requirements analysts may prefer working with text descriptions, domain experts or clients often need representations closer to the realization of a product. Based on our experience with projects in medical, communications, and automation domains, we identify prototyping practices that can result in rapid requirements evolution and resolution.

9.1   Background

Requirements elicitation and analysis are very much people-oriented activities. Stakeholders are encouraged to share their vision of the new product, understand each other's viewpoints, negotiate tradeoffs, and eventually come up with a common view of the features of a product such that it will be competitive in the market. As long as the requirements can be interpreted in more than one way, their ambiguity creates various risks to the product development.

It's difficult to unambiguously retrieve and interpret ideas from another person without first converting them into a shared representational medium [Berry et al. 2003]. This medium is most commonly a human language, and in some cases more formal textual or modeling representations are used. The less formal the representation is, the more likely it is to have inherent ambiguities. On the other hand, increasing formality and unambiguousness of a representation may lead to increased complexity of the representation. Additional effort may be necessary to precisely define requirements that at least some stakeholders view as obvious. In general, stakeholders who represent the end users tend to prefer to work more at the informal, prose end of the communications spectrum, while engineers in many domains tend to use more formal, automatable representations. Neither side is particularly adept at translating between these representations without some loss of information. Using formal requirements modeling in combination with stakeholder training in modeling could address these issues, but it may not be practical because of potentially additional learning curve costs, as well as possible resistance from stakeholders. Another difficulty with modeling is that the current state of modeling tools is relatively poor; i.e., the difficulty of using the tools sometimes defeats the communication intent of the models.

Prototypes have the potential of being more easily comprehensible both to stakeholders and developers, without much special training. We have found that rapid prototyping allows us to quickly make representations of the target system that help minimize or remove ambiguity from the requirements analysis process. Thus, prototypes can help address the complexity that is caused by uncertain requirements and by differing stakeholder views.

We identify the situations where prototyping can be effective in shortening the time it takes to improve the common understanding between the stakeholders, and in uncovering the incompleteness of the requirements with respect to the target business domain. Prototyping may also be used during early phases of product development; for example, by building a vertical slice of the architecture to check for potential performance problems [Paulish 2002]. Prototyping must be *rapid* in that the prototypes should be frequently available early in the development process and be easily modified as stakeholders provide feedback.

For prototyping to be rapid, prototype developers of software products often do not consider reuse. In such cases, the prototype can be viewed as "throwaway code" and would not become part of the product development. Managers that encourage code reuse will often require that the prototypes have the possibility of becoming the shipped product. This is difficult to achieve in an environment where product requirements are continuously and quickly changing. From our experience, we encourage the use of some of the anticipated product development tools to develop the prototypes. This encourages the software or systems engineers to learn the new tools early in the development life cycle, ensuring effectiveness in the target technologies when product development begins.

Exploratory prototypes are used when the functionality is evolving or being discovered during the project. Agile approaches such as Scrum [Schwaber et al. 2004] may work well on software projects for such situations, where the functionality is added incrementally. Scrum may be applied both to early phase activities such as for rapidly developing a throwaway prototype, or during implementation where the development is broken down into monthly sprints.

9.2   When to Prototype

Rapid prototyping is generally used when requirements are not well understood, and there is a need to better understand what the envisioned product will do; e.g., by viewing the user interface. The primary goal of prototyping is to answer specific questions regarding the target system, and in doing so to decrease the complexity and risk involved in its implementation. Lack of clarity about what the system should do, either due to its novelty, or due to stakeholder conflicts, or due to a shifting competitive landscape, increases the complexity and the risk that significant changes will become necessary in later stages of the development life cycle.

We recommend prototyping as a good way of quickly evolving from fuzzy high-level requests toward realistic and viable system and feature requirements. Prototyping is commonly used as a way to validate technical solutions or to explore an unknown problem or engineering domain. Prototyping is also used very widely throughout engineering and manufacturing organizations to validate future products or production processes. In many cases, software prototyping is a lower-cost alternative to producing real physical prototypes, and software prototypes are often sufficient for representing many functions.

Formal requirements inspections coupled with prototyping are effective in reducing requirements defects [Jones 2008]. However, the size of prototypes becomes an issue (see the following "Prototyping and Size" sidebar). If the size of the prototype implements less than about 10 percent of the total application, the prototype cannot replicate many of the key features. But for very large systems in about the 100,000 function point range, a 10 percent prototype would be a major system in its own right. Therefore, prototyping becomes less effective for very large applications such as ERP packages in the 300,000 function point range [Jones 2008].

Some example areas where prototyping supports requirements engineers are given under the headings that follow.

Early Requirement Elicitation

The initial requirement elicitation for prototyping tasks is generally similar to the approach of many agile methodologies. The tasks must be structured around specific scenarios of interest, and in the context of specific user types. When the requirements are discussed in the problem domain, the end users are much better able to reason and communicate useful information about the business goals, constraints, and preconditions that they perceive. The function of the desired features of the product must be put in context of the agreed-upon scenarios in order to be considered in the prototyping process.

Once specific scenarios are identified, with some agreement on their preconditions and constraints, the next step is to introduce candidate user interactions. These can come from the domain experts and be based on their knowledge of existing systems in the market or availability of reusable or standardized components. Developers and designers can often suggest alternatives, based on their experience with existing or emerging technologies. Interactions can be defined at multiple levels, both at a high granularity describing long-running interactions, and at a low level describing the interactions of individual user controls.

Once the scenarios are defined, with specified context and users, they are prototyped in a lightweight form. Such prototypes can be reviewed by the stakeholders, providing a stable basis for accepting or rejecting specific user interaction details and for formulating specific change requests. Continuing with a simple representation or proceeding to an executable prototype then becomes a decision about optimizing the progress based on the quality of representation and the prototyping effort. Some benefits of using prototyping in the context of requirements elicitation were quantified in the industrial case study described in [Verner et al. 2004].

Conflicting or Nonprioritized Requirements

There are many potential conflicting stakeholder requests that will arise as a new system is being defined. There are inevitable conflicts between the localized interests of individual stakeholders and the overall interests of the entire organization. Conventional, text-based requirements representations may provide inadequate support for conflict detection and resolution.

Modeling of system requirements provides a better analysis infrastructure to be used for detecting and resolving conflicts, particularly if the model is sufficiently formal to allow certain automated consistency checks. However, this still may not solve the problem, because domain experts and stakeholders may not be proficient in the modeling techniques used by system architects and developers. As such, domain experts and stakeholders may be unable to fully understand the proposed system as it is being presented, and thus may not be able to identify conflicts or errors.

We can use prototypes to execute unambiguous representations of relatively complex user scenarios for the system. By incorporating some scale and complexity into the prototypes, we expose more stakeholders to a high-level view of the system and enable them to identify domain inconsistencies of a global nature. Once the requirements are better understood on a global level by the stakeholders, there is more opportunity for conflict identification, and subsequent negotiation about prioritization and tradeoffs. Additionally, the prototypes can represent the viable implementation options. This helps the designers better quantify the risks of implementation choices and gives stakeholders hands-on experience with such choices.

Bridge the Skills of Stakeholders and Developers

Stakeholders often know *what* they want a new system to do, but they don't know *how* to implement the features. Developers know *how* to implement new systems, but they rarely have a full understanding of *why* a given solution is chosen. Technical skills play an important role in determining an optimal implementation approach.

Despite the lack of clarity about the constraints and capabilities of available technologies, stakeholders commonly specify *how* their needs should be satisfied, instead of concentrating on a clear description of *what* these needs are. Once a request is specified as a desired solution, it creates constraints that may limit the alternatives for the entire system.

Many software developers lack broad domain and business knowledge, since they tend to concentrate on technology-centric work. Job mobility in the software industry is relatively high, and developers often jump across industries and domains, thus making their technology knowledge their most portable asset. As a consequence, developers may not have the requisite domain insights to be able to internally identify business-related shortcomings in the specifications, regardless of the representation methods used. As an example, specifying that a money transfer requires an amount is a technical issue, but understanding that the transfer has a different impact on savings or loan accounts is a business issue. Prototypes provide a language for both stakeholders and developers to express their capabilities, alternative solutions, proposals, and requests.

Capture Detailed Requirements

High-level requirements often abstract away some aspects of a system in the effort to simplify the representation. Requirements engineering best practices suggest that requirements should be implementation independent, so it often becomes easy to overlook implementation-related issues. Sometimes, domain-related special cases are overlooked. Decomposition of high-level requirements into lower-level requirements and system specifications is not a straightforward technical task, since it often involves a significant potential for uncovering conflicts and different interpretations of the high-level requirements.

Prototypes ensure that at least a part of the system requirements is decomposed very early with respect to a candidate technology, and that the stakeholders can evaluate these artifacts as they refine and negotiate the majority of system requirements. Stakeholder agreement on prototype validity provides a common area of interpretation for the high-level requirements still being elaborated.

Time-to-Market

Any activity that can be eliminated, shortened, or performed concurrently is an important source of development process improvements. If requirements engineering activities take a long time, and they are used as a precondition for starting development, the time-to-market may be undesirably long.

Early phases of project inception suffer from a high degree of uncertainty, both about the feature set and about the details of how the system will satisfy the requests of stakeholders. It is not uncommon to have uncertainty even about who the stakeholders are for a specific project, since at this stage many infrastructure and technology issues are unconstrained. For example, the type of applications planned for a new product determines whether the data center, security, and

Prototyping and Size

During some private communications with Capers Jones, he suggested some interesting guidelines for prototyping, depending on the size of the future product. For small applications below 100 function points, the entire product can be built as a disposable prototype to try out features such as interfaces and algorithms. Disposable prototypes are safer than evolutionary prototypes due to the common use of shortcuts and sloppy methods. Prototypes are usually about 10 percent of the size of the applications themselves, so prototypes are very useful for applications in the size range of 1000 to 2000 function points. This is where you are most likely to find "time boxed" prototypes developed in a month or so. When applications reach 10,000 function points, it is difficult to do a 10 percent prototype because 1000 function points is a nontrivial application in its own right. Therefore, for these cases, prototypes are usually only for interfaces or a few key algorithms. When applications reach 100,000 function points, it is not feasible to build a 10 percent prototype, so the best you get are small prototypes for specific topics such as user interfaces and critical algorithms. Thus, prototypes are usually under 500 function points in total size no matter how big the application is. Because the difficulty of constructing meaningful prototypes increases with application size, this is one of the reasons bigger applications tend to have more requirements creep and worse quality than smaller applications.

licensing staff are stakeholders or not (see the section "Selecting Significant Stakeholders" in Chapter 5). The length of this early-phase time period, where the risks are very high and generally nonmeasurable, directly impacts the total duration of the project.

Most software and systems projects suffer from some requirements-related problems. In general, these problems manifest themselves in development, testing, or quality assurance activities and thus tend to cause large rework costs and schedule delays. Obviously, the earlier that these requirements problems are identified, the better chance the project team has to mitigate the risks.

9.3   Practices and Experience

As we've discussed, in certain situations there is much value in developing a prototype that is used to discover and evolve the features of an envisioned new product. Some specific recommended prototyping practices are given under the headings that follow.

Requirements Engineering and Prototype Development in Parallel

Requirement elicitation and analysis are generally a precondition for successful development work. Conversely, progress on developing the system leads to improved understanding of the problem and solution domain, and thus contributes to the evolution of the requirements toward a viable and useful set. Concurrent work on requirements and prototype development has been widely accepted as a best practice, and in many situations it may be the best approach. An example concurrent process is given in Figure 9.1 [Song et al. 2005], and an example overlap of prototype development, prototype testing, and feature analysis across multiple iterations is given in Figure 9.2.

Here are some tips for concurrent requirements engineering and development:

- Work on each activity with the goal of achieving some progress, such that the work results can contribute to other project activities.

- When using paired programming, the team member who is more experienced with the domain works more on requirements and domain understanding, while the other team member works on the implementation details in close collaboration.

- Both requirements and development staff meet periodically to exchange information. An even better practice is if a single collocated small team is doing both requirements engineering and prototype development (see Chapter 10).

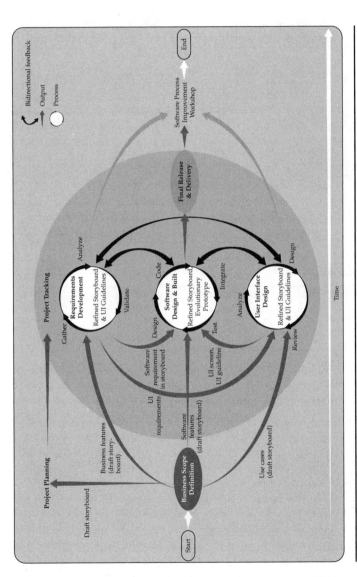

Figure 9.1 Concurrent rapid prototyping process for workflow-driven web interfaces

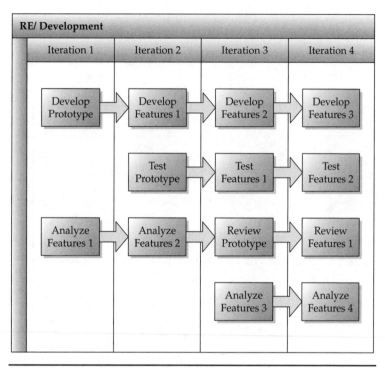

Figure 9.2 Concurrent RE and development

- Domain experts and/or customers review the outputs of both RE and prototype development, and the feedback is used as inputs for both processes.

- Simplicity and unambiguousness of the presentation reviews are important for smooth progress of the prototype development and requirements engineering processes. An example could be the review of the outputs of a Scrum sprint at the end of the month for a set of features implemented in the prototype user interface. Prototypes are reviewed in the context of relevant and agreed-upon business scenarios, and the stakeholders are expected to provide specific feedback. The feedback related to a review should be as fine grained as possible, particularly if some prototype aspects are rejected.

- Multiple functional proposals are elaborated by the requirements engineers for review and selection by the customer (end user). In some cases, it may be more cost effective to create customized versions of the prototype and make a selection among these.

- Prototyping should not continue for an extended period of time without specific selections among the alternatives. Concurrent analysis or development of multiple variations tends to quickly increase the complexity of interactions and increases the risks of unidentified problems in the design. Thus, the requirements decision making should be time boxed, so that project progress can continue.

- Multiple features can be implemented and reviewed within a single developer/RE team. This way, if some features are blocked waiting for feedback, the staff can redirect their efforts to other features.

- The output of prototyping is considered to be a throwaway, since no emphasis is put on architecting and designing the implementation for anything more than the currently known scope of the requirements. Since the requirements are evolving, the normal activities involved with developing a maintainable product would likely be a wasteful effort. However, within the context of the known requirements and expected evolution, the architecture of the prototype should support quick refactoring and evolution.

Identify and Eliminate Stakeholder Conflicts

There are numerous sources of conflict in systems development projects. Stakeholders may want the system to serve their incompatible interests. The needs of individual stakeholders must always be balanced with the goal of optimizing the effort and resources needed to develop and deploy the system. We want to identify incompatible stakeholder requests as early as possible in the project, in order to support the evolution of the individual requests toward a set of compatible requirements. For example, the requests of insurance companies and medical providers in electronic patient records are often incompatible when it comes to billing and approval information, yet they are stakeholders that can benefit from the introduction of a shared format. Patient privacy issues play a role in what information becomes visible to the other stakeholders and when.

The construction of a use case with conflicting requirements can start from an agreed high-level sunny day scenario. Stakeholders are prompted to expand the scenario with specific details related to the actors and events. As the level of detail increases, conflicts are likely to manifest themselves in the form of data to be shown or hidden, requests for different action sequences, and differences in the availability and visibility of required actions or data views. Another practice for collecting incompatible requirements information is to elicit from the stakeholders their expectations of where the conflicts are, since many of them are likely to be already known. That information can be used to guide the targeted process of identifying specific conflicts.

A practice to achieve a simplified representation of functionality when prototyping is to concentrate on a small subset of system aspects, coupled with transparency to others. By not trying to address all the issues the eventual system needs to deal with, we can select a representation that is particularly good for meeting most of our goals. For example, a storyboard or an activity diagram provides a good representation for user-driven interactive web applications. However, for an asynchronous web application using Ajax, for example, this representation would not be as useful in capturing the richness of system interactions driven by asynchronous updates. Using this representation in the asynchronous web applications (or for example in avionics or process control software) would imply that while our prototype is useful in understanding the user-driven interactions, it may not be applicable to the requirements related to asynchronous and event-driven behaviors.

Early phases of requirements discovery are characterized by a great deal of uncertainty and generally inconsistent views among the stakeholders. The goal of requirements discovery is to understand these inconsistencies, and to reduce the uncertainty by creating a common understanding of the system needs, capabilities, and potential conflicts among stakeholders. We are not targeting the conflicts that are already known to some of the stakeholders, since those are likely to be already documented by them. Our emphasis is on understanding the conflicts that will be brought to the surface by the development and deployment of the target system.

Rapid Iteration of Requirements/Stakeholder Feedback

Scheduling a meeting with the goal of identifying inconsistencies among stakeholders is not a very productive approach in our experience, since we don't know a priori what all the inconsistencies are. A more constructive approach to requirements discovery is to elicit requests from individual stakeholders, present these requests in a common and unambiguous form, and then collect feedback from the stakeholders. Conflicts and inconsistencies can be detected in two ways: either the harmonized view can't be constructed due to our perception of conflicts, or the harmonized view gets rejected by some stakeholders because their perception of the system differs from our assumptions. Either way, when such conflicts are detected, they must be openly presented to the stakeholders, for a resolution to be jointly determined. Goal modeling, as described in Chapter 4, can be an effective way of communicating high-level requirements conflicts to stakeholders.

The iterative nature of this prototyping process allows us to concentrate on manageable units and to make quick progress toward a common and unambiguous representation. This also helps the stakeholders to progressively evolve their perception of real requirements based on the evolving presentation of the proposed solution. This aspect of requirements prototyping has a great deal of similarity to the work done in an agile development project, with the notable difference that our process generally does not try to produce a finished product, and thus it can iterate very quickly, as soon as the feature modifications are complete [Schwaber et al. 2001].

We have had success on projects where prototype review and elicitation sessions were strictly and periodically scheduled, and also on projects where there was no a priori schedule for the requirements review sessions. Updates on the prototype's representation of requirements can usually be done very quickly, in a day or less in most cases. The review sessions can be scheduled on demand or in advance with a specific schedule. It is important to have frequent updates and reviews [Matos 2007]. We recommend that each stakeholder involved in a specific aspect of a system should be involved in a review session at least once a week during prototype development.

Reviews can be done one on one with specific stakeholders, or preferably with the participation of multiple stakeholders in order to reduce the duplication of presentation effort and to foster communication among the stakeholders. The presence of multiple stakeholders is strongly encouraged in the early reviews, because these are an opportunity for uncovering large and fundamental discrepancies. The probability of discovering discrepancies also goes down with subsequent iterations unless new aspects or details are being added to the requirements representation.

Sufficient progress in prototyping relies on feedback of domain experts and other product stakeholders. Their feedback on the prototype reviews needs to be informative, timely, and actionable. The review comments should be as specific and detailed as practical, explicitly accepting or rejecting specific parts of the prototype. Whenever possible, the rationale for a given comment should be given in order to capture the implied assumptions, particularly when some approach is rejected. Noncommittal evaluations should be avoided whenever possible, even if the right choice is not clear. In this situation choosing to go forward with prototyping multiple approaches in parallel may be superior to saying that the current approach "may be okay."

Experienced domain experts with a broad understanding of their markets, environments, and other critical aspects of the product context are rare, and they are unlikely to be available for extended periods of time in the early stages of product planning and development. Our approach to prototyping as a means of eliciting requirements relies on using the domain experts' feedback for evolving the understanding of the important requirements of the planned system. We emphasize maximizing the value of the feedback collected during the periods when the domain experts are available. This can be done by presenting intermediate results to the domain experts, and then collecting their comments on the value of certain feature implementations and necessary improvements.

Storyboarding

We define a prototype as any artifact that unambiguously represents a certain aspect of a system with sufficient detail to draw meaningful conclusions or to make decisions. We don't necessarily have to develop executable software to prototype an aspect of a system. We can use a number of lower-cost intuitive techniques that give very good results for their respective domains. For example, we often use *storyboards* to illustrate the specific interaction sequences for a system.

Storyboards are a visual and textual medium that allows multiple stakeholders to produce, modify, and comment on the content, and thus foster rapid communication and evolution of common understanding, as well as the identification of possible conflicting areas. Storyboards can be used for high-level modeling of user stories over multiple events/interactions, and they can also be used to model the low-level user interface (UI) interactions that occur for a specific application or even one of its user screens. The choice of the level of representation is driven by the stakeholders and by what needs to be modeled for the evaluation. We have found that PowerPoint often provides the right level of fidelity to represent the UI and workflow, combined with ease of annotation and usage by all stakeholders. Storyboards are easy to create in most commonly used presentation editing tools, but WYSIWYG document editors work as well. We have mostly used PowerPoint, but Visio was also successfully used for this purpose. An example storyboard is given in Figure 9.3, illustrating simple visual and textual entry, scenario sequence, usage of captured images, and direct annotation.

In addition to visual sequences and text comments about the content of specific slides, storyboards can be expanded to include

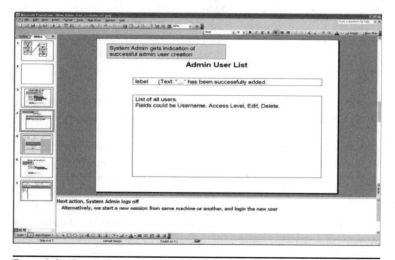

FIGURE 9.3   Example storyboard

several other evaluation aspects. If the storyboard contains several optional workflows, it can be marked to illustrate their start and end points, including preconditions and postconditions. This allows us to represent these multiple workflows in one artifact, simplifying maintenance and analysis. Also, storyboards can be used to show different variations of the proposed solution. Both the selected and dropped variations can remain in the document, allowing later reconsideration of the choices.

Visual prototyping is most commonly used in the context of UI design. Storyboards provide useful support for this type of prototyping. It is very easy to import a screenshot of an existing application to be used as an initial placeholder for the desired functionality. If executable prototypes are involved, screenshots of the actual prototype can be used as a further approximation in the storyboard description. Also, this type of prototyping commonly goes on in parallel with UI design. While the UI design itself is unlikely to be done using PowerPoint, the screen designs from any specialized UI design tools can always be imported into the storyboard to improve the representation of the target system.

Storyboards focus the discussion between requirements engineers and various stakeholders on the specific requirements of an agreed scenario of interest. They enable them to elicit, elaborate, and organize the system requirements within a single artifact. The intuitive nature and representation capabilities of the storyboard generally allow any stakeholder to contribute to the evolution of the requirements. They can do this individually or in coached groups, by simply annotating the relevant parts of the document. While we don't advocate a specific process for handling storyboards, there are some specific aspects of requirements that can and should be explored.

- The graphical part of the storyboard slide should describe the visual aspect of the application, and only the most important user interactions. User interactions are described by highlighting the visual elements that enable them. Highlighting and callouts are also used to emphasize the contents or the role of specific areas of the display.

- Notes associated with a storyboard represent other details, including optional interactions, unavailable interactions, further stakeholder requests not associated with the primary scenario, and general notes associated with a specific step. Notes allow multiple stakeholders to formulate conflicting change requests, and to keep track of them in a well-structured form associated to the context where they are relevant.

- Each step of the system interaction should be represented in the storyboard. This completeness of the sequence is important to ensure the unambiguous representation of the system for multiple stakeholders. In general, it is better to put simple placeholder representations of the seemingly irrelevant steps to enable stakeholder review. The level of detail used for individual steps varies according to the stakeholders' need for clarification, such that the most novel, uncertain, or risky steps will be explored most thoroughly.

- If the storyboard describes a nontrivial dynamic behavior, it should be summarized in the form of a behavior model. Most stakeholders will understand the semantics of simple state-based models, such as state machines, particularly if no cyclic behaviors are involved.

- When a requirements engineer elaborates a storyboard together with a domain stakeholder, the following questions should be addressed with respect to each step of a storyboarded scenario:

  - Are all allowed/optional interactions enumerated? Are their effects described?

  - Are all disabled or forbidden interactions enumerated? Are the reasons clarified?

  - Does the stakeholder agree with the enabled and disabled interactions? Why not?

  - Are all the visual items proposed for this screen/step consistent with the user's needs? Would different presentations be useful?

  - Are there visual items that are missing? What would the stakeholder want to see and why?

  - Is there proper emphasis on the important data aspects in a given step? What is the important data and why? This level of discussion is most likely to involve UI designers, but it is very important for the developers to stay involved in order to provide input on what screen representation technology can or can't do.

Executable Prototypes

Certain aspects of application behavior can be modeled using a descriptive notation, and then enacted by an engine that interprets the model. This type of prototyping is similar to using 3-D modeling software to represent physical models. For example, the prototype can give an overview and flythrough capability, and even provide some analysis if the model allows it.

Fully executable prototypes are the most generic alternative for creating a realistic and unambiguous representation of some aspect of the application. The primary benefit of developing executable prototypes is that they include some ability to verify the solution, as well as directly introducing realistic elements into the analysis of requirements and potential solutions. For web applications, developing an executable prototype can even be faster and cheaper than developing a visual but nonexecutable prototype.

Executable prototypes can be classified on several dimensions. A common decision is whether the prototype is going to be a throwaway or an evolutionary step toward the final product. This decision depends on a number of technological factors, including actual technology selection, technology support for quick changes, and how familiar the developers are with the implementation technologies and tools. The most important factor in deciding whether an evolutionary prototype or a throwaway one is the better approach is based on the current maturity of the existing set of requirements. If the requirements are very fuzzy, it is highly improbable that the majority of architecture and design decisions made during the prototyping process will be applicable to the actual product development.

Branch prototypes are the most common type of prototyping used by many software development organizations. A branch prototype is created every time a development team starts to work out some uncertain issue by modifying the existing product code without necessarily planning to add the changes to the product. If the prototyping works out and the solution is deemed satisfactory, the prototype is generally close enough to the main development trunk that it can be merged back without large disruptions. In many cases, the main benefit of a branch prototype will be the ideas and knowledge gained, and these may be applied directly in the development of the product, while making sure to harmonize their usage with the system architecture (or adjusting the architecture, if required).

Creation of fully executable prototypes is occasionally required in order to understand the technological viability of the planned solutions. In such situations, it is very advantageous to develop a realistic target scenario on top of the viability prototype in order to create a full vertical slice of the target system in the target technology [Paulish 2002]. This does not require the prototype to be evolutionary, even though many lessons from the prototype will probably be carried into the implementation, and some of the code may even end up being reused.

The primary driver for requirements elicitation using prototyping techniques is to gather useful information as efficiently as possible. In some situations, a simple prototype can serve as an intermediate step in collecting information that will help create a more complex, executable prototype that can be fully evaluated by customers (users). In most cases, the initial prototype takes the form of a user story or storyboard, but it contains enough detail to allow the elaboration of necessary detail for a more complex prototype. This approach is commonly used in agile software development projects, but without looking at the user stories as a form of prototyping. We think that as long as the stories are representative and unambiguous in defining the desired functionalities, they can serve as a simple prototype.

Transparency

High-level agreement on requirements may conceal conflicts at the lower levels of a complex system. We concentrate on uncovering and verifying the details, by incorporating them into the prototypes as early as possible. Domain experts need to clarify both the general rules and their exceptions as early as possible. Software or systems engineers need to provide good visibility into their assumptions about the implementation and the associated constraints.

There are a few important activities that contribute to achieving satisfactory transparency. No time should be spent on preparing a smooth presentation with a rough prototype; rather, it is more important to showcase the most recent and questionable additions to the prototype. Also, the prototype should be created around scenarios that are relatively complex, in order to bring any potential problems to the surface. We want to amplify the "demo effect"; that is, "unexpected things will happen." This is somewhat of a challenge to many developers, who consider a smooth presentation to be of intrinsically higher value. It sometimes shows even in agile product developments, where teams devote significant time to preparing a smooth end-of-iteration presentation, using workarounds or even code patches to ensure that errors stay hidden. In prototyping, this is strictly counterproductive and should not be done.

Another important aspect of transparency is the extrapolation of the undocumented requirements from the documented ones. All significant participants in the prototyping process should use their own interpretations of the system, as represented by the prototype or existing requirements, and extrapolate it independently to define what they see as complex user scenarios. By comparing the extrapolations and assumptions from multiple sources, additional conflicts are likely to be uncovered.

The complexity card game, as practiced in many agile methodologies [Schwaber et al. 2001], can serve as a good introductory step for the extrapolation activity. When multiple stakeholders on the development side make wildly divergent complexity and effort estimates for some tasks, it is very likely that they are basing their estimates on significantly different assumptions about the system requirements. The outliers in terms of complexity estimates are good candidates to start the process of presenting their assumptions and the derived complexity issues.

Testing

In early stages, it is useful to practice test-first development [Beck 2002], [Sangwan et al. 2007]. In addition to commenting on prepared prototypes, the domain expert can help the developers construct a small number of representative test cases to be used to internally verify the model or prototype until the next opportunity to present the results to the domain expert. Unlike the common use of test-first development, we don't want to produce a test suite that verifies the quality of any produced software. Our goals are limited to having an oracle that unambiguously verifies if the ideas or systems we are experimenting with will satisfy the requirements given by the domain experts.

Obviously, the quality of the feedback collected from the verification against such tests is determined by their representativeness. We consider the tests to be representative if they model the behavior in situations where the requirements are not well understood. Also, the predefined tests should be sufficiently specific as to make the verified system unambiguous. This level of detail is the responsibility of the domain experts, and the prototypers usually don't have sufficient domain expertise to formulate such domain-specific questions. This approach is only used as an interim step, and its results must be validated with the domain experts, in the form of a prototype, before being considered "accepted."

The set of tests that satisfies our goals has the following characteristics: it is representative of the important requirements of the system, and it is unambiguous. A prototype models the target system, while the set of tests models the expectations of the system's impact on its environment.

Modification Optimization

A primary optimization goal for our prototyping approach is to emphasize the collaborative aspects of interaction among the stakeholders and to maximize the emergent shared understanding. We assume that the prototyping effort is taking place early in the development project for certain features that are unknown, such that the total complexity can't be accurately estimated or planned. However, early determination of stable requirements is a critical issue that will allow subsequent optimization on development efforts. We believe that limited early effort aimed at fostering this shared understanding and trust eliminates wasted effort and reduces the risk inherent in development later on.

The prototyping process is centered on artifacts that unambiguously represent some aspect of the planned system or feature. It is rarely the case in practice that the issues of interest for evaluation are very easy to integrate into one artifact, primarily because their interplay is unknown at that time. Creation of multiple artifacts forces some overhead in creation and updates, but it provides the necessary degree of freedom for the individual artifacts to evolve toward the best representation of the desired aspect of the system. With multiple artifacts in concurrent evolution and analysis, the feedback loop on each artifact is shortened and is decoupled from any problems that may slow the progress for some other artifact.

The consistency between multiple artifacts is the responsibility of the involved stakeholders, who must be actively involved with all artifacts that relate to their area of interest and expertise.

The desire to optimize the prototyping process around the fastest possible feedback loop has a significant impact on the nature of the chosen prototype. A mock-up prototype is usually easier than an executable prototype to manipulate by multiple stakeholders, and this makes such mock-ups the logical first step in developing consensus. An executable model is likewise usually faster to modify and evolve within its boundaries than an executable prototype, and should take precedence for the supported aspects of system functionality. The choice of technology and prototyping process is also subject to the goal of optimizing the feedback, particularly by minimizing the prototype development time and effort. A target product technology may be skipped in favor of another technology that models the behavior in a satisfactory way, while providing a faster or more powerful prototype development and code generation environment for a throwaway prototype. Also, evolutionary prototyping requires the developers to concentrate very early on architecture and quality issues. Throwaway prototypes are likely to provide faster progress on requirements understanding, since they are easier to modify. When creating throwaway prototypes, care must be taken to manage stakeholder expectations; e.g., the customer should clearly understand that the deliverable is not a viable product.

While the speed of collecting feature solution feedback is the paramount goal in requirements prototyping, many other aspects of product development still play an important role in this process. In order to provide reliable feedback, the prototype needs to be representative of the desired feature and unambiguously understood by the stakeholders. This implies that a certain minimum level of quality of presentation must be achieved and maintained. Also, the complexity of the prototype may grow beyond levels where ad hoc hacking can maintain the prototype at the needed quality level. Expected and attained complexity should be used as a guide in defining the architecture and prototyping practices.

9.4   Tips for Prototyping

To summarize some of the prototyping practices described and make them more prescriptive for the practitioner, we suggest the following rules for prototyping. These tips for prototyping are adapted from the rules for software development using agile principles found in [Poppendieck et al. 2003].

- **Eliminate unnecessary work**   Many quality processes strive to find defects early in the development process. For rapid prototyping, extensive testing of a prototype and writing extensive documentation about how a prototype is implemented is unnecessary. Development of executable prototypes is wasted effort if simple storyboards will suffice. Animated web or scripting applications are often easier means than the target technologies to develop the prototypes. Creation of reusable structures is wasted effort if limited replication is sufficient. Conversely, when prototyping is combined with feasibility studies or product development activities, reusing some prototyping artifacts for development may be appropriate.

- **Accelerate learning** Quick prototype turnaround and transparency helps the stakeholders, REs, and developers learn about the product and its implementation. New technologies and tools can also be learned as needed to implement the prototypes.

- **Decide as early as possible** Make certain that prototyping is concentrated on a concrete example. Decisions that focus the prototyping progress can thus be made incrementally, possibly on one important feature at a time. If the implementation of a particular feature solution fails, backtrack as quickly as possible. When prototyping, we have the opportunity to implement features in multiple ways, in order to verify which is better.

- **Deliver as fast as possible** Don't wait for customers or users to ask for results, but proactively elicit their feedback based on one or multiple prototype versions. Deliver intermediate results as soon as a sufficient difference is visible, and don't wait to implement a complete solution. Prototype development iterations should be very short; e.g., much shorter than the one-month iterations typically used for product development with Scrum.

- **Empower the team** Don't spend time defining formal roles or processes, predefined representations, or document formats. Keep the prototyping team and key stakeholders small in number, and collocate everyone in one work area if possible. Allow the team to customize the interactions and artifacts or reuse standard models or solutions for the problem at hand. Stakeholders have very little direct control over the prototyping process and progress. But, if they have clear and frequent transparency into the prototyping progress, they can evaluate whether progress is being made. Stakeholders can also determine if prototyping specific aspects of the system requirements is valuable, or whether the efforts should be directed elsewhere to other features. Staff the team with experienced cross-functional experts and encourage collaboration at the lowest granularity level.

- **Trade off reuse requirements with prototype speed**   Do not over-engineer the prototypes, either for evolutionary purposes or for maintainability. In many cases, a copy-paste approach works well enough to enable requirements elicitation and evaluation. But, developers are always free to define reusable components if they expect them to improve the effectiveness of the prototyping process; for example, when a large number of related prototypes are being considered.

- **Develop bottom-up**   Implement the parts, and then understand how they combine into the whole. The primary goal of rapid prototyping is to create a sufficiently unambiguous representation that will allow the stakeholders and developers to eventually better understand the whole picture. If the whole is understood at the start, then prototyping for requirements elicitation is not needed.

9.5   Summary

Product requirements that are unclear or are highly user-visible can be quickly developed and visualized with a storyboard paired with a running system prototype. Improved stakeholder communications centered on the prototype will result in more rapid elicitation and validation of product requirements. Highly concurrent work and rapid feedback keep the entire small team engaged and focused until the requirements are better understood, correct, and unambiguous.

9.6   Discussion Questions

1. When should working prototypes be implemented as compared to non-coding-based approaches such as storyboards?

2. Under which conditions should one consider reusing prototype code for the product development as compared to throwaway prototypes?

3. How frequently should iterations of prototype feature development and review occur?

4. When is the best time to stop prototyping and move on to full-scale product development?

References

Beck, K., *Test-Driven Development: By Example*, Addison-Wesley, Boston, MA, 2002.
Berry, D., Kamsties, E., and Krieger M., "From Contract Drafting to Software Specification: Linguistic Sources of Ambiguity," University of Waterloo, 2003.

Gunaratne, J., Hwong, B., Nelson, C., and Rudorfer, A., "Using Evolutionary Prototypes to Formalize Product Requirements," *Proceedings of the Workshop on Bridging the Gaps II: Bridging the Gaps Between Software Engineering and Human-Computer Interaction*, ICSE 2004, Edinburgh, Scotland, May 2004.

Hofmeister, C., Nord, R., and Soni, D., *Applied Software Architecture*, Addison-Wesley, Boston, MA, 2000.

Hwong, B., Laurance, D., Rudorfer, A., and Song, X., "User-Centered Design and Agile Software Development Processes," *Proceedings of the Workshop on Bridging Gaps Between HCI and Software Engineering and Design, and Boundary Objects to Bridge Them*, 2004 Human Factors in Computing Systems Conference, Vienna, Austria, April 2004.

Jones, C., *Applied Software Measurement*, McGraw-Hill, New York, 2008.

Matos, G., "Use of Requirement Stability in Optimizing Iterative Development Processes," *Proceedings of ENASE 2007, 2nd International Working Conference on Evaluation of Novel Approaches to Software Engineering*, Barcelona, Spain, July 2007.

Nikolova, G., "Reference Process Definition for Agile Development with S-RaP," Master's thesis, Technical University of Munich, January 2006.

Paulish, D., *Architecture-Centric Software Project Management*, Addison-Wesley, Boston, MA, 2002.

Poppendieck, M., and Poppendieck, T., *Lean Software Development*, Addison-Wesley, Boston, MA, 2003.

Sangwan, R., Bass, M., Mullick, N., Paulish, D., and Kazmeier, J., *Global Software Development Handbook*, Auerbach Publications, New York, 2007.

Schwaber, K. and Beedle, M., *Agile Software Development with Scrum*, Prentice-Hall, Upper Saddle River, NJ, 2001.

Schwaber, K., *Agile Project Management with Scrum*, Microsoft Press, Redmond, WA, 2004.

Song, X., Matos, G., Hwong, B., Rudorfer, A., and Nelson, C., "People & Project Management Issues in Highly Time-Pressured Rapid Development Projects," *Proceedings of the EuroSun 2004 Conference*, Cologne, Germany, November 2004.

Song, X., Matos, G., Hwong, B., Rudorfer, A., and Nelson, C., "S-RaP: A Concurrent Prototyping Process for Refining Workflow-Oriented Requirements," *Proceedings of the 13th IEEE International Conference on Requirements Engineering*, IEEE Conference Publishing Services, August 2005, pp. 416–420.

Verner, J., Cox, K., Bleinstein, S., and Cerpa, N., "Requirements Engineering and Software Project Success: An Industrial Survey in Australia and the U.S.," *9th Australian Workshop on Requirements Engineering*, 2004.

## CHAPTER 10

Distributed Requirements Engineering

by Daniel Paulish, Hans Ros

Paul just learned that his next assignment would be requirements analysis for a large transportation system project with a high-profile customer. He knew that there were already a few thousand requested features in the requirements management database, and it was still growing. What was unique about this project is that the requirements engineers with whom Paul would be working were located at different offices around the world in so-called "competence centers." For Paul's new project, he was expected to work with established groups of requirements engineers, some of which were located far away from his workplace, specifically in India, China, Slovakia, Hungary, and Brazil. He had never met any of these remote requirements engineers. Paul was understandably apprehensive about how he would efficiently collaborate with these remote requirements engineers, stakeholders, and domain experts. He was relieved to read that the existing features were described in English, and that the customer was located in his city. He suspected that he would be doing much traveling for this project, and he checked his personal calendar for the next few months.

This chapter deals with requirements engineering for globally distributed projects. It discusses some of the organizational and technical issues involved with doing global development. It describes techniques that have been successfully used to elicit and analyze requirements across multiple locations and manage the requirements after the elicitation phase is over.

10.1 Background

Coordination and control become more difficult due to distance, time zones, and cultural differences as development project teams are geographically distributed. Some tasks can be distributed among collaborating staff located far away from each other, but some tasks are better done locally at a single site or with staff sitting together in one room. An everyday example is plumbing. If you have a water pipe leak in your house located in the United States, you do not want to call someone from Bangalore, India, to repair it. You prefer to work with someone local who can get to your house quickly to stop the flooding and restore your water service with repaired pipes.

The initial motivation for software companies to outsource work was to reduce development costs. Managers realized that software engineers living in countries such as India, China and Slovakia were paid less than engineers living in the United States. Since software engineering is a labor-intensive activity, in theory it should cost less to develop products using engineers in lower-cost countries. However, our experience has shown that labor cost savings can often be offset by the learning curve costs for a new remote team to develop know-how about the applications domain and by the coordination and communication overhead costs [Sangwan et al. 2007]. Thus, we encourage such companies to plan their projects for the long term to be able to realize any cost savings after domain competence is developed at the low-cost sites.

As computing speed has been enhanced and memory costs have decreased, the trend has been to add more features to a product through software. Therefore, development team sizes are growing to be able to develop large systems with increasing feature content within a reasonable time-to-market. Large teams may not be available at a single development site, and the necessary domain expertise may likely reside at many sites around the world. Thus, most new projects today to develop large systems are staffed with engineers from around the world.

Development work that is being done by distributed teams creates new challenges for project managers. An example of a software and systems engineering task that is best done by a small collocated team is architecture design. System architects do much of their creative work while discussing possible design tradeoffs by drawing proposed design diagrams on a white board, and then discussing and modifying the design until it is stable enough to be documented within an architecture design document (ADD) [Clements et al. 2003]. For example, using an *extended workbench model* for distributed development, a small architecture team is part of a central organization with members assigned full-time from both local and remote sites [Sangwan et al. 2007]. The team operates as a project, with a chief architect as its leader and a project manager responsible for the entire product life cycle. Furthermore, these central team architecture design tasks are staffed with some members of the future remote development teams, who have temporarily relocated to work at the central site. Ideally, the time spent at the central site (e.g., six months) is used to "train" the future remote team member on the application domain, architecture, tools, and processes that will be used during the development. These team members will hopefully become leaders of the remote development teams upon returning to their home sites. The design artifacts created by the central architecture team will be given to the remote teams for them to understand the architecture of the system that they will be developing.

Ideally, requirements engineering like architecture design is best done by a small collocated team. However, requirements engineers must either have personal application domain expertise or have access to such subject matter experts. For large, complex systems, it is not very likely that all the domain experts necessary to define a product or product line will be living in the same city. Thus, requirements engineering processes for distributed projects must recreate the highly interactive and efficient communications of, say, the architecture design team gathered around the white board.

10.2   Requirements Engineering for Global Projects

Requirements engineering for distributed projects requires enhanced processes in two primary areas as compared to collocated projects.

- **Higher-quality artifacts** On distributed projects, many engineers will learn about the requirements for the system they are building from reading functional and other specifications. Thus, the artifacts generated from the RE process must be readable and understandable. Remote team members will not be able, as easily as in collocated projects, to ask for clarification from the domain experts that defined the requirements. For such projects, models will likely be used to describe the requirements, since some team members may not be able to easily read long specifications written in English, if their English language skills are limited. Defects introduced in requirements engineering may not be so easily discovered by remote teams working on downstream processes. When remote teams with limited domain know-how develop the product code, they may implement exactly what is described in the functional specification even though it may be incorrectly specified.

- **Improved collaborations** On distributed projects, REs may not have the possibility for quick response communications and casual communications with distant REs. In fact, an RE working at one site may be working while another RE at a different site in a different time zone is sleeping. An example common situation is that RE A has a question about a requirement that was defined by RE B at another site. RE A e-mails his question to RE B, who is sleeping while RE A is working. RE B comes to work the next day and answers the question by e-mail when RE A is sleeping. With such asynchronous communications, one can see how responses to questions can take substantial time before the requesting engineer receives an answer to proceed with her work, thus disrupting the overall workflow. Although REs in distributed sites will adjust their work hours to allow some workday overlap, we have noticed that most REs prefer to sleep when it's dark. Thus, collaboration tools are used to reduce the response times between question and answer communications, as well as to persist the communications content so that questions and answers (e.g., decisions) are not lost in a stack of e-mail messages.

10.3   Organizations for Distributed Projects

Good communications are important for good requirements engineering. In a large survey among professionals on their experiences with distributed development, communication, particularly face-to-face meetings, was frequently mentioned as a solution to diverse RE problems [Illes-Seifert et al. 2007]. We have observed that project managers for globally distributed projects will often carefully monitor their travel costs [Sangwan et al. 2007]. When there's an unexpected increase in travel between two development sites, it's often a good indicator that there is some type of project problem involving the two sites.

Project managers can use many organizational structures for doing requirements engineering across multiple development sites. Some of the project organizational approaches that could be considered include organizing by product structure, process steps, release, competence center, and open source. In a *product structure* organizational approach, the requirements engineers and architects allocate features to components and the components are allocated as work packages to the different sites. In a *process steps* structure, work is allocated across the sites in accordance with the phases of the development process; e.g., requirements engineering may be done at one site, development at another site(s), and testing at yet another site. In a *release*-based organization approach, the first product release is developed at one site, the second at another site, etc. Often, the releases will be overlapped to meet time-to-market goals; e.g., one site is testing the next release, another site is developing a later release, and yet another site is defining the requirements for an even later release. In a *platform* structure (see Chapter 6), one site may be developing reusable core assets of the product line and other sites may be developing application-level software that uses the platform. In a *competence center* organizational approach, project work is allocated to sites according to the technical or domain expertise located at a given site. For example, perhaps all user interface design is done at a site where usability engineering experts are located with experience designing similar products. In an *open source* structure, many independent contributors develop a software product in accordance with a technical integration strategy. Centralized control is minimal except when an independent contributor integrates his code into the product line. These organizational approaches may change over time. For example, components may be allocated at first with the intent that the remote site will develop the skills over time to become a competence center in the functionality that component provides [Avritzer et al. 2008].

We will illustrate two example organizations that were used on the Global Studio Project (GSP). During the first two years of the GSP, a product structure approach was used to organize the project and an extended workbench model development process was used [Sangwan et al. 2007]. This resulted in a hub-and-spoke organizational structure (Figure 10.1) where the remote component development teams communicated mostly with the central team roles (e.g., chief requirements engineer, chief architect, project manager) at the headquarters or central site.

Requirements information is transferred from the central team to each remote component development team in the form of models and specifications. The documentation package is used to help communicate to the remote teams the work that will be done in accordance with the development plan. The work to be done is scoped to be implemented by a relatively small component development team (maximum of ten engineers). The roles of the development team members are multifunctional, including domain, design, development, and testing expertise. Thus, with the extended workbench model, requirements definition and analysis are done by the central team at a single site; however, domain expertise is developed over time at the remote sites. One way to build up this remote domain expertise is to have the requirements engineers at the remote sites work as temporary members of the central site's RE team and then serve as the domain experts in the remote team.

This hub-and-spoke organization is typically used when a central organization is utilizing remote development sites for the first time. It often will take a year or more to be able to develop the domain expertise, RE, and development skills in the staff in the remote teams. Thus, the central team transfers some of their know-how to the remote teams over time such that they are able to take on a bigger role in the development project. We recommend to organizations starting distributed development for the first time to take a long-term view, since there will be a substantial learning curve time necessary for the remote teams to become productive contributors to the development project.

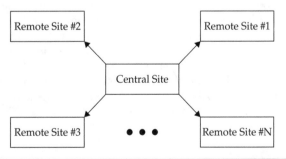

Figure 10.1 Example extended workbench model global development organization

Using the extended workbench model approach, the overall project RE organization will consist of experts in remote development teams that will fit within the organizational structure of their local company and report to a central team made up of experienced REs. The remote teams *supply* software components and other artifacts to the central team, who use them to build a product. Thus, over time, with an exchange of technical artifacts and staff, the remote team may become a *competence center* of the central organization. Over time, the remote organization will develop more applications for the central organization and become increasingly more involved in early-phase RE and other activities. For such a relationship to be successful over time, we recommend the exchange of staff as short- or long-term delegates between the central and remote sites. For any organization, but especially for ones crossing national and geographic boundaries, its success will depend on the trust among peers and their reporting relationships. Such trust across, up, and down the organization can only be built up over time and is based upon personal interactions. Given the current state of software engineering practice, we doubt that an approach where requirements specifications are sent to a remote site and the central team waits for the code to be delivered back to them without ongoing communication will be successful [Herbsleb et al. 2005].

Figure 10.2 gives an example organization showing the relationship between the central and remote teams for an extended workbench model. The project manager has the overall responsibility for the life cycle of product development. The chief requirements engineer is the head of the RE team and also has overall responsibility for technical decisions affecting the product's functionality and performance. The members of the remote component development teams report to a local R&D resource manager at their site. The remote teams report to the project manager at the central location, primarily through their assigned supplier manager, who serves as a bridge between the sites.

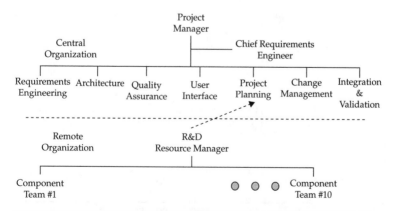

FIGURE 10.2   Relationship between central and remote teams

It may be valuable for sites to share best practices information as experience is obtained. This could be helpful to bring on new teams or for teams to learn about processes used by other teams. However, this should be initiated carefully over time, since the various sites may initially be viewed as competitors of each other until the competence centers build up their unique expertise and trust is established. An example process description summary for an extended workbench model is given in Figure 10.3.

During the third and fourth years (versions 3.0–4.0) of the Global Studio Project, a *system of systems* approach was used for distributed development [Avritzer et al. 2008]. With this approach, the software development process is still defined and managed centrally, but the architecture and requirements engineering teams are extended with key domain experts resident at the remote sites. Specialized domain knowledge drives the overall requirements and software architecture specification efforts as early phase activities. Frequent communication between the central and remote teams and

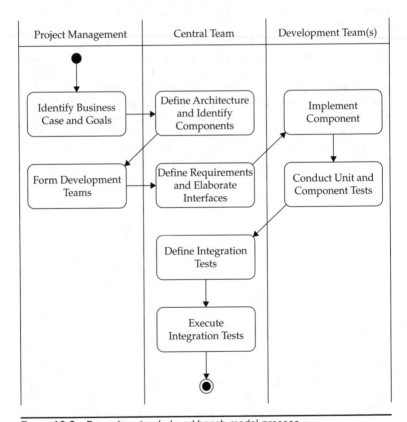

FIGURE 10.3   Example extended workbench model process

among the remote teams is encouraged. Unlike the extended workbench model approach, this approach does not require the central team to coordinate the communications among the distributed teams.

The GSP version 3.0–4.0 project team was organized as a central coordinating team, a distributed requirements engineering/ architecture team, several remote development teams, and a remote integration testing team. The central coordinating team was responsible for product identification and assignment of components to the distributed development teams. An example process description summary for a system of systems model is given in Figure 10.4.

For GSP versions 3.0–4.0, more of an open source approach was used as compared to GSP versions 1.0–2.0, with competence centers located at the remote sites. The system of systems approach worked well for a project of the size of the GSP and with staff from similar cultures. The extended workbench model with its hub and spoke organization is difficult to scale for very large projects, since as the project gets larger, the central team requirements engineers can often become overloaded with communications from the remote teams. As the central team requirements engineers must answer all functionality and performance questions from the remote development teams, they can quickly be viewed as communication bottlenecks. Thus, distributing RE expertise to remote sites seems to help optimize communications for very large projects. However, for many RE tasks

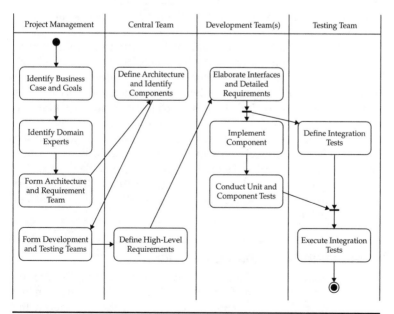

Figure 10.4 Example system of systems model

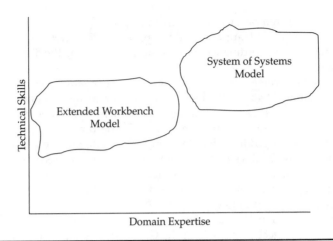

Figure 10.5 Extended workbench vs. system of systems models

such as definition, review, and analysis, collocated RE teams perform best. In the real world, the lack of collocation is compensated for by bringing the distributed REs together periodically for RE workshops and reviews and encouraging personal networking among them to build a "virtual RE team."

Many practices are used to make such RE workshops and reviews more efficient. For the case of REs coming together from different parts of the world, jet lag can be a major concern. One practice to combat jet lag is to collocate the RE team for three weeks at a time, and then they have two weeks at their home work site to work individually on documentation and catch up with their obligations to their local development team. We have been told by traveling REs that the 3/2 week schedule is preferable to the more common practice where a weekly RE workshop is held every month. In this case, REs can lose efficiency as their bodies must more frequently adjust to different time zones.

Figure 10.5 compares the extended workbench model with the system of systems model. In practice, central organizations working with a remote development site for the first time will likely apply the extended workbench model and then migrate to the system of systems model as the domain and technical expertise of the remote site team members increases.

10.4   Managing Distributed RE Efforts

Perhaps the most critical roles on any development project are the project manager, the chief architect, and the chief requirements engineer. The chief requirements engineer is concerned about the various technical requirements of the project, the chief architect is concerned about the design parts, and the project manager is concerned about the project management parts, e.g., schedules, budget, organization, staffing, status. For global development projects, the project manager, chief architect, and chief requirements engineer must make decisions for a team that is geographically distributed and not under their direct control. Thus, in addition to the usual required management and technical skills, they must be able to work effectively with staff from differing company and country cultures. Their communication skills will be stretched as they attempt to lead and interact with staff whom they may have never met and who may have performance incentives different than their own. We recommend that staff assigned to these roles for global projects have intercultural experience or are given intercultural sensitivity training early in the project. Furthermore, they will need to be flexible and adaptable as projects progress and as status changes due to events beyond their control; for example, political conditions in the countries where their development teams are located [Sangwan et al. 2007].

The best practices used in distributed RE projects are often similar to those used in large projects. RE and design artifacts must be high quality, since the author of a specification may not be so easily accessible to answer questions from the readers (users) of the specification. High-quality artifacts will likely have a review process associated with them such that stakeholders and technical experts can review the documents before they are distributed to a large group of distributed engineers.

In general, large, complex projects are made more manageable by breaking them into smaller projects. Thus, distributed software projects are often planned as development iterations made up of monthly sprints. The features to be implemented for each sprint are planned centrally using a build plan. Using techniques such as Scrum [Schwaber 2004], project plans can be communicated at a high level and then detailed planning can be done by each component team for each sprint. Delivery dates are fixed, but there will be some feature migration between sprints. Such techniques tend to focus the development on a small subset of features each month and build development discipline within the teams. With a fixed, one-month time period to develop a set of features, there is much effort to prioritize the features and focus on getting an operational system working by the end of each month. With such techniques, the feature content is developed a little at a time with more visible progress than if all the features are integrated at the end of the development project.

10.5   Requirements and Collaboration Tools

For large or distributed projects, the use of a requirements management tool (e.g., Teamcenter) is required. Such tools typically have a collaboration feature with which engineers distributed around the world can view and edit the requirements in the database using a user interface of the web browser client type.

Scrum teams will likely conduct daily stand-up meetings to help coordinate the activities within the team. These short meetings typically address the three questions: What have you done? What do you plan to do? And is there anything standing in the way of making progress? For global development we recommend a weekly coordination teleconference facilitated by the product or project manager with a representative from each component development team, called a "scrum of scrums." The audio portion of the weekly teleconference can be augmented with a desktop sharing tool so that presentation charts, diagrams, or documents could be viewed by all the participants.

We recommend using videoconferences for "special" meetings. These would include iteration kickoff meetings, review meetings, or meetings where technical documentation is exchanged or discussed between the central team and a remote team. Since the videoconference equipment is usually a shared resource, these meetings would likely be scheduled in advance. In contrast, the weekly teleconference would be scheduled for the same time slot each workweek. If staff members are not at their workplace during the fixed time slot, they can call into the teleconference. When participants are not available due to vacation or illness, they should assign a proxy to participate in the weekly scrum of scrums meeting.

Although we prefer that some members of the central team be present at the iteration kickoff meeting at the remote sites, clearly for large projects with many remote teams, this is not possible. In this case, we recommend that videoconferencing be used. We also recommend that, whenever possible, central team members visit some of the remote sites to review the sprint deliverables. Again, this is probably not possible for every sprint for every site, but we have observed that periodic contact between the remote and central teams is valuable for motivating all the team members.

Many of the communications between the central and remote teams will necessarily be in the form of e-mail. This is particularly likely between sites, for example, in the U.S. and India when one team is likely to be working while the other team is sleeping. It is suggested that a secure intranet and virtual private networks be set up for such e-mails and development tools. This will provide some degree of protection for your proprietary project communications and artifacts.

We recommend that a collaboration web site (e.g., wiki) be set up for all team members to view decisions made on the project, store key documents, and support asynchronous discussions (e.g., forums). This collaboration site should also contain the tool set that will be used on the project and relevant training information. Although we have no problem with differing processes used at different development sites, we stress the importance of using a common tool set across the project. For example, we wouldn't want different teams to use different requirements management databases or change management tools during the project.

The collaboration web site would also link into the development site. Here, team members would be able to, for software projects, submit code to a build, run regression tests, and generate release notes describing which features are implemented in each version of the software. For such projects, we recommend continuous integration techniques. Ideally, anyone on the project should be able to view the current status of the development by running the current or most recent build.

Another area where telephone and video communications may be helpful is in recruiting and interviewing remote team members. We recommend that at the beginning of a new project, the central team should interview candidates and select the key staff who will be assigned to the remote team. Depending on the size of the project, this may not be possible, but all key staff should be interviewed and selected. This would include the requirements engineers who would work periodically with the central requirements engineering team, but who would eventually become the domain experts at their development site. The working language of the project should be selected, and central staff should determine if the language and technical skills of the remote staff are adequate for effective technical communications via telephone. These interviews may be group or one to one. Sometimes, the remote person's manager may be included in the interview as an observer. The advantage of this is that the remote resource manager will get insights into the desired skills that the central team is seeking for the remote development teams. The central team should be aware of any cultural issues that may arise; e.g., what happens to a remote site employee who interviews but is not selected for the distributed project? Over time, when there is a good working relationship and common understanding between the central team and the remote resource managers, staffing decisions can be delegated more to the remote sites.

10.6   Communications, Culture, and Team Size

As you have seen, for distributed projects distance and time zones can make communications among requirements engineers, stakeholders, and other team members more difficult. The informal "water cooler" communications are lost when team members are located at different sites. Thus, these lost communications must be compensated for with better specifications, collaboration tools, and periodic face-to-face meetings.

Intercultural and language differences can also hinder effective communications among REs. Requirements may have to be described in written and oral forms, including using models (e.g., described in UML) that everybody on the team understands. Remote engineers may be asked to develop features for products with which they have no personal experience; e.g., for new automobiles being introduced into local markets where that model has never been sold. Work habits, educational backgrounds, and value systems will vary among the REs working at distributed sites. Central site REs will need to have some understanding of cultural differences to be able to effectively work with remote REs residing in other countries.

Team size is a concern not only for a distributed project but for any project that has more than a few team members. As the team size gets larger, there are more communication paths among the team members. Thus, adding people to a project may be a way to get more work done, but individual productivity will decrease as team members have more people who they will need to communicate with to accomplish their work. For very large projects, some team members (e.g., supplier managers) are likely spending most of their time communicating and little time on developing project artifacts. Ideally, project managers recognize this negative productivity impact and strive to keep their development teams as small as possible. However, there is great pressure to bring new products to market quickly, and most project teams likely will be larger than desirable. One solution to this problem is to break the project work into pieces that can each be done by a small team and then have another team integrate the pieces. The resulting organization is a collection of small teams that communicate with each other for predefined reasons or have specialists who do the communicating. Drawing on our experience with large projects, we recommend the rules of thumb that no individual team be larger than ten members, and the team members have their workplaces within 50 meters of each other [Allen 1984]. Furthermore, each team should have a work or conference room in which they can all fit for joint work tasks or stand-up meetings.

10.7   RE with OEMs and Suppliers

Requirements are often developed by a central team that must transfer the feature information as specifications, models, or verbal communications to a remote organization that develops the features and delivers the resulting product component to the central team or a third party. Thus, the RE processes used for dealing with suppliers and OEMs are very similar to those generally used for distributed development. That is, the requirements artifacts must be higher quality and more formal than for a project where the engineers are sitting within 50 meters of the REs and stakeholders working for the same company.

There are competitive situations where the central team may be looking for the "lowest-cost" supplier or evaluations of the suppliers' competencies. For distributed development, we have found that a remote development organization working in a domain for the first time has a difficult time generating a realistic estimate of the cost and schedule to develop the requested functionality. Thus, we recommend that the central organization do their own cost estimates as they would if they were developing the features using their experience with past similar projects. These internal estimates can be used to "validate" the estimates received from the suppliers. In such situations, we have observed that the "lowest-cost" supplier may indeed be the "most naïve" supplier. As domain expertise requires the longest learning curve for a new supplier, selections of vendors should be primarily driven by domain experience or the ability to learn a new or related domain. Cost and schedule estimation methods can be found in [Jones 2007]. Cost and schedule estimation methods for globally distributed projects can be found in [Sangwan et al. 2007].

10.8   Tips for Distributed Requirements Engineering

The following tips are suggested for distributed requirements engineering:

- Plan your distributed projects for the long term to be able to realize any cost savings after domain competence is developed at the low-cost sites.

- Staff your RE team with some members of the remote development teams, who have temporarily relocated to work at the central site. These team members will become the domain experts at the remote sites.

- Begin a new project with a new remote team using a process like the extended workbench model, and then migrate to more of a system of systems model as the domain and technical know-how of the remote teams is developed.

- Monitor your travel costs as an early indicator that a problem may be developing across two sites.

- Exchange staff as short- or long-term delegates between the central and remote sites.

- Bring the distributed REs together periodically for RE workshops and reviews and encourage personal networking among them to build a "virtual RE team."

- To combat jet lag, collocate the distributed RE team for three weeks at a time, and then allow them two weeks at their home work site to work individually on documentation and catch up with their obligations to their local development team.

- Provide intercultural sensitivity training to team members early in the project.

- Set up a collaboration web site (e.g., wiki) for all team members to view decisions made on the project, store key documents, and support asynchronous discussions (e.g., forums).

- In the beginning of a new project, the central team should interview candidates and select the key RE staff who will be assigned to the remote teams.

- No individual team should be larger than ten members, and team members should have their work places within 50 meters of each other.

10.9   Summary

Distributed projects must compensate for the large communication paths from the central team requirements engineers to distant teams. Requirements engineering is most efficiently done by a small team located at a single site, but today's need to rapidly develop new products will require that teams collaborate with each other across national boundaries. You will likely view the relationships with your suppliers as long term, where over time they become extensions to your own organization and build up similar or complementary domain expertise.

10.10   Discussion Questions

1. How long should one expect the learning curve time to be for a remote team to become productive working in a new domain?

2. What are some of the intercultural communications problems that may arise on a globally distributed project?

3. What kinds of "soft skills" must requirements engineers have to effectively work on distributed projects?

4. How might the requirements engineering artifacts differ for distributed projects as compared to collocated projects?

References

Allen, T., *Managing the Flow of Technology: Technology Transfer and the Dissemination of Technological Information within the R&D Organization*, MIT Press, Cambridge, MA, 1984.

Avritzer, A., Cai, Y., and Paulish, D., "Coordination Implications of Software Architecture in a Global Software Development Project," *Proceedings of WICSA 2008*, 2008.

Clements, P., Bachmann, F., Bass, L., Garlan, D., Ivers, J., Little, R., Nord, R., and Stafford, J., *Documenting Software Architectures Views and Beyond*, Addison-Wesley, Boston, 2003.

Herbsleb, J., Paulish, D., and Bass, M., "Global Software Development at Siemens: Experience from Nine Projects," *Proceedings of the International Conference on Software Engineering (ICSE 2005)*, 2005, pp. 524–533.

Illes-Seifert, T., Herrmann, A., Geisser, M., and Hildenbrand, T., "The Challenges of Distributed Software Engineering and Requirements Engineering: Results of an Online Survey," *Proceedings of GREW '07*, 2007, pp. 55–66.

Jones, C., *Estimating Software Costs*, McGraw-Hill, New York, NY, 2007.

Sangwan, R., Bass, M., Mullick, N., Paulish, D., and Kazmeier, J., *Global Software Development Handbook*, Auerbach, New York, NY, 2007.

Schwaber, K., *Agile Project Management with Scrum*, Microsoft Press, Redmond, WA, 2004.

## CHAPTER 11

Hazard Analysis and Threat Modeling

by Brian Berenbach

eems like it is based on the assumption that this hypothetical user with no experience will somehow have access to a body of knowledge about the applications, users, and environment that they gloss over as 'already known information'—just enter it into the tool, it's that simple. Entering it into the tool is the easy part. Knowing what questions to ask, and where to go to get that information, is the hard part. OK, they probably have a template for the information gathering. In which case, you have a tool into which inexperienced people can enter information they don't understand (and might have guessed at if it's too hard to track down), in order to generate results they don't understand."—A security expert with over 20 years of experience.

This chapter describes two topics, hazard analysis (HA) and threat modeling (TM). Threat modeling is part of the broader subject of security analysis. Skill in these areas may occasionally be needed by the requirements analyst, but the topics are rarely described in basic RE texts. The role of the requirements analyst will most likely be that of integration and coordination. As hazard analysis and threat modeling are complex subjects, learned over time and performed by experts, this chapter focuses on their relationship to Model-Driven Requirements Engineering (MDRE) as well as on how to integrate their activities into traditional RE processes. For more information on HA or TM, we suggest you look at the references, or one of the many texts available on the subjects.

11.1   Hazard Analysis

Hazard analysis is performed whenever there is a potential risk to the health and safety of the user of a product. In many cases, the thoroughness and output of an analysis have to meet certain minimum standards that are domain and location specific. In the United States, for example, the Food and Drug Administration (FDA), the Federal Aviation Administration (FAA), and the U.S. Department of Transportation's Federal Transit Administration (FTA) each have guidelines for performing hazard analyses.

Terms Used in Hazard Analysis

There are certain terms that are used in hazard analysis that are common across domains. Some of the more frequently used terms[1] are defined here:

- **Hazard**   A condition, event, or circumstance that could lead to or contribute to an unplanned or undesired event.

---

[1] FAA Order 8040.4

- **Hazard analysis** Identification of a substance, activity, or condition as potentially posing a risk to human health or safety.

- **Risk assessment** The process of identifying hazards and quantifying or qualifying the degree of risk they pose for exposed individuals, populations, or resources (severity) and the likelihood that the hazard will occur (probability of occurrence). The term also refers to a document containing the explanation of how the assessment process is applied to individual activities or conditions.

- **Safety-critical system** A system that has been designated by a regulatory body as needing a hazard analysis before being put into operation.

- **Severity** The actual categorization of severity is usually domain specific. For example, the categorizations for the Food and Drug Administration (FDA) and the Federal Transit Administration (FTA) are compared in Table 11.1.

Other domains and regulatory bodies have their own definitions of terms. The reader is encouraged to review the appropriate guidelines for their specific area of concern.

Severity alone is not sufficient when analyzing a hazard, as not only is the severity important, but also the likelihood or probability of occurrence. For example, a car company manufacturing a convertible might determine that there is a risk that the vehicle might roll over, causing injury to its occupants; however, the likelihood is very low because of the vehicle handling characteristics and low center of gravity. In such a situation, after performing a *risk assessment*, a decision is made not to include a roll bar with every convertible sold.

Hazard Analysis Processes

The process of identifying hazards may be different for different domains. Regardless of domain, the basic steps are the same (see

Type of Hazard	FDA Classification	FTA Classification
Potential for death	Major	Category I
Potential for serious injury	Major	Category II
Potential for minor injury	Moderate	Category III
Design flaws are unlikely to cause injury	Minor	Category IV

TABLE 11.1 Comparison of FDA and FTA Categorizations of Risk

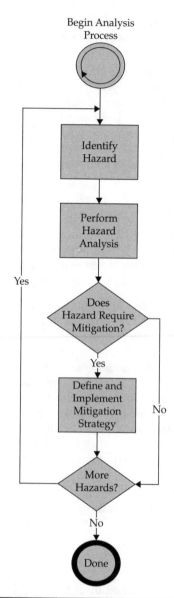

FIGURE 11.1 Hazard analysis

Figure 11.1). When a hazard analysis is performed in the context of requirements elicitation and analysis processes, all the processes must be tightly integrated. The level of integration is often dictated by regulation, usually requiring traceability.

Requirements in a domain considered safety critical need to have special attributes so that they can be mined for metrics. These are some of the attributes:

- Is the requirement part of a safety-critical system?

- Has this requirement been checked to see if a hazard analysis needs to be performed?

- If so, is the requirement associated with a hazard analysis (hyperlink to hazard analysis)?

- Does the requirement need mitigation (traces to mitigating requirements)?

The attributes should be filled out at the appropriate level so that a query will provide valid metrics. The attributes are usually associated with the highest level requirement associated with the hazard. Typical metrics that might be associated with hazard analysis for a product or system are shown in Table 11.2.

Note that the metrics shown in Table 11.2 rely on the assignment of levels to requirements, and level-sensitive queries to return metrics. We know from the requirements pyramid that there is an explosion of lower-level system requirements from higher-level customer requirements, both functional and nonfunctional. Conducting a hazard analysis at the wrong level might result in either overlooking potential hazards or an overwhelming amount of effort needed.

The maturity of organizations' RE processes can have an impact on the effort to conduct a hazard analysis. Consider two situations

Metric	How Calculated	Interpretation
% of requirements checked for a potential hazard	Total requirements at designated level vs. requirements checked at that level	This metric provides an estimate of the amount of work necessary to complete the hazard analysis. It also provides an indication of how stable the system architecture is. If the ratio is low, any architecture may need to be changed significantly to support mitigating functional or nonfunctional requirements.
% of requirements that need a mitigation	% of requirements at designated level that have been identified as needing mitigation	The higher this number is, the greater the potential risk of building the product or system. A high percent of requirements needing mitigation may be an indication of an unsafe design.

TABLE 11.2   Sample Hazard Analysis Metrics

(from our experience), where situation #1 is a positive situation and situation #2 is a negative situation. The two situations illustrate the differences between well-organized and poorly organized requirements necessary to conduct a hazard analysis. In situation #1, the requirements are well organized, let's say in three levels: business requirements, customer requirements, and system requirements. The traces between the requirements exist and are correct, and the customer requirements are tied to a preliminary architecture. We assume a ratio of 1:10 between the customer requirements and the system requirements (often, the ratio is higher). This means, ten system requirements exist for each customer requirement. Let's assume there are 500 customer requirements. This would mean we have 5000 system requirements. For a hazard analysis, we would need to analyze the 500 customer requirements. If we assume that the analysis of each customer requirement requires 1 person hour, it would require 500 person hours.

In situation #2, we assume poorly organized requirements; e.g., requirements are not organized in levels and are listed randomly. Traces do not exist, and only some requirements are tied to a preliminary architecture. In this situation, we need to analyze all 5500 requirements because we do not know which of the requirements belong to which level. Applying the previous assumptions, it might take 5500 person hours in this case to determine which requirements need to be analyzed for hazards.

Reflecting Actions into the Requirements Database

Hazard analysis activities are "reflected" in a database whenever mitigating action is required (see Figure 11.2). In Figure 11.3, an analysis has resulted in identification of risk, justifying the addition of new requirements. For example, a train door might close on a passenger,

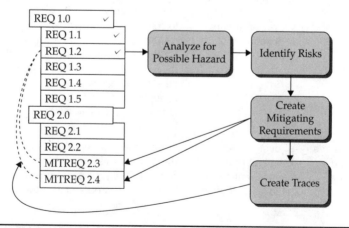

FIGURE 11.2 Mitigation "reflection" in requirements management

Example Quality Assurance Script for Hazard Analysis Reviews

A quality assurance script to ensure compliance with regulatory requirements might read as follows:

Loop for each requirement in the database

Does the requirement have a hazard associated with it? If the requirement has a hazard associated with it, is the risk severe enough to warrant mitigation? If the risk is severe enough to warrant mitigation, then does the requirement trace to complementary mitigating requirements? If not, then add the requirement that appears not to have been mitigated to a published list of requirements requiring further investigation.

Loop End

resulting in injury, and to prevent that from happening, requirements are added to the database to ensure that sensors in the door detect resistance and prevent closure on the passenger. The reflection process is then completed by creating traces from the hazard requiring mitigation to the mitigating requirement.

Hazard Analysis and MDRE

Extending a modeling tool to support hazard analysis helps support performing visual inspections and conducting reviews. Furthermore, any traces in the model are intrinsic to the relationships. An example is shown in Figure 11.4 of an X-ray machine use case, along with potential hazards and mitigating requirements. Note that the symbols used to indicate hazards can be domain specific, e.g., radiation, toxic material, biohazard, high voltage, and so on. The use of domain-specific symbols helps to move the analysis effort from the analyst's domain into the subject matter expert's or customer's domain, enabling client and expert reviews (see Chapter 4).

Requirement	Hazard Analysis Completed	Requires Mitigating Requirements	Mitigating Requirement	Is a Mitigating Requirement	Mitigates	
REQ103.7 Door closes on Engineer signal	Yes	Yes	REQ101.5 REQ103.7.1 REQ103.10.3	No		
REQ101.5 Door sensor to detect obstruction in door	Yes	No		Yes	REQ103.7	Door Close Hazard Analysis

FIGURE 11.3   Database attributes supporting hazard analysis

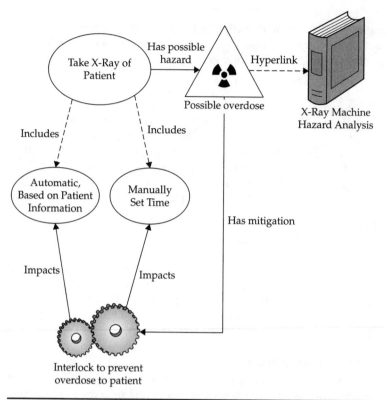

FIGURE 11.4   Example use case with hazards and mitigating requirements

When extending any process model to support hazard analysis, some new symbols and relationships are needed. Some suggested extensions to the modeling tool used for analysis are described in Table 11.3.

Importance of Hazard Analyses

Hazard analyses are sufficiently important that they are mandated by regulatory agencies in various domains. Furthermore, for a product to be accepted by the agency, the appropriate traces must be in place (see the section on traceability in Chapter 7) and due diligence must be performed to determine that

- Processes are in place to support hazard analyses.
- It can be proven that a full coverage check for needed hazard analyses was done.
- The analyses have been completed.
- Where necessary (high risk = f(severity, probability of occurrence)), hazards have been mitigated.

Symbol or Relationship	Description	Comment
Hazard	This is a placeholder for a hazard analysis.	When activated, would either hyperlink to a hazard analysis or open the hazard analysis if the model and analysis are in the same tool.
Mitigating requirement	Identifies a requirement is needed to mitigate the risk of a potential hazard.	The requirement could be entirely in the model or could be a placeholder for a hyperlink to the requirement in a requirements database.
Mitigates	A mitigation relationship between a hazard and a mitigating requirement.	This relationship can take the place of manually entered and maintained traces.
Impacts	An impact relationship between a mitigating requirement and another requirement.	Indicates that the mitigating requirement may constrain or otherwise impact another requirement.

TABLE 11.3   MDRE Extensions for Hazard Analysis

A Cautionary Tale

On July 12, 2006, the ceiling of a portion of a tunnel (the "Big Dig") in Boston fell on a woman's car, killing her.[2] An investigation revealed that the wrong glue had been used to fasten the ceiling panels. Each of the organizations and staff that were involved in the construction of the tunnel blamed other parties. Finally, the company that supplied the glue was charged with involuntary manslaughter.[3] As there were no traces from requirements through construction, it was not possible for project management to trace from the installation back to the correct type of glue needed (the correct glue needed was known and recorded at the start of the project). We can learn from this tragedy:

- People can be held criminally liable for failure to follow best practices.
- Hazard analysis coupled with effective trace mechanisms can potentially save lives.

---

[2] July 12, 2006, edition of the *Christian Science Monitor*.

[3] August 9, 2007, edition of the *Boston Globe*.

11.2   Threat Modeling

Threat modeling differs from hazard analysis in where in the life cycle it occurs. While hazard analysis tends to occur after a significant part of the high-level requirements analysis effort has been completed, threat modeling usually occurs in parallel with initial elicitation and analysis. Although there are many different approaches to modeling threats, the use of scenarios is very common. It is, therefore, a simple matter to extend MDRE techniques to support threat modeling. Just as hazard analysis requires experienced hazard analysts, threat modeling is best accomplished by experienced security analysts. The role of the requirements engineer is to merge the threat modeling processes into the larger requirements elicitation and analysis effort so that there are no discontinuities between analysis and threat models; e.g., full traceability and metrics are in place. Of course, the easier it is for nonexperts to understand the models, the easier it will be to conduct reviews with stakeholders.

Basic Terminology

There are just a few basic terms the requirements engineer needs to know about threat modeling:

- **Asset**   An item that needs to be protected or secured. It can be because of the potential for financial (e.g., bank account information) or personal (e.g., medical information) loss.

- **Threat**   The type of attack (e.g., service denial) that may cause a potential risk of lost, destroyed, or stolen assets.

- **Treatment**   A modification to a system that will help prevent or mitigate the effect of an attack.

Example Scenarios Where Threat Modeling Would Have Helped

"One case involved child-support payments in California, where one of the flaws in the application was updating the wrong father's records. Due to this flaw, some fathers who paid child support were not getting the payments recorded, while some other, unrelated father was falsely credited with payment. There were even a few arrests made due to this defect."

"Another case involved a financial application where a defect caused the plaintiff to have to restate prior year earnings. This caused a disruption of bank credit. Another interesting aspect of this case is that the defendant made 4 unsuccessful attempts to fix the defect. Each attempt not only left the defect in the software, but accidentally injected new defects as well! The defect was finally fixed on the 5th attempt, about 10 months after it had been reported. The point is that software can cause business damage as well as harm in a physical sense."—Capers Jones

Threat Modeling and MDRE

While the driving force behind hazard analysis is regulation and the potential for harm, the motivation for threat modeling is generally financial. (There are, of course, exceptions, such as the early release of a criminal because of corrupted data in a database where the criminal, after being freed, commits crimes.) An MDRE tool would need just a few additional symbols and relationships to support threat modeling (see Table 11.4).

Symbol or Relationship	Description	Comment
Threat	Identified threat to the user or owner of a product or system	The description can be as short as one line or as lengthy as an entire document. For external descriptions, a hyperlink would be used.
Treatment	Identifies a requirement or set of requirements that are needed to protect the asset(s) against the threat	The treatment can be as complex as a process (use case), or as simple as a single requirement. Treatments are marked with an icon and attribute that identifies them as treatments.
Attacks	A relationship between an asset and a threat	The relationship indicates that the threat applies to the specific asset.
Asset	The object that needs protecting	This is identified by an icon that indicates something of value, e.g., currency sign, pot of gold.
Avoid	A relationship between a treatment and an unwanted incident	Through the treatment, the incident can be avoided.
Impacts	An impact relationship between a treatment and another requirement	This indicates that the treatment may constrain or otherwise impact another requirement.
Unwanted Incident	The threat may be realized by an unwanted incident occurring	The incident is a use case or event.
Realized	A relationship between a threat and an unwanted incident	A threat may be realized by an unwanted incident.

TABLE 11.4   Suggested MDRE Extensions for Threat Modeling

Threat Modeling Metrics

Threat modeling metrics may be simple or complex, depending on the methodology used to perform the security analysis. Simple metrics are relatively easy to add to an MDRE model; for example, percent of use cases or features that may be associated with unwanted incidents. If this number is large, it might be indicative of a system that is inherently unsafe and needs a redesign.

11.3 Summary

In this chapter, we have shown the relationships of hazard analysis and threat modeling to requirements engineering processes. Hazard analyses take place late in the requirements analysis phase, while threat modeling should occur at an earlier point in the life cycle.

It is important to use an integrated approach to requirements engineering, hazard analysis, and threat modeling. If a seamless set of processes and artifacts are not in place, traces may break, or, even worse, not get created. When that happens, there is the potential for catastrophic consequences to customers, users, vendors, or owners of a product or system.

11.4 Discussion Questions

1. Give some examples of systems where inadequate hazard analysis can lead to potential loss of life or personal injury.

2. What types of additional tooling are necessary for threat modeling?

3. What is the difference between a hazard and a threat?

References

Burns, S., "Threat Modeling: A Process to Ensure Application Security," SANS Institute, January 5, 2005.

Ingalsbe, J., Kunimatsu, L., Mead, N., and Baeten, T., "Threat Modeling: Diving into the Deep End," *IEEE Software*, Vol. 25, No. 1, January/February 2008.

Swiderski, F. and Snyder, W., *Threat Modeling*, Microsoft Press, June 2004.

CHAPTER 12

Conclusion

by Brian Berenbach, Juergen Kazmeier, Arnold Rudorfer

Requirements engineering (RE) is only one part of a project's effort, and it can never be done in a vacuum. Life-cycle activities such as project management, quality assurance, validation, configuration management, system architecture, design, implementation, and maintenance are all important activities. RE is cross-cutting, and it helps enable each of these project areas.

The goal of this book is to discuss and share experiences from many requirements engineering projects (of different sizes, technologies, business domains, application areas) with practitioners in the field. All of the authors of this text have had significant experience in their various domains outside and within Siemens, and they have presented techniques they have personally used and are appropriate for large, real-world projects. But, also through collaborations with universities and "RE best practices sharing events," the individual experiences were checked and benchmarked against both RE theory and industrial practice. Furthermore, this book is not just about requirements engineering. Rather, it looks at how RE relates to other software and systems engineering disciplines such as architecture, testing, and validation.

In Chapter 1, we introduced some basic terminology and concepts, as well as exploring some common myths of requirements engineering. We hope that the discussion of terminology will lead to, at least within the reader's organization, a better understanding of the different types of requirements and a more uniform set of terms.

In Chapter 2, we provided the architectural foundation of requirements engineering, that is, the artifacts on which the field is based and how they can be represented with Requirements Engineering Artifact Models (REAMs). Furthermore, we also highlighted how taxonomies can be used to define and clarify the relationships between various types of requirements. In our experience, taxonomies and artifact models have proven to help support building domain-specific, useful, and scalable RE approaches.

Chapter 3 is all about eliciting and accurately capturing requirements. Some of the key takeaways are tips on how to gather requirements most effectively, how to define the right level of requirements granularity, and how to train staff members to be effective communicators when they are involved in the elicitation process.

Model-Driven Requirements Engineering (MDRE) techniques are explored in Chapter 4. These techniques, while challenging and requiring some skill on the part of the participants, offer significant benefits over the traditional textual approach. Model-driven approaches utilize graphical structures, based on syntactical and more or less formally defined semantic rules for model creation. It is possible to perform verification and validation on such models to a level that is not feasible with natural language text descriptions.

Pictures generally convey more information than text and so are easier for professionals to create and manage. Also, model views can be more easily understood by all stakeholders, and thus they facilitate more rapid and effective reviews.

The role of the system architect in requirements engineering is the management of quality attribute requirements (QARs) or nonfunctional requirements (NFRs) as discussed in Chapter 5. A key point of this chapter is that nonfunctional requirements need to be analyzed and managed by senior architectural staff to identify the architecturally significant requirements (ASRs), starting as early in a project as possible. Furthermore, the management of nonfunctional requirements needs to be fully integrated with functional requirements activities.

In Chapter 6, techniques for handling platform requirements were discussed. Since platforms can be an integral part of a large product line, we see that the handling of product line and single product requirements can differ somewhat; e.g., one can expect that requirements management for product lines will be a more challenging undertaking than for single products.

Chapter 7 dealt with requirements management and traceability. A tracing strategy is a necessary precondition for coverage, impact, and derivation analysis—the key enablers of proper change management. One major cause of project cost escalation is requirements churn, which is why effective requirements management is important for project success.

A benefit of a well-defined requirements hierarchy is a simplified test phase. Test plans must derive from requirements. A formal approach to defining requirements can result in generating sets of test cases from the requirements model. Chapter 8 describes techniques for deriving and generating test cases from UML activity diagrams, which significantly reduces the effort to produce and perform high-quality tests.

Innovative product development and user interface design often starts with fuzzy requirements. To make fuzzy requirements more concrete, there's a need for a high degree of interaction with all the stakeholders that cannot be adequately handled with visual models or textual descriptions due to high volatility and complexity. In such cases, evolutionary prototyping can be of great value for requirements visualization and analysis, as described in Chapter 9.

In today's complex product development environment, the effort is almost always done by a global project team that is spread across different sites in different countries. Distribution introduces a new set of challenges. Chapter 10 describes experiences with distributed product development and provides some best practices when eliciting and managing requirements in global projects.

An often overlooked aspect of requirements engineering is that of dealing with safety-critical and secure systems. While RE staff may not have deep expertise in this area, it is important to understand the implications of safe and secure systems (or other systems that may be in regulated domains) in terms of RE processes and artifacts. Chapter 11 discusses the relationship of hazard and safety analyses to RE artifacts, and some of the necessary extensions to the requirements management process.

In summary, excellent requirements engineering can be a unique competitive advantage for organizations, because it supports optimizing the value chain as well as delivering what the market expects. We wish you only success with your future software and systems engineering projects.

Configuring and Managing a Requirements Database

This appendix contains suggestions for creating and managing a requirements database (RDB).

A.1   Introduction

A requirements engineering database is different from a traditional relational database in that it is optimized for the storage and management of requirements. It consists of a front end component that is optimized for requirements and a back end server that is only accessible through the front end. A typical configuration is shown in Figure A.1. One possible configuration has the RE management software on the server, using a browser to access it. Another configuration, which is faster but requires that software be installed on the client, is to have a client application on the user PC accessing the database on a server. Most commercial databases support both approaches.

The unique attributes of an RE database (as contrasted with a traditional database) include

- Schema predefined to support the storage of requirements of different kinds

- Version control at the requirement (record) level, with user views of the history of a requirement

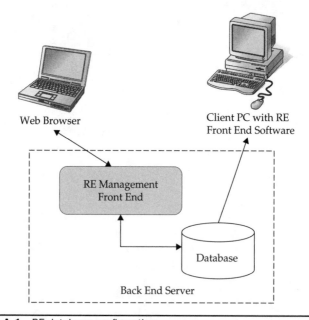

FIGURE A.1   RE database configuration

- Intrinsic support for tracing, that is, a "drag and drop" mechanism that is easy to use and supports creating traces manually between requirements

- Generation of requirements specifications and reports directly from the repository. The preferred method of working is to create and edit requirements in the database, and then to use the documentation facility of the database to create a filtered and formatted set of requirements in a requirements specification, usually as either a Word or PDF document.

Commercial requirements databases vary in terms of features, but all of them have certain core features in order to comply with corporate mandates (such as achieving a CMMI level) as well as various sets of regulations. For example, one common attribute of requirements databases is version control at the requirement level, so that changes to requirements can be audited.

Prerequisites for the Use of a Requirements Database

A requirements database is a tool to support the requirements management process. As such, requirements processes should be defined prior to the selection and installation of the RDB, keeping in mind issues of productivity, scalability, and usability. For example, not defining requirements levels when creating traces can result in a large, unusable report when generating a trace matrix. Some of the prerequisites for effective use of an RDB are described next.

Glossary of Terms

There needs to be a uniform approach to the definition of terms in order for specifications to be understood across organizations and projects. In addition, where consultants are used or implementation is outsourced, the ramp-up time is much lower if everyone understands the same term to mean the same thing. Furthermore, when outsourcing development, a standardized glossary can significantly reduce ambiguity. A glossary has other advantages in that it can enable the structuring of a requirements hierarchy (see the next heading). Multiple glossaries with a defined precedence are used where the same RDB is used for multiple organizations or projects. An example hierarchy is given in Table A.1.

If an RDB is shared across projects or organizations, it is important that there be no name collisions. The use of specific project or product logins can help to prevent that from happening by keeping project or product glossaries in separate name spaces.

Hierarchical Requirements Structure   A hierarchical requirements structure is necessary for effective use of trace and query mechanisms. With requirements decomposition resulting in an expansion of a single product feature into hundreds (or thousands) of requirements,

Type of Glossary	Description	Sample Term	Precedence (1=highest)
Corporate glossary	Standardized terms across all business organizations	Stakeholder: A corporate officer, who may be a member of the board of directors.	3
Organization glossary	Terms that are unique to a specific organization within a corporation	Stakeholder: An organization manager of rank department head or above.	2
Project or product glossary	Definitions that are customer, domain, product, or project specific	The product manager, designated customer representatives, and project management staff.	1

TABLE A.1   Example Glossary Hierarchy

a well-thought-out hierarchy is necessary to manage scale and support coverage and impact analysis. An example requirements hierarchy is shown in Table A.2.

By rigorously defining requirements levels and defining rules for traces, queries relying on trace mechanisms can be considerably more effective. For example, an impact analysis is performed to determine the cost of a change to a product feature. The feature traces to level 6 system requirements, and the system requirements trace to a specific level of design, resulting in a reduced set of objects coming back from the query, i.e., only those directly impacted by the proposed feature change. Furthermore, restricting and enforcing traces by levels increases the number of metrics available for RDB analysis.

Metrics Definition   Metrics must be defined in advance in order to configure some requirements attributes and business rules for evaluating metrics. Table A.3 shows typical metrics and their implementation in an RDB.

Requirement Type	Possible Levels	Can Trace Only to Level
Stakeholder request	1	2
Customer requirement	2–4	3
Product feature	3–5	6
System requirement	6–9	Design Component

TABLE A.2   Example Requirements Hierarchy

Metric	RDB Implementation
% Ambiguity	Ambiguity pass/fail attribute
% Modifiable	Modifiable pass/fail attribute
% Complete	Depends on level
% Traceable	Depends on level
% Feasible	Feasible pass/fail attribute

TABLE A.3   Example Metrics and Implementation

Note that since other database attributes such as the assignment of a requirement to a release are known, completeness, correctness, ambiguity, etc., for a specific specification or release can be computed once the appropriate reviews have been conducted.

A.2   RDB Basic Features

Key features for an RE database are listed here:

- All fields/attributes should be definable on a per-company or per-project basis, such that the same corporate data dictionary is used on multiple projects for consistency, but each project can still have its own glossary of terms, keywords, etc.

- At a minimum, the following requirements attributes should be available:

  - **Priority, Stability, Status, Author, Title, Category** Attributes should be user definable on a per-project basis.

  - **Keywords (note: multiple items dragged/dropped into one field)**   As the ability to do queries is of critical need, a keyword mechanism is mandatory.

  - **Requirement type (see the preceding discussion of levels)**   It should be possible to create requirements of different types with different attributes and business rules.

  - **Project-specific tags (graphics, GUI, etc.)**   It should be possible to create attributes that are project specific, so that if more than one project is stored in the same database there are no name space conflicts.

- It should be possible to have a parent-child relationship, and where there is such a relationship, it should be possible to have a parent and children of different core requirement types, for example,

FEAT101

SECRQT101.5

PERFRQT 101.3.3

Note that some commercial databases do not allow parent-child requirements to be of different types, which can increase the amount of tracing that has to be done in the database.

- The tool used shall enable end-to-end traceability, as well as vertical and horizontal traceability. This may require integration with other tools such as IDEs and/or modeling and testing tools.

For example,

- Requirement to requirement
- Requirement to test case
- Requirement to PDF
- Requirement to external document (In this case, the need is to extract a requirement from text and to drag and drop it into a new requirement; then when the requirement is selected, the document pops up with the text highlighted. This is used when extracting requirements from large, complex documents. Note that it is important to keep links from getting broken when a document is updated.)
- Bidirectional tracing to and from CASE tool artifacts (hopefully synchronized)
- What components implement this requirement? (Impact Analysis)
- What requirements caused this component to be developed? (Development QA)
- Who is implementing this requirement?
- Automatic generation of warning indicators should a trace become suspect
- Protection of critical traces with locks that prevent them from becoming suspect

- It should be possible to generate ad hoc reports based on advanced searches using combinations of the attributes; e.g., "give me all requirements where priority=high and status=approved OR subsystem=graphics".
- It should be possible to extract all detailed requirements that are approved and used to generate/update the test plan.
- It should be possible to create hyperlink references to Word documents, web sites, etc.

- It should be possible to baseline and perform change control on requirements.

- Performance should be reasonably good in a fully populated database (that is, one with several thousand requirements).

- The database should be easy to use; i.e., intuitive with minimal need to refer to documentation.

- Bidirectional dumps should be possible to and from another format such as Access and/or Excel (csv).

- It should be possible to work offline; one should be able to take requirements home, review them, change them, and roll them back into the database later.

- It should be possible to generate requirements documents automatically from the database (e.g., Functional Requirements Specification, System Requirements Specification).

- Rich text and graphics should be supported in a requirement description.

- Product line support should be available (e.g., create subsets of requirements that can be reused for different projects and products).

- It should be possible to create rich traces, that is, to attach a rationale to a trace and to define traces hierarchically.

- Global support should be available. The ability to have distributed requirements analysis is more than just the ability to have people at different locations entering requirements. It implies the ability to fold in rules to determine routing, review procedures (e.g., workflow), and scripting for user guidance and quality assurance.

A.3   RDB Advanced Features

Requirements databases can be augmented with business rules to assist in managing problems of scale. Some example advanced features are described under the headings that follow.

Automatic Upward Propagation of Attributes

Product features are fully described by successively lower levels of requirements, tending from the abstract down to the concrete. At the leaf level, every requirement is testable. We can then define a business rule, for example, that a product feature is testable only if it has level 6 requirements (see Table A.2) for each of those requirements or all its children that have been reviewed and found testable. In other words, the trace mechanisms form a tree structure, starting with the product requirement at the root. The tree is fully traversed in a downward direction, and where the leaves are testable, that attribute is propagated upward to the root node. Thus, the extractable metric would be that the feature is testable, and that is true if and only if all the leaves in the tree formed by its downward traces are testable (see Figure A.2).

Automatic Downward Propagation of Attributes

Just as some high-level attributes of a requirement can only be determined by traversing all of its downward traces, so too can some requirement attributes be calculated with an upward trace. However, whereas downward tracing is through a tree structure, upward tracing is through a directed graph. For example, certain safety-critical features in medical products fall under FDA regulations that require that a hazard analysis be performed on the requirement. However, a product feature may have several hundred derived system requirements. If the analysis can be performed at the feature level, then, by implication, all of the derived requirements inherit the analysis. But it is not that simple; a low-level system requirement may trace back up a graph to several product features. If any one of those high-level features has not been marked as having a completed hazard analysis, then the low-level system requirement cannot be set to "analysis completed." Downward propagation can then be used to improve productivity by reducing the workload of analysts; e.g., automatically marking hot spots and propagating attribute values where appropriate (see Figure A.3).

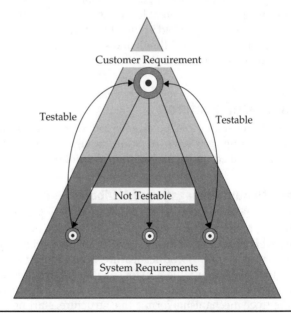

FIGURE A.2   Upward propagation—for the Customer Requirement to be considered testable, all of its system requirements must be testable

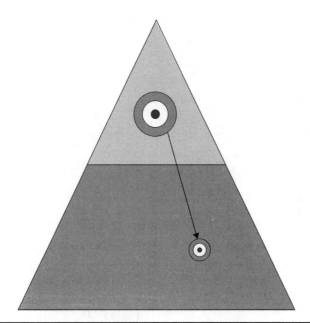

Figure A.3   Downward propagation—if a requirement attribute value is set at a higher level, it is automatically applied to all derived lower level requirements.

A.4   Unique Needs for a Product Line RDB

Product lines can impose additional burdens on an RDB (see Chapter 6). Just a few issues will be described here. As always, it is best to plan for the RDB implementation through process definition and an artifact model (see Chapter 2).

Multidimensional Support

A product line consists of several products with some shared features and some divergent features. This means that the relationship between product release, product definition, and product line definition is three-dimensional. In Figure A.4 you see that products in a product line may or may not implement a requirement. Furthermore, even if a product is destined to implement the requirement, it may take several releases before it does. In order to support a product line, then, it must be possible to support the generation of three-dimensional structures.

Generation of Product Maps

A product map shows, for any given product line, which product features will be in a specific product (Figure A.5). As many requirements may be associated with a product, it is important that when maps containing product reports are created, they be filterable so that the generated map is understandable; e.g., only has requirements at the same level shown.

FIGURE A.4   Three-dimensional nature of product line requirements and databases

Camera Feature		P1	P2	P3	P4
Lithium Ion Battery		X	X	X	X
In-camera Red-eye Remover		X		X	X
Video Capability				X	
Anti-Shake			X		X
Continuous Shooting Mode				X	
18X Zoom Lens					X
3-inch Display Screen			X		X

FIGURE A.5   Example product map

A.5   Summary

In this appendix, we have shown that advanced planning is extremely important in order to get the most out of a modern RDB. Although defining a process, its metrics, and the structure and content of generated material may not seem all that important when a project is initiated, careful planning is the key to effective database management as the project size increases. Furthermore, when selecting a database, needed features should be prioritized. All the current commercial RDBs can do a reasonable job if used effectively, but not all RDBs will have all needed features. Sometimes, a missing feature (such as attribute propagation) can be implemented using the extensibility features of the database. If a desired RDB feature is not available, then the purchaser must decide for each case just how important it is.

Index